# Karl Barth &
# Evangelicalism

## Gregory G. Bolich

InterVarsity Press
Downers Grove
Illinois 60515

InterVarsity Press is the book-publishing
division of Inter-Varsity Christian
Fellowship, a student movement active on
campus at hundreds of universities, colleges
and schools of nursing. For information
about local and regional activities,
write IVCF, 233 Langdon St.,
Madison, WI 53703.

Distributed in Canada through
InterVarsity Press, 1875 Leslie St.,
Unit 10, Don Mills, Ontario M3B 2M5,
Canada.

ISBN 0-87784-615-4
Library of Congress Catalog
Card Number: 79-2716

Printed in the United States of America

*Gratefully dedicated to Dr. Arthur M. Climenhaga,*
*whose faith in me triumphed over any doubts.*

The last word which I have to say ... is not a term like "grace," but a name, "Jesus Christ." *He* is grace, and he *is* the last, beyond the world and the church and even theology.... What I have been concerned to do in my long life has been increasingly to emphasize this name and to say: There is no salvation in any other name than this. For grace, too, is there. There, too, is the impulse to work, to struggle, and also the impulse towards fellowship, towards human solidarity. Everything that I have tested in my life, in weakness and in foolishness, is there. But it *is* there.

*Karl Barth*

# Preface

Some two thousand years ago the apostle Paul spoke of "an acceptable time" of salvation. Today is another "acceptable time"—in this case, for reform and renewal in evangelical Christianity.

I see movement in this direction in the new attention being focused on Karl Barth, an enigmatic figure to many evangelicals. Certain articulate evangelical spokesmen are using Barth's theology in their suggestions for renewing the evangelical faith. But no study of any breadth or depth has yet surfaced that has as its major concern the relation of Karl Barth to American evangelicalism *in the light of the need for reform and renewal*. For better or worse, this is the object of my own contribution.

It is my hope that the reader will be as patient in reading through this one short work as I was forced to be with each of the many I had to consult to draw forth this model of what I term "constructive" theology. Certainly, apart from the careful study of a multitude of voices I could never have found adequate expression for my own voice. I began with a nonverbal need to express something positive in a community setting that appeared to me increasingly negative and introspective. But what could I say?

The answer came to me from a completely unexpected confluence of two independent researches. On the one hand, the current situation in evangelicalism demanded that I pay close attention to its history. On the other, my personal desire to become something approximating a "theologian" necessitated a study of Karl Barth. As I steadily progressed in the one, I found myself increasingly immersed in the other. A host of unforeseen and unanticipated points of contact began to emerge. Eventually I found myself with a task that could be my voice to the evangelical community. The result, of course, is entirely my own responsibility, although I must acknowledge my heavy indebtedness to all those whose labors became my own as I reasoned with them.

# Part I

## Evangelicals & Crisis

# 1

# Introduction:
# The Present
# Crisis

If evangelical Christians do not join heart to heart, will to will
and mind to mind across their multitudinous fences, and
do not deepen their loyalties to the Risen Lord of the Church,
they may well become—by the year 2000—a wilderness cult in a
secular society with no more public significance than the
ancient Essenes in their Dead Sea caves.[1]
Does this warning, written more than a decade ago, bear any
relevance for the evangelical community of the late seventies? Its
author, Carl F. H. Henry, obviously thinks it does. He repeated it
in his more recent book *Evangelicals In Search of Identity* (Word,
1976) and added: "I think that both the Watergate era without and
mounting evangelical dissension within suggest that we are far-
ther along the bleak road to those lonely caves than many evangelicals realize."[2]
Henry is not an alarmist. His warnings have been echoed by
other evangelical leaders as it has become evident that contemporary evangelicalism stands at a point of crisis. Harold J. Ockenga, in the foreword to Harold Lindsell's controversial *The Battle for the Bible* (Zondervan, 1976), noted: "As evangelicalism
grows, it becomes more and more threatened with incipient division."[3]

Certainly no one in touch with the religious life of America can deny that evangelicalism continues to grow. At the same time, however, problems inherited from a former time are joined with current troubles. Old bridges built among themselves by "fundamentalists" of a half century ago in their common defense against "modernists" were never as strong as many wanted to believe. Eventually they fell under the weight of never-resolved, inherent differences. Although the bridges collapsed, the problems were partially obscured by events that culminated in new alliances among conservative Christians. Old problems persisted but again were left unresolved.

Those problems stemmed from essential differences in church polity, Christian life and, of course, doctrine. The pressures of combating liberal inroads brought together Christians who were united in upholding certain "fundamentals" even while retaining significantly different points of view. What is surprising is not that those differences were never fully reconciled but that a remarkably effective unity was attained, at least for a while.

Can workable unity among evangelicals, one that respects differences, exist today? Are evangelicals threatened with "incipient division"? Indeed, is division already so deeply ingrained that any unity is only apparent? Such questions lie at the heart of the evangelical crisis. With evangelicalism's rise to prominence have come doubts of the suitability of maintaining an "evangelical faith"—as well as of the ability to do so. Now, as perhaps never before, the right questions must be asked and adequate answers must be formulated if the fate envisioned in Henry's warning is to be avoided.

Accordingly, the crisis facing evangelicalism can be termed a need for reformation and renewal. The vigor of a new beginning is needed. Rather than starting over, this must be a starting forth, a "setting out." The need is, as Henry put it, "that we who will one day stand together in Christ's presence may yet find and support each other in these days of tragic human need to identify and implement evangelical duties and incalculable opportunities."[4]

Surely the opportunity is here for a beginning toward change. The dimensions of the beginning can be as small or as great as the evangelical community permits, but faith must be its *sine qua non*. Faith in the living God must determine the boundaries of change.

The evangelical community must make a fresh start in meeting old needs. As a point of departure, evangelicals must affirm a vision of constructive, dynamic and dogmatic theology. Thus the foundations laid in the apostolic age and repaired by the Reformers will once more become evident.

Exercising faith is a positive venture. The nature of faith includes change and indicates the direction that change must take. Faith is *constructive:* it builds. Faith is *dynamic:* it exhibits an eternal freshness of power. Faith is *dogmatic:* it conforms to its own logic with a divine consistency. Apart from faith there is no hope for successful renewal and reformation of evangelicalism.

By faith the current crisis can be overcome and a workable unity with high visibility before the eyes of a hurting world can be brought about. The present situation points to the necessity of developing a positive theology, one formed by action, not reaction. Evangelical action can, by faith, begin building roads of communication as well as walls to defend the gospel. Such action, proceeding in the power of God's Spirit, can manifest a freshness and vitality of the church's proper authority. Positive action can do that just as well as the weighty intonations of canon law. Indeed, it can even prove itself dogmatic in the best sense of that word as evangelicals strive anew—and together—to make the proclamation of the gospel a faithful mirror of the Holy Scriptures.

## A Positive Theology

For a positive evangelical theology to emerge, several events must occur. First must come a recognition of the need to change and to change in a particular direction. The need for theological reform and renewal is already being demonstrated to some extent by leaders like Carl Henry who have a clear grasp of the current situation and the prospects for the future.[5] Those who recognize the desirability of movement in that direction are agents of change. The initial stimulus to develop a better theology, or to revitalize an old theology, generally comes from change agents at the top of the ecclesiastical structure; to maintain such a movement requires broad support within the community.

Before support can develop, two important facts must be communicated. First, change agents must indicate how reform and renewal can take place and why it should. So far there have been more warnings about the consequences of not changing than programmatic proposals about how change can occur.[6] Many prominent evangelicals have addressed the subject only indirectly. The significant efforts of Francis A. Schaeffer, for example, have their chief value in the analysis of the contemporary Western culture in which evangelicalism finds itself. It is true that in his books Schaeffer puts forward a solution to the disillusionment and disorder of modern culture. The answers, however, are directed to changing the world; the address to the evangelical community is to hold fast the received truth of the gospel. Schaeffer's approach has been taken up by others with varying degrees of reasonableness. Their common theme is that the only change evangelicals need is a renewed interest in the old and true answers, together with a reformation of personal lifestyle to become more Christlike.

There is great good in this theme. Nothing about it contradicts the development of a positive evangelical theology. Yet its expression is not always developed positively. It may be cast in a defensive, even irrational manner; sometimes its appeals to piety replace appeals to sound rationality. Schaeffer himself steers far from such dangerous shores, but sometimes his presentations seem conducive to incipient division. His work could be criticized for its essentially reactionary character.

Schaeffer's legitimate concern to conserve truth has made it difficult for him to establish meaningful communication with nonevangelicals. Enough walls have already been built by evangelical apologists. It is time to listen to dialog with and learn from nonevangelicals as well as evangelicals. Positive theology can engage in polemics, but only as a means to build truth. It cannot decry those who seek truth. The theme which Schaeffer advances is one central to positive theology; but it must be expressed correctly. When the received truth is revived through personal conviction and revealed through every avenue properly open to the Christian church, then and then only does it serve to free human beings and their society. Then it can truly be said that not even the gates of hell can prevail against it.

A positive evangelical theology adequate for the current crisis must be the result of formal theological endeavor. If the work of Francis Schaeffer and others has laid some of the preparatory groundwork, then whatever its flaws, it has performed a useful purpose. If it spurs others on to better work, it will deserve praise. With evangelical faith now thrust into the bright glare of society's examination, evangelicals must come together to say what they have always said—but better than they have ever said it before.

Not long ago Donald Dawe described the current scene in Christian studies like this:

> Since the fading of the hegemony of neo-orthodoxy, theology has developed kaleidoscopically. A new insight would emerge to hold out momentarily the prospect of ordering theological thinking in some new pattern. There were speculations as to whether this or that theologian was to be the new orderer of our disorder. It was almost as if we were looking for a Tillich or Barth *redivivus*. Theological fashions changed with rapidity, like the images in a kaleidoscope, each one dazzling in its momentary beauty but evanescent. The only order that it was possible to impose on this parade of theologies was a temporal one. Each successive theology was said to put its predecessors out of fashion, so that theological discourse degenerated into a kind of nervous one-upmanship.[7]

Now that evangelicals are "front and center stage," will they abdicate the opportunity to present responsible, scholarly studies? Is evangelicalism only a shallow, broad, populist religion, or can it demonstrate the depth and power of the gospel it espouses? The challenge to replace disorder with order stands before the evangelical theological community. So does the temptation to continue the degeneration of theological discourse.

The second important matter to be communicated to the evangelical community at large is that change is desirable. Development of a positive theology is simply the pursuit of the best expression of the gospel of Jesus Christ. Positive theology promotes meaningful discourse in order to make sense, to promote understanding. But more important, positive theology exists to further the church's mission.

Today evangelical understanding of the Christian mission stands in a position it has rarely if ever before occupied. As an integral and prominent part of evangelical faith, missions must be scrutinized, renewed and justified within the church. People outside the church are now looking with interest at the thought and practice of all who maintain a staunchly biblical faith. Missiology in the wider circles of the Christian religion has been steadily eroded by the winds of a syncretistic ecumenism. What remains of that missiology is so confused as to provide virtually no points of contact with evangelical understanding. Hence now is "the acceptable time" to present a model of the Christian mission decidedly different from the debacle of so-called Christian humanism. Now is the time to exercise a working model of that mission, a model soundly biblical, proclaiming Christ to all who are at this moment watching the evangelical community.

Missiological motivation is essential to positive theology. There is truth in asserting that mission begins at home with each individual. Without a renewal of interest in sound doctrine and reformed lifestyles the missionary work of the church will be only so much hot air, devoid of the mighty wind of the Spirit's coming. But motivation deprived of content and context is wasted energy.

Unfailing loyalty to the Bible as God's personal address to humankind has given to evangelical theology an unchanging content. The Bible is appealed to as the final authority. Thus the missionary motive instilled by the Bible finds its direction, scope and methodology in the Bible. In other words, the Bible provides the content which the missionary motive energizes. This is the fundamental logical circle of the Protestant view on the Scriptures. Karl Barth once remarked:

> We have to admit to ourselves and to all who ask us about this question that the statement that the Bible is the Word of God is an analytical statement, a statement which is grounded only in its repetition, description and interpretation, and not in its derivation from any major propositions. It must either be understood as grounded in itself and preceding all other statements or it cannot be understood at all. The Bible must be known as the Word of *God* if it is to be *known* as the Word of God.[8]

Beginning from this foundation, evangelicalism has proceeded in its theological studies with the confident belief that the experience of the world, of the natural and the supernatural, and of every aspect of human existence validates the claims of the Bible. Because of this confidence in the Bible's absolute authority, the rise of higher criticism and the challenge to the doctrine of scriptural inerrancy created substantial conflict between evangelicals

and others. Rightly or wrongly, many evangelicals found their
confidence threatened by the use of historical-critical tools. For
some, this feeling continued even after eminent evangelical
scholars like George Eldon Ladd wrote books on the matter and
advised:

> Although much critical biblical study displays a negative at-
> titude toward the biblical doctrine of divine self-revelation both
> in redemptive history and in the Scripture, it has shed great
> light on the historical side of the Bible; and these historical dis-
> coveries are valid for all Bible students even though the pre-
> suppositions of the historical-critical method have been often
> hostile to an evangelical view of the Bible. Contemporary evan-
> gelicals often overlook this important fact when they condemn
> the critical method as such; for even while they condemn his-
> torical criticism, they are constantly reaping the benefits of its
> discoveries and employing critical tools.[9]

Although many evangelicals have come to an appreciative if cautious use of the higher-critical methodology, the line of conservative orthodoxy has been drawn by some right through this point.
What was once a solid criterion for dividing evangelicals from
others has become a highly publicized conflict among evangelicals
themselves. Led by Harold Lindsell, many who defend the doctrine
of inerrancy as essential consider it still the hallmark of evangelical theology. They agree with Lindsell's assessment: "I regard . . .
biblical inerrancy to be the most important theological topic of
this age."[10]

The inerrancy conflict is part of the crisis facing evangelicalism.
The need to rediscover the right motive and to redefine the content of evangelicalism remain at the heart of the task of formulating a positive theology. Beyond these is a third, less visible concern. The missionary motive, which finds its content in the Bible,
finds its context in the church. Mission begins at home, with the
training of disciples. But as Larry Richards has observed:

> A great trap into which evangelicals have fallen in the past has
> been to assume that since we have a true *content*, we need only
> make that content known. A search for a biblical theology of
> communication leads us to see that equal consideration must
> be given to the person in the communication setting. Bible
> teaching is also concerned with the best ways to open the ears of

hearers to the living Voice of God, and with support of the hearer as he or she steps out in faith to try out the new lifestyle to which God in Scripture calls us all.[11]

Only when motive, content and context have been clearly fixed and set in right relation to each other can the Christian mission become what it must be to reach the world for Jesus Christ. These three elements correspond to the aspects of the crisis already described.

First, the missionary motive of the church demands of evangelicals a willingness to work together to realize the goal that is their raison d'être. Thus a need for unity is the primary point of crisis.

Second, the content given for the motive is the Bible and, because the authority and veracity of the Bible are challenged, the actual existence of evangelical Christianity is challenged. Accordingly the most visible point of crisis is whether evangelicals can demonstrate the validity of what they uphold. They can try to do this through the kind of scholarly work that will indicate they represent something other than a historical anachronism. Among other matters, this requires a resolution of the inerrancy debate. They can succeed only by returning full attention to the faithful proclamation of the gospel.

Third, since both motive and content demand context, the most hidden point of crisis is a need to redefine evangelicalism. As Carl Henry's title suggests, evangelicals are in search of their identity. In essence this means determining what acceptable forms of communication are to be used by those who call themselves evangelicals. Ultimately the form of communication is related to the content of evangelical faith; sound doctrine defines the limits of acceptable proclamation and behavior.

Perhaps the crisis will go away. More probably it will produce either a strengthened evangelicalism or an evangelicalism of the caves. The call for reform and renewal is a cry to develop a positive theology to help bring about a stronger evangelical faith. It is a plea for faith in God activated in love and purposeful work.

## A Possible Approach

How is a positive theology to come about? There is no one right way. There are many possible ways.

It is the object of this study to suggest one approach that confronts the crisis at each of the levels delineated above: motive, content and context. The features of this approach accentuate theology as a constructive, dynamic and dogmatic exercise of faith. The approach takes the form of theological discourse with scholars both inside and outside the evangelical camp. It attempts to be responsible and academic, yet simple enough for easy comprehension. Above all, it tries to be "methodologically redemptive."

"Redeem what has been lost" is perhaps a fitting rubric for the proposed approach, which attempts to use sources from both the past and the present. The proper use of sources is often a matter of rescuing them from obscurity, disrepute or even canonization. Such "redeemed" materials may inform theology concerning the basis, nature and execution of the Christian mission. The sources open to investigation are innumerable. Among them are the writings and examples provided by the important theologians of the church.

An important aspect of this approach is establishing that theologians need be neither feared nor ignored, no matter what their theologies might be. At the same time certain limitations are already inherent in evangelicalism. The perimeters of evangelicalism, for instance, exclude all non-Christian religions as proper sources to draw on in formulating expressions of the gospel. But those perimeters must be wide enough to allow consideration of all theologies within the church, including those that are not evangelical. Only a few such extra-evangelical sources will finally be included for their contribution toward a positive theology; this approach must be both selective and redemptive.

To be redemptive means to possess legitimate communications of the gospel even while recognizing that to do so means bearing the cost of change. But this is precisely what is entailed in renewal. No honest renewal comes without reformation. Resolution of the present crisis depends on an openness to examine the sources, evaluate them and integrate them in whole or in part into the life and proclamation of the evangelical community.

In this study one specific example is used to illustrate the proposed approach. A subject has been chosen that fits comfortably within the boundaries for legitimate examination. The purpose of the study is to promote the achievement of a positive theology. Accordingly, the specific goal is to indicate how the person and work of Karl Barth can provide inspiration and direction for a healthy renewing and reforming of evangelical theology today.

The introduction of Barth requires several preliminary comments. First, Barth was a theologian, in fact the most acclaimed theologian of this century. Yet in America Barth was slow to gain a hearing and was never as well received or understood as he was elsewhere. Second, Barth has been feared or ignored by vast numbers of evangelicals.[12] This is especially regrettable in view of the tremendous potential available in Barth for recovery and use in developing a positive evangelical theology. Some theologians who should know better have failed to appropriate any good from Barth. Rather, they have dismissed him with a label and a critique. Third, Barth's person and work can both reveal strengths at the very points where evangelicals and their theology are weakest.

Four arenas help define why Barth is particularly valuable. First, his place historically and theologically is one of great relevance to evangelicals. Barth claimed to stand squarely in the middle of the Reformation tradition. His echoing of vital ideas and themes from the Bible drove people back to listening to the Scriptures as God's Word. Second, Barth's method was biblical and dogmatic. His exegesis stimulated a major movement in biblical theology. His understanding and use of dogmatics was among the most creative and comprehensive of any theologian since Aquinas. Third, Barth's work was constructive and kerygmatic. He utilized the best thoughts of church history to communicate the gospel message. Fourth, Barth's challenge to others was always both Christocentric and relevant. He saw himself as a witness to only one Lord, Jesus Christ. This witness he always sought to communicate by word and deed in a manner appropriate to the situation at hand. Such facts justify Barth's place at the center of an investigation intended to strengthen evangelical life and thought.

The present investigation is aimed primarily at informing and assisting those men and women who are change agents. As a model this work is concrete in form but ready to be expanded, adapted and completed where and when opportunity should arise. The intent is first to report, then to suggest ideas based logically on the findings. The direction of the study is from the concrete to the possible, from the past to the future, from "what is" to "what if."

Several features of this approach might be mentioned. First, it is meant to be educational, to promote understanding. Second, its incorporation of dialog with theology and the theologians behind it should contribute to meaningful communication and to learning. Third, it attempts to be constructive, appreciating the work of others and building on it. (This is one reason for the extensive use of quoted material.) Fourth, it integrates two separate investigations, both bearing on the crisis of evangelicalism. Studies of Barth and surveys of evangelical history both abound. In this work they are both pursued with the specific purpose of interrelating them and of applying the findings to the solution of problems. Specifically, the goal is to show ways in which Barth can aid evangelicals in effecting a workable unity, proving their validity and discovering their fundamental identity.

Since evangelicalism is the area of concern, its roots are explored before tracing in its developing story those lines that have produced the current crisis. Since the thesis is redemptive application of the figure of Karl Barth as a guide to evangelicalism, a close examination of the evangelical response to Barth is made. Barth's life and thought is then presented, with particular emphasis on his theological methodology. The final step is the setting forward of a scenario in which what has been learned from Barth is applied to what has been learned about evangelicalism.

# 2

# Some Preliminary Definitions

Before launching into the study proper—that is, before beginning to explore the roots of evangelicalism, the events leading up to the present crisis and the significance of Karl Barth to that crisis—it may be helpful to define certain key terms which will arise repeatedly in the discussion. Precise definitions of the terms *theology, dogmatics* and *evangelicalism* are hard to come by. Even harder to come by are definitions acceptable to all. The following, however, should provide a context for understanding how I wish to use the terms in this study.

### Theology
In a broad sense "theology is the literature in which the faith of Christians finds intellectual expression."[1] Although the almost inevitable product of human reflection on faith is framed in writing, this definition is inadequate. It is too limited by its sociological and phenomenological orientation.

Somewhat better is this: "By theology we mean the rich diversity of analytic and synthetic undertakings by which Word of God and world of men are understood and brought into confluence.... In this sense, everyone who speaks a word of witness is a theologian.... But Christian theology ... testifies that one strand of history is particularly meaningful."[2]

The problem with this second definition is twofold. On the one hand, it is so broad as to include material not usually recognized as theological. The boundaries are too loosely defined to provide the pragmatic guidelines needed by most men and women who do theological work. At the same time, despite its broadness, the accent is on human labor. Thus on the other hand, it is too limited. It leaves inadequate room for the divine element. John Macquarrie insists that "theology cannot fail to talk of God, for the very word 'theology' means 'God talk.' "[3] The tendency of modern theologians to talk more about history, even "salvation history," than about Jesus Christ has vexed the evangelical church. So, too, have reconstructions of a non-Christological Jesus and a Christ without history. "God talk" used to mean a sense of communication between the divine and human that took place in history but was more than just *a* history, or the sum of all history, or history itself. Evangelicals must call the church to Christ in a manner that does not displace history but removes it from its throne to a more proper role in theology. Theology is not simply the study of history.

"God talk" is God talking as well as God being talked about. Definitions preoccupied with the faith response give only half the picture. Theology, as an operation of grace, proceeds from God to the more or less accurate and trustworthy perceptions of human beings. Therefore theology is not simply "the systematic conceptual elaboration of the faith response to revelation or revelatory events."[4] Theologians are more than "persons who ask the question of our ultimate concern."[5]

What then is theology? Barth captured some of the challenging complexity of "God talk" when he reflected in his *Church Dogmatics:*

> The old Lutheran theology . . . made a very sensible distinction between the *theologia archetypos* [original theology] which God has and in fact is Himself, and *theologia ektypos* [derived theology], as with the exception of Christ according to His humanity and the angels it may belong to men as well, where too the *theologia hominum* [human theology] possible to us has once more one of two meanings, as *theologia patriae* [theology of the homeland] in the eternal redemption and as *theologia viatorum* [theology of journeying, or theology along the way] in this world,

and here in this world a different one *ante* and *post lapsum* [before and after the Fall], again a different one *post lapsum* as *theologia naturalis* and *supranaturalis* [natural theology and supranatural] and as *supranaturalis* once more a different one as *theologia immediatae* [immediate or direct theology] and *mediatae revelationis* [mediated revelation]; the former only for prophets, apostles, and evangelists, the latter for us, as persons directed to their writings.[6]

The result is, according to Barth, that "we shall have to understand by *theologia ektypos mediatae revelationis hominum viatorum post lapsum* [derived theology of mediated revelation which in its humanness is a continuing journey after the Fall] on the one hand Church dogma, and on the other hand . . . the scientific work of dogmatics."[7]

This formula presents theology "in its completion as the Church's concrete work of thought completed in time and always completed at a particular time, the work of the Church and in the Church, the inquiry after the relation laid upon us for the sake of Church proclamation."[8] In that "relation," dogma is the object of inquiry. The movement is from God to humankind and includes both hiddenness and disclosure. There is nothing static about theology. Dogmatics is always valid in its continual relation to dogmas.

Barth's statement that the goal of theology is proclamation makes the understanding of theology profoundly missiological. The movement from God to human beings is motivated by divine mission. Theology inquires after "that attitude towards the Bible as the Word of God which is essential to Church preaching."[9] There is no presumption that church proclamation is identical with the content and meaning of Scripture. Indeed, history has often demonstrated how far apart the two may become. Rather, within theology is an inner necessity for correspondence between its understanding at any given time and its communication to contemporary listeners. The crucial part in this correspondence process is played by dogmatics.

## Dogmatics

The usual understanding of the term *dogmatics* seems to focus on it "as the organized and systematic presentation of the dogmas of the Christian Church."[10] This definition obscures the vitality of theology as Barth defined it. "Dogmatics," says Barth, "is the science in which the Church, in accordance with the state of its knowledge at different times, takes account of the content of its proclamation critically, that is, by the standard of Holy Scripture and under the guidance of its confessions."[11]

Reduced to simpler terms, "Dogmatics is the scientific test to which the Christian Church puts herself regarding the language about God which is peculiar to her."[12] These two statements on dogmatics together comprise the idea of a function vital to theology. Moreover, they avoid any false separation of theology and church. "Dogmatics is a theological discipline. But theology is a function of the Church."[13] Thus there are two spheres that constitute the proper context for theology: the Christian canon and the church.

Of course, many theologies boldly claim to operate within the contexts proper for Christian theology. To dispute such claims is not the purpose of this exercise in positive evangelical theology. Since Barth's descriptive remarks, which serve to introduce his thought, are in no way inimical to an evangelical understanding of theology, they are accepted here as a solid starting point.

## Evangelical

It is proper to understand evangelical theology "as the science and doctrine of the commerce and communion between God and man, informed by the gospel of Jesus Christ as heard in Holy Scripture."[14] An evangelical is "one who is devoted to the Good News— or 'Evangel'—of God's redemptive grace in Jesus Christ."[15] Thus " 'Evangelical' means informed by the gospel of Jesus Christ, as heard afresh in the 16th-century Reformation by direct return to Holy Scripture."[16]

The term *evangelical,* however, has also come to represent a more restricted and particular perspective. Today the term in the United States signifies a distinct group with clear doctrinal characteristics:

> Evangelical Christians are thus marked by their devotion to the sure Word of the Bible; they are committed to the inspired Scripture as the divine rule of faith and practice. They affirm the fundamental doctrines of the Gospel, including the incarna-

tion and virgin birth of Christ, His sinless life, substitutionary atonement, and bodily resurrection as the ground of God's forgiveness of sinners, justification by faith alone, and the spiritual regeneration of all who trust in the redemptive work of Christ.[17]

It is entirely appropriate to delineate American evangelicalism within the context of the theologically conservative group described above, although the existence of an identity crisis has already been mentioned. This crisis has not arisen because the above descriptive definition has been discarded; it is scarcely challenged. Rather the problem lies in the negative character of the evangelical face toward the world.

Positive theology, shaped by constructive action, is dynamic in its aggressive proclamation of the good news. It confronts the world rather than waiting to be confronted by the world. It is confidently but carefully dogmatic. That evangelical theology is inherently positive is evident, since the fundamental truths are good news indeed. Yet evangelicalism seems clouded over by uncertainty, division and negativeness.

The ambiguity of evangelical identity is a direct result of the historical attempt to maintain the gospel and at the same time to build a reactionary front on the world. The evangelical claim to be bearers of a right appreciation and understanding of Holy Scripture has been brought into severe examination. Inconsistencies have been posed by evangelical theology as scholars sought to preserve correct doctrine within an impossible context. Walls built by the evangelical community have been found increasingly to inhibit the Christian mission. So in this day of mounting crisis, as the cracks in the wall appear more visible, the task of reform and renewal is not only a necessary matter, but is itself a good and glad task.

# 3

# Walls
# Go Up

Any reforming process within evangelicalism must include the effort to understand its present in light of its history. Among recent efforts toward this kind of self-understanding are Donald Dayton's *Discovering an Evangelical Heritage* (Harper & Row, 1976) and George Marsden's more restricted *The Evangelical Mind and the New School Presbyterian Experience* (Yale Univ. Press, 1970). What follows is not a comparable attempt at in-depth analysis, but I do want to trace the particular historical developments which in my view have contributed to the present crisis in American evangelicalism.

## The Forging of American Evangelicalism

Evangelicalism, as Sydney Ahlstrom writes, "is a battle-torn flag that has waved over many different Protestant encampments ever since the Reformation, sometimes over more than one at the same time."[1] As a distinctly American phenomenon evangelicalism belongs not only to the Christian West,[2] but particularly to the United States. Although its roots are solidly entrenched in many of the fundamental doctrines of church orthodoxy, evangelicalism has acquired its uniqueness from another source—the fundamentalist-modernist controversy which gave birth to the contem-

porary conservative movements collected under the single designation "evangelical."

Of course a rich and varied heritage extends backward in time
from this twentieth-century controversy to the colonial Puritans.
What began, strictly speaking, as the Pilgrims' attempt to embody
in the New World the New Testament church soon outgrew even
that magnificent effort. The Puritan way became a road down
which traveled both Calvinist and Methodist in a great evangelistic movement to form a new Christian society. In the interest of
the Christian mission, revival movements like the Great Awaken-
ing (1740-42) brought about a curious blend of Calvinist and Ar-
minian theologies. The resulting evangelical theology was forged
in the hot fires of controversy, with many dissenters, but became
a broad union within which the Great Commission could be pursued on a majestic scale.

Revivalism, not theological reflection and debate, increasingly
formed the evangelical charter. "In the nineteenth century, revivalism was not a type of Christianity in America; it was Christianity in America."[3] The Puritan orientation to sound doctrine
became an evangelistic preoccupation with an inward life of piety,
a life begun in that crisis moment of conversion called the "new
birth." The revivals emphasized the urgency of a clear-cut decision between being "born again" or going to hell. In the period
just before the Civil War the evangelical character blossomed into
the great voluntary societies, a natural outgrowth of revivalism
that sought the evangelization of the nation, the remaking of
society and the expression of Christian benevolence through a
multitude of good causes.[4] But the setting of brother against
brother, daughter against son, brought evangelical optimism to a
sudden crushing halt.

Evangelicalism lost its initiative in the confusion surrounding
the Civil War and Reconstruction. And though great evangelists
like Dwight L. Moody still proclaimed the gospel and large numbers of people responded, there were not the widespread revivals
of earlier days. A strange new mood pervaded the land, a mood
deepened by the changes entailed in postwar society.

## Response to Biblical Criticism
Evangelicalism came under major attack from the new biblical

criticism finding its home in the United States. In the 1890s a series of sensational heresy trials brought to the fore the conflict between conservatives and liberals or "modernists" as the proponents of the new theology were sometimes called.

Eugene Osterhaven characterizes the era as follows:

As in the closing decades of the seventeenth century when new streams of thought ... overwhelmed the earlier British Christian tradition, so in the closing decades of the nineteenth century a flood of ideas that had gathered strength and prestige throughout several generations swept from Germany to inundate the convictions of many American theologians. ... By 1900 the transition had virtually been completed and the "liberal" era in American theology had arrived.[5]

While evangelicalism was still struggling to recover from the effects of the Civil War, the incoming liberal theology brought with it an optimism founded in a peaceful Europe and the hope for a brighter day for America. As the decades passed from late nineteenth century to early twentieth, the industrial boom in America, a world mostly at peace and a progressive, broad-minded theology all seemed to go rather well together. The outcome was predictable. Despite evangelical resistance the day belonged to liberalism.

As Harold Linsell suggests:

So strong was the influence of the modernists that few defenses remained for the fundamentalist. As early as 1910 most of the denominational theological seminaries had been captured by the modernists. As a consequence, new seminaries were formed by the Bible literalists, but the development of these new institutions was to take time before their influence could be felt. In many instances the attack against the old faith was so powerful that whatever strongholds were left to the literalists became hideaways from the enemy rather than bases from which to launch a counter blow. For the greater part the modernists were able to ride roughshod over the prostrate bodies of their helpless "brethren."[6]

The widespread evangelical inattention to positive theology was taking its toll. The factions that had jointly comprised the great evangelical mission were not prepared to wage effective battle on theological ground. A swing in evangelical concern from mass evangelism to theological controversy began to make itself visible. Early reaction to the liberal movement consisted mainly in strongly worded confessions and, when necessary, heresy trials.

The Presbyterians, from the first a focal point for viewing the conflict, on several occasions affirmed the orthodox formulations of Scripture as posed by Westminster. The General Assembly in 1892 adopted the Hodge-Warfield doctrine of a Bible inerrant in its original autographs. That position was reaffirmed in 1893, 1894 and 1910. The General Assembly's action in 1910 was decisive and far-reaching. The doctrine of an inerrant Scripture was placed alongside the doctrines of the virgin birth, satisfaction theory of the atonement, bodily resurrection, and miracles of Jesus as the most fundamental and essential teachings of the church.[7]

## The Fundamentals

"The desire to arrest the drift from old moorings led," notes Sydney Ahlstrom, "to one other major event in the history of pre-World War Fundamentalism—an event, some would say, that gave the movement its name."[8] This event was the product of an intervention by two evangelical laymen into the struggle. Lyman and Milton Stewart created a $250,000 fund to provide for evangelical leaders a series of booklets by conservative scholars on the issues of the debate. *The Fundamentals,* as the booklets were entitled, began appearing in 1910. Three million copies had been distributed by the time the twelfth and final volume appeared some three years later.

With Amzi C. Dixon, Louis Meyer and Reuben A. Torrey serving as editors, *The Fundamentals* were composed of articles on a wide variety of subjects. Of the ninety articles, four were specifically concerned with the inspiration of the Bible, one with the virgin birth, one with the resurrection of Jesus, one with the deity of Christ, one with the atonement and none with the Second Coming.[9] The distinguished scholars who contributed included James Orr, B. B. Warfield, H. C. G. Moule, A. T. Pierson and G. Campbell Morgan.

The importance of *The Fundamentals* can hardly be overestimated. They appeared at a moment when the evangelical position desperately needed an organized and coherent exposition of orthodox scholarship. The attitude reflected by the authors was far from panic-stricken. In fact, as Harvie Conn notes, "the spirit of the work was typical of the spirit of early fundamentalism—calm, determined, intending merely the reaffirmation of fundamental truths."[10]

The books had at least two important effects. First, they promoted a great interdenominational witness by conservatives. This witness rested squarely on strong convictions that were expressed firmly and honorably. For the time, at least, a remarkable unity was formed to support an agreed position. Second, this unity encompassed, as Ahlstrom notes, "two fairly incompatible conservative elements: a denominational, seminary-oriented group, and a Bible institute group with strong premillennial and dispensational interests."[11]

United by a common cause and in a common confessional stance, the evangelicals were able to present a fairly unified and reasonable case for their faith. Yet the old differences tended to persist. The evangelical theology that was being brought to bear against modernism was rich in diversity. "Doctrinally, a great many elements were part of this early fundamentalism. The sweep of its campaign brought together Calvinists and Arminians, Baptists and Presbyterians. Dispensationalists were also strong leaders in the program."[12]

From the beginning the divergence in doctrine showed itself to be an obstacle. The united front presented in the conflict was never far removed from profound and crucial differences. Thus the success of *The Fundamentals* in bringing about an unprecedented union of differing theologies into one evangelical theology actually served a negative function as well. The call to unity "despite clashing interpretations of countless scriptural passages"[13] effectively masked disunity of doctrine. In later years, renewed calls to Christian union in the conservative cause would continue to denigrate attempts within evangelicalism for interdenominational respect and understanding.

But *The Fundamentals,* despite the doctrinal diversity represented, were instrumental in defining the points of conflict between orthodoxy and modernism. Every arena of contention could be seen in light of the issue of authority. Evangelicals found themselves espousing a common front of biblical inerrancy in order to unite on that issue. Gradually the matter became a highly visible point of battle. Eventually every wing of the fundamentalist coalition found it necessary to affirm some understanding of the doctrine of biblical inerrancy, not only in the interest of evangelical unity, but because of pressures to avoid any false accusations of sympathy with the modernists who so vigorously ridiculed the ideas of inspiration and inerrancy.[14]

Although *The Fundamentals* focused the scholarly powers of the evangelicals, it took a greater power to deliver the blow that eventually brought liberalism to its knees. In 1914 the war in Europe introduced those elements of human existence so deadly to the kind of optimism upheld by modernists. Yet when the war ended, the death of liberalism was not nearly as evident in America as it was in Europe. On the Continent a new theology was raising its head and offering hope for a disenchanted people. But in America the liberals continued to parade their theology. Of course, they were a little less exuberant and were more restrained in their optimism, but still they were confident of an eventual historical vindication of their doctrines.

## Postwar Struggles

The fundamentalist-modernist controversy was renewed in intensity. The World Christian Fundamentals Association was formed in 1919. In 1920 evangelical delegates to the Northern Baptist Convention vowed "to re-state, re-affirm and re-emphasize the fundamentals of our New Testament faith."[15] An editorial in the Baptist *Watchman-Examiner* wrote about "Fundamentalists" who were prepared to fight for the "fundamentals" of Christian orthodoxy. The designation was quickly adopted by many evangelicals and also picked up by modernists, who often used it in a pejorative manner.

The struggle was broadened somewhat in 1923 with the formation of the Baptist Bible Union. This group directed itself to combating the teaching of evolution as well as aiding other fundamentalists in the defense of orthodoxy. Although evolution, as understood by the modernists, had been an issue for some time, the 1920s marked a special interest in keeping evolution out of public schools and universities. The existence of new organizations like the Baptist Bible Union showed the growing concern of many conservatives to protect the younger generation from a speculative theory deemed inconsistent with Scripture. In this regard, the conflict reached its climax in 1925 with the famous Scopes trial. The trial turned the evangelical cause into a travesty. Although a few local crusades against the public school teaching of evolution were decided in favor of the fundamentalists, the Scopes trial resulted in the discrediting of the whole fundamentalist movement in the minds of many people.

Meanwhile the controversy was keen on other fronts. Within certain denominations the struggle for ecclesiastical control was fierce. A few groups, like the Lutherans and many southern churches, were relatively peaceful. In the Southern Baptist Convention liberals constituted no threat at all. But the Northern Presbyterian bodies and those of the Northern Baptists were in the middle of the conflict. To a lesser extent so were the Disciples of Christ. In Congregationalism and Northern Methodism the liberals were in strong control.[16]

One particularly significant struggle was centered at Princeton. That institution had long been the bastion of orthodox Reformed theology. In the nineteenth century, Charles Hodge, perhaps the greatest American theologian of that period, taught at Princeton. His position of influence was inherited by his son, A. A. Hodge, and B. B. Warfield. Those men represented the strongest expression of the doctrine of inerrancy. Warfield had engaged C. A. Briggs in a landmark debate of the 1890s. When Warfield died in 1921, John Gresham Machen became the leader of Princeton orthodoxy.

Machen was faced with a difficult situation. During the years from 1921 to 1929, Princeton was experiencing pressures that eventually led to a realignment within the school in pronounced favor of the liberals. But Machen turned his considerable talents to the fray and produced the most powerful evangelical work of the period, *Christianity and Liberalism* (1923). Machen also was instrumental in establishing an independent foreign missions board. In 1935 he was tried and found guilty by a presbytery convened at Trenton, New Jersey, on charges brought by the General Assembly of the Presbyterian Church. Accused for his activities with the mission board, Machen was forbidden to defend himself and was suspended from the ministry. In 1936 Machen and one hundred ministers banded together to form the Presbyterian

Church in America. Two years later that new denomination was faced with division.[17]

Shortly after its creation the denomination was renamed the Orthodox Presbyterian Church. Within the new church an intense struggle arose over certain points of doctrine. A faction led by Carl McIntire opposed a move by Machen's colleagues at Westminster Seminary that dispensationalism be avoided. McIntire perceived that move as, ultimately, an attack on premillennialism. When no agreement could be reached, McIntire led the defection to yet another new denomination, the Bible Presbyterian Church.

The division exemplified a growing split within fundamentalism. On the one hand were those like Machen who had never felt comfortable with the term *fundamentalist* and who believed that the extremes represented by groups like the dispensationalists should be avoided. On the other hand were the strongly premillennial, dispensational evangelicals who had formulated a distinctive framework around a unique hermeneutic. More and more frequently the fundamentalists found themselves faced by difficulties within as well as without. As the period between the two world wars drew to a close, an uneasy peace prevailed in evangelicalism.

## The Challenge of Neo-orthodoxy

During those years a new theological wind seemed to be blowing into the United States from the Continent. Few Americans were ready to assess the new theology, which was being called "neo-orthodoxy." Instead, the American people were struggling to cope with the collapse of the economy, a depression lifestyle and a growing dissatisfaction with all of the old answers. The churches were again mostly conservative, but many wondered if the cause was more the liberal uncertainty than the evangelical message.

By the end of the second world war, neo-orthodoxy was firmly entrenched in America. Liberalism, for the moment, was laid low. Evangelicalism was in grave danger. The diversified elements in fundamentalism had been controlled by union against a common foe. With the fall of modernism, the evangelicals came face to face with their internal problems.

Perhaps the most pronounced change was a growing identification with dispensationalism. Reformed evangelicals with their

Calvinistic heritage were understandably reluctant to associate themselves too closely with that shift. Many evangelicals withdrew from the movement. Some were attracted to neo-orthodoxy. Others were left waiting for a new development to bring evangelicals together in a workable unity.

The reason for fundamentalism's existence as it had appeared in the preceding decades had passed. Fundamentalism had possessed a unity essentially different from that of the pre-Civil War period. Then the common cause joining evangelicals had been the salvation of souls. During the fundamentalist-modernist controversy, evangelicals had joined forces to save sound doctrine. Their effort had been reactionary in character. The cause which had sustained their coalition for so long proved itself inadequate to effect a lasting union. Fundamentalism had made only a half-right start.

As Frank Mead observes:

But in due time fundamentalism made one capital mistake. This is why it converted from a religious movement to a religious mentality. Unlike the Continental Reformers and the English dissenters, the fundamentalists failed to develop an affirmative world view. They made no effort to connect their convictions with the wider problems of general culture. They remained content with the single virtue of negating modernism. When modernism decayed, therefore, fundamentalism lost its status. Neo-orthodoxy proved too complex for it to assess. It became an army without a cause. It had no unifying principle.[18]

## The Rise of Neo-evangelicalism

Fundamentalism after World War 2 could be defined from a number of directions. First, fundamentalism represented an attitude that led many to define the fundamentalist as "a person with orthodox convictions who defends them with an anti-intellectual, anti-scholarly, anti-cultural belligerency."[19] Second, fundamentalism was essentially a separatist position. In taking a strong stand against liberal or neo-orthodox leadership in the traditional denominations, the fundamentalists withdrew to form separate denominations or independent congregations. Third, fundamentalism repudiated higher criticism and "with obscurantism" held to the verbal inspiration and inerrancy of the Bible. Finally, fundamentalism was generally identified with the *Scofield Reference Bible,* dispensationalism and premillennialism.[20] Eventually even a leading evangelical, E. J. Carnell, could write:

> Fundamentalism is a lonely position. It has cut itself off from the general stream of culture, philosophy, and ecclesiastical tradition. This accounts, in part, for its robust pride. Since it is no longer in union with the wisdom of the ages, it has no standard by which to judge its own religious pretense. It dismisses nonfundamentalistic efforts as empty, futile, or apostate.... Status by negation must be maintained or the *raison d'etre* of fundamentalism is lost.[21]

That judgment, harsh though it may sound, became a motivating factor for many evangelicals to create some form of instrument to indicate evangelical unity, openness and action. During the latter part of the 1930s it became evident to many that simply remaining in a fundamentalist union could not solve the problems that persistently raised their heads. Therefore in 1941 evangelical leaders called together by Ralph T. Davis and J. Edwin Wright met at Moody Bible Institute in Chicago. Like many conservatives they were dissatisfied with the newly formed American Council of Churches, a politically oriented, exclusivist organization founded under Carl McIntire. Most evangelicals, however, were in sympathy with McIntire's desire to find some corporate expression by which to counter the Federal Council of Churches, an organization with decidedly nonevangelical convictions. So in 1942 a group numbering nearly 150 met at St. Louis to continue the work begun the previous year. As a result the National Association of Evangelicals was founded. A strong creedal statement was formulated, and in 1943 they held their first convention. By 1956 the association claimed over a million and a half members.

Other expressions of a new evangelical awareness began to take place. Fuller Theological Seminary was founded in 1947. In 1948, during the opening exercises for Fuller, its first president, Dr. Harold Ockenga, introduced a new word to the theological world: "neo-evangelicalism." The term was quickly adopted by some to express their ties to the past while at the same time making clear their separate identity from fundamentalism or, as some preferred, "neo-fundamentalism." Men like Carl Henry,

Gordon H. Clark, Bernard Ramm, Harold Lindsell and Edward J. Carnell—whether they chose the new name as their own or not—became prominent and influential spokesmen for the new evangelicalism. But the man perhaps most responsible for presenting the new outlook to wide groups of people was William Franklin Graham. A Los Angeles tent-meeting revival in 1948 thrust him into national prominence, and the name *Billy Graham* became synonymous with *evangelical* for many Americans and people around the world.

In 1951 the National Association of Evangelicals, closely identified with the new evangelicalism, helped organize the World Evangelical Fellowship. Then in 1956 the periodical *Christianity Today* brought added cohesiveness to the movement. All these varied expressions had in common the desire to avoid the pitfalls that befell fundamentalism. Rather than separating themselves from the nonevangelical theological world, they welcomed open and honest dialog. Social concerns were given new attention. The new evangelicals were active in bringing their message to the world by every means and in every way open to them.

Ahlstrom observes:

Still another aspect of this "new evangelicalism" which gained public notice during the fifties was its effort to overcome the powerful anti-intellectual and anti-scientific spirit that had discredited the older Fundamentalism. This did not involve much (if any) modification of the movement's commitment to scriptural infallibility or its emphasis on the conversion experience. Nor, for the most part, did it involve an effort to transcend the many serious doctrinal issues that divided the "third force." But it did result in a considerable body of critical and apologetic literature attacking modernism, exposing Neo-orthodoxy as but another form of modernism, and defending conservative theology as a rational option for modern man.[22]

The new evangelicalism was an important return to a positive missiological orientation. But the theology of the movement was, for the most part, still marked by the fundamentalist-modernist debates. Although the new theologians successfully sought to emulate the scholarship of earlier evangelicals, they did not mold their theology to the mission of the church. It essentially remained a theology for controversy.

# 4

# Tumbling Walls?

Evangelicalism, still divided by sharp exchanges between its fundamentalist and neo-evangelical wings, seemed as baffled as everyone else at the turns in American society in the 1960s. Although the decade marked continued growth for evangelicals, the growth was hidden and hushed by the reign of the silent majority. For the most part conservatives were on the defensive as representatives of the status quo. Anything new or different became suspect. Harold Lindsell himself noted: "Many Christians still hold to the faith of our fathers. . . . Not having shifted theologically, these people are still adrift because they have been unable to make the change which changing times require."[1]

That was true, to some extent, from the leadership downward. The evangelical openness of the 1950s was possible, at least in part, because of the general character of American society. The evangelicals had once more become an American fixture, accepted as an institution that belonged. This created a security that permitted the new evangelicals to carry forward their programs without any effective opposition. Only growing apathy and inertia posed a threat in those days. But the 1960s changed that dramatically.

Suddenly society's attention was drawn to radical new voices in theology. Not many wanted to hear the evangelical gospel; after all, it had had its chance and had not proved itself—or so the discontented could claim. And who could fault them? Evangelicals appeared at a loss. On the one hand, it was hard to deny their relative ineffectiveness. Many were defecting from the old standards of morality, and a host of different evangelical voices were each proclaiming that they and they alone had the gospel truth. On the other hand, they found themselves forced to defend the societal status quo against alternatives that were far from New Testament teaching. The outcome of this dilemma was a vast evangelical silence. The evangelical voice was drowned out by the strident voices of extremists both right and left.

Not all the protesting in the world, however, could quench the deep thirst for stability and security. People wanted some kind of change but not what they were being offered. Thus in the midseventies the old desire for a God above and beyond human creaturely reality reestablished itself. Not surprisingly, the evangelical churches reaped the greatest benefit from this turn.

## The Restless Seventies

By the year 1976, the bicentennial for the United States, evangelicalism was once more a popular and acceptable alternative for Americans. Then the evangelical "silent majority" found its voice. As *Newsweek* observed, "With the strength of growing numbers, evangelicals are also discovering what they can do for themselves."[2] The new publicity prompted this reflection by David Kucharsky: "Evangelical recovery has taken fifty years. During the fundamentalist-modernist controversy, biblical orthodoxy retreated to the cultural periphery. But it has again come to the center as theological alternatives have fallen on very hard times."[3]

The accepted institution of the 1950s, the ridiculed institution of the 1960s, had become the restless institution of the 1970s that at last erupted in a multitude of highly visible persons and acts. Most prominent was the sudden publicity for evangelicalism in the midst of the nation's search for a president. Both candidates claimed a "born again" experience. Gerald Ford, the incumbent, was an Episcopalian; his challenger, Democrat Jimmy Carter, a Southern Baptist. Carter's testimony to his faith occasioned new interest by the news media in evangelicalism. Pollster George Gallup conducted a national survey to uncover some of the facts and statistical dimensions of evangelical Christianity in America. Among his findings were these:

A far higher proportion of persons of the evangelical group of churches than among the nonevangelical or mainline denominations have had a "born again" experience, hold a literal interpretation of the Bible, and witness to their faith.

The greater missionary zeal of the evangelical group of churches may be an important reason why these churches are experiencing a spectacular growth in membership while certain mainline churches are experienceing serious membership losses.[4]

Researchers reported in *Eternity* magazine that "the evangelicals in the mainline denominations, if totaled, would exceed or compare favorably with the smaller denominations outside the larger ones."[5] James A. Taylor, a committed liberal, summed up his feelings and those of others like him when he wrote:

Frankly, I don't know how to cope with these evangelicals. Nor, it seems, does my church, the United Church of Canada—nor for that matter any of the other mainline churches. These new evangelicals can't simply be lumped together with the old fundamentalists. For a while we tried ignoring them as an aberration that would somehow go away if we pretended it wasn't there. Now, with the election of an evangelical president in the U.S., and with the obvious growth of evangelical churches, particularly those attracting large numbers of youth, we have no choice anymore. The evangelicals are here.[6]

The election of Jimmy Carter signaled the emergence of the evangelical community into the mainstream of the American consciousness. Signs of political muscle-flexing by evangelicals began to show. At least thirty candidates for Congress included in their platform the testimony that they could be trusted to bring morality to public office because of their evangelical commitment. At the same time, a nationwide revival called "Here's Life, America" brought a great number of people into direct and personal encounter with the evangelical community. In politics, sports and elsewhere evangelicals suddenly stood up and were recognized. *Newsweek* commented:

For the first time in this century, large numbers of evangelicals
are stepping out of cultural isolation and assuming the burdens
of political responsibility once exercised largely by mainline
Protestants in consort with Jewish and Catholic leaders. . . .

With typical evangelical fervor, groups of "New Evangelicals" are asserting alternate forms of leadership. Beginning
in 1973 with its historic "Chicago Declaration," an ecumenical
group of scholars and activists called "Evangelicals for Social
Action" has functioned as a goad to repentance, reform and
radical social witness within the wider evangelical community.[7]

The traditional strengths of evangelicalism stood the new publicity as well as ever. Fidelity to an authoritative Bible, fervor
for evangelism and orthodox convictions were all submitted again
and again to investigation by those outside evangelical circles.
But all these matters were also being reconsidered within evangelicalism. Of course to some extent that had been happening for
many years, but suddenly, in the flash of unexpected attention,
these things were brought out into the open. The same *Newsweek*
article noted:

Despite the evangelical's newfound strength, a number of serious divisions have opened up within their ranks. Evangelicals
are sharply divided over fundamental religious issues such as
the infallibility of Scripture and what they think the Gospel
requires of them as born-again Christians. Searching for more
authentic Christian life-styles, younger evangelicals are rejecting the salvation-brings-success ethos of establishment
evangelicals. And in their hour of political ascendancy, the
evangelicals are exhibiting new and often sharply divergent
views on how the church should relate to public affairs.[8]

### Tension over Inerrancy

The issue of scriptural inerrancy as the basis of biblical authority surfaced to a new visibility during the seventies. Once it had
been a focal point of battle between conservatives and liberals.
Now the issue became a cause of controversy within evangelicalism. Harold Lindsell's *The Battle for the Bible* announced itself with the confession, "This is a controversial book."[9] It was
indeed. As Clark Pinnock warned in his review of it: "What con-

cerns me is the fact that evangelical commonality is being wrenched apart by a number of issues, one of which is a controversy over the interpretation of biblical inerrancy. The dispute has been fanned into flame by the publication of Harold Lindsell's book, ... and it threatens to create a new wave of bitterness and controversy on account of its militant tone and sweeping attacks."[10]

Lindsell's defense of his work was centered in his understanding that "the battle that rages over the Bible today centers around the question of infallibility. ... I am of the opinion that this is a watershed question and must be seen as such."[11] The importance of the battle, and Lindsell's central thesis, was the conviction that "embracing a doctrine of errant Scripture will lead to disaster. ... It will result in the loss of missionary outreach; it will quench missionary passion; it will lull congregations to sleep and undermine their belief in the full-orbed truth of the Bible; it will produce spiritual sloth and decay; and it will finally lead to apostasy."[12]

Carl Henry noted that despite Lindsell's arguments "scores of young evangelicals emphasize that scholars uncommitted to inerrancy are producing substantial evangelical works. They repudiate the 'domino theory' that a rejection of inerrancy involves giving up 'one evangelical doctrine after another.' "[13] More important, Henry remembered that

> for all their commitment to inerrancy, scholarly evangelicals earlier in this century—Hodge and Warfield included—avoided wholly resting Christian theism upon it. With New Testament balance, their doctrine of Scripture emphasized first of all the divine authority and then the inspiration of Scriptures, much as did the apostles. While scholars disagreed as to whether inerrancy is explicitly or only implicitly taught in Scripture, they did not make inerrancy a theological weapon with which to drive those evangelicals not adhering to the doctrine into a non-evangelical camp.[14]

Lindsell, on the other hand, in his "final appeal" in *The Battle for the Bible* spoke of evangelicals no longer holding to inerrancy as still "relatively evangelical" but insisted: "I do not for one moment concede ... that in a technical sense anyone can claim the evangelical badge once he has abandoned inerrancy."[15] By taking such a stand together with such other evangelical luminaries as

Francis Schaeffer, Lindsell successfully forced the issue into the harsh light of full exposure in both religious and secular presses.

## Propositionalism Challenged

Along with the furor over biblical inerrancy, other standard doctrinal understandings were being challenged. The concept and categories of revelation had come under sharp scrutiny by evangelicals, as by others in the theological world. Not every evangelical was willing to remain content with propositional revelation, and adjustments were made by some. But the more or less uniform understanding of revelation within evangelicalism remained strongly oriented to propositionalism.

In the first two volumes of a projected four-volume series entitled *God, Revelation and Authority,* Carl Henry offered a strongly rationalistic appeal for propositional revelation in the Bible.[16] Using a simple test for truth based on the maxim "a proposition and its denial cannot both be true at the same time," Henry encountered criticism from evangelicals whose commitment to propositionalism was tempered by a more personalistic view of revelation. Such a view reemphasized that "Scripture cannot be looked upon as a pure deposit of revelation but as the cognitive element of the more comprehensive program of salvation."[17] This comprehensive program also included an understanding of revelation as the acts of God in history so that revelation is seen as the balanced self-presentation of God in word and deed.

Accordingly, proponents of the propositional-personal view of revelation protested Henry's reduction of truth tests for revelation to the law of noncontradiction. They insisted on a more complete understanding of revelation and a better comprehension of propositional revelation as well. In his review of Henry's two volumes, Bernard Ramm pointed out the complexity of the matter:

> I think that there is a great deal of propositional revelation in Scripture. That is not where I part company with Henry. But in that he defines the test for a revelation to be reason, that which cannot be stated in propositions cannot be tested by reason. Hence all the literary genre of Scripture (poetry, drama, parable, apocalyptic literature, fables, symbols) and all figures of speech (simile, metaphor, hyperbole, etc.) must be reduced to propositions or they cannot be tested.

Henry is really in a predicament here. If he proposes to reduce all such materials to propositions, the whole world of scholars of literature will protest. Wilbur Urban has discussed this issue in his book, *Language and Reality,* and shows (in my opinion correctly) that symbols, metaphors, etc., cannot be restated in propositions without significant loss. If, however, Henry cannot do this then he has to admit that there is more to revelation than propositions and therefore other criteria of truthfulness must be used along with the law of non-contradiction.[18]

## Evangelism versus Social Issues

Serious as the doctrinal debates of the period were, they were nevertheless overshadowed by the evangelical enthusiasm for personal evangelism. Some individuals may have wondered if there was more to evangelicalism than a fight over nonexistent autographs, a "born again" experience and Jimmy Carter. Yet it was plain to much of America that evangelicalism still meant Billy Graham crusades, Oral Roberts evangelistic meetings and a host of other attempts to induce them to turn their lives over to Jesus Christ by an act of personal commitment. Some leaders in the mainline denominations complained about a preoccupation with personal salvation and biblical literalism, while vital ministries were being neglected by the evangelicals. Was there a connection between, on the one hand, the flourishing of fundamentalism, the Lutheran Church-Missouri Synod controversy, the charismatic renewal, and attacks on the National and World Council of Churches and, on the other, the growing neglect of social issues such as racial justice, world peace, and the abolition of hunger and malnutrition?[19]

"Here's Life, America" in particular received some heavy criticism. That evangelistic campaign was condemned in *The Christian Century* on seven points: (1) for allegedly having a faulty understanding of the gospel and the meaning of salvation; (2) for manifesting a faulty understanding of witness; (3) for depending on gimmicks for results; (4) for having a rigid attitude toward both the ends and means of evangelism; (5) for depending on emotional exploitation of persons technologically sophisticated but theologically naive; (6) for its latent political significance; and (7) for using the gospel as a means to an end.[20]

Such criticisms were entirely overlooked or dismissed by many evangelicals. But the fact remained that, as the evangelical community moved into a period of tremendous potential as the leading element in American religious life, not all was well. Many internal problems beset evangelicals. Threatened by internal division and external criticism, sensitive evangelical leaders renewed efforts to effect reform and bring about a stronger evangelical coalition. Evangelicalism had not adequately coordinated its theology with its zeal for the Great Commission. The resulting crisis of identity went as deep as the old bifurcation between unity and theological credibility initiated in the fundamentalist-modernist controversy. Evangelical unity had never depended on a genuine reconciliation of doctrinal differences, or on the kind of respect and understanding that might have kept them working together in a coalition for the Christian mission even after that great controversy had died down. Some, like Carl Henry, suggested guidelines for evangelical advance. But change comes hard.

As the decade of the 1970s came to an end, both past and present confronted evangelicals with a responsibility for positive change. The burden had been laid upon them to set their house in order. Yet even as the work toward reform and renewal began, the warning of the world remained unanswered:

Evangelical Christianity has been growing quietly for ten years—often at the expense of played-out mainline churches. During that period, evangelicals have zealously sought out the young, offering the certainties of a fired-up faith as an alternative to secular disillusion. But as it happens, just as the nation is at last taking notice of their strength, evangelicals find their house divided. The Presidential election has only exacerbated latent differences in doctrine and social attitudes. As a result, 1976 may yet turn out to be the year that the evangelicals won the White House but lost cohesiveness as a distinct force in American religion and culture.[21]

# Part II

## Evangelicals & Karl Barth

# 5

# The Specter of Karl Barth

Even before Karl Barth's death in 1968 theologians in the United States were confidently asserting that the day of "Barthian" influence had passed. The vestigial trappings of his reign were still visible on the Continent and to a lesser degree in America. But the initiative had passed from Barth and Brunner to Bultmann in the postwar era of the fifties.[1] Particularly among evangelicals the passing of Barth's influence was marked with a sigh of relief.

Then, as the seventies moved toward the decade's midpoint, an odd revival began to take shape. In the *Reformed Journal,* late in 1974, a two-part article by Donald W. Dayton exposed seven indications of what Dayton termed a "steady growth in the impact of Barth's thought on American theology."[2]

First, a new depth in the understanding of Barth by Americans was surfacing. Second, this better understanding was accompanied by an increasing respect and appreciation. Third, the founding of the Karl Barth Society of North America, with headquarters in Toronto, Ontario, focused American investigation and discussion. This group was joined by others with similar interests. Fourth, new concerns in American biblical studies, exemplified in Brevard Childs's *Biblical Theology in Crisis* (1970), directed a second look at Barth.[3] Fifth, a new cultural situation in America created greater openness to Barth's message. Sixth, a controversial new interpretation of Barth, one seeking to use him in connection with radical politics, had risen in Europe and traveled to America. Finally, calls for an American "Barmen Declaration" had caused many to reappraise Barth's theology.[4]

In the midst of this reappraisal it was surprising to find a group of evangelical scholars participating and assuming leadership positions. They produced some of the best and most appreciative books on Barth. Yet it had been assumed that Barth belonged more comfortably with thinkers like Tillich and Bultmann than with evangelicals. That assumption was shaken by keen participation from men like Bernard Ramm, who demonstrated a willingness to learn and profit from Barth while refusing to identify with Barthian theology. Carl Henry, Donald Bloesch and other conservatives in theology were among those who participated in the Karl Barth Colloquium convened at Union Seminary in New York during December 1970.[5] Evangelicals were also represented at the colloquiums of the Karl Barth Society of North America. Kenneth Hamilton presented a paper entitled "Barth on Creation" at the second colloquium in 1972.[6] Evangelicals were also prominent in the leadership of the society, with Donald Dayton the membership secretary.[7]

With attention drawn to evangelicalism in 1976, such activity, questionable at best in the minds of many conservatives, became a potential issue for controversy. Yet for those who participated in the colloquiums or otherwise showed a new interest in Karl Barth, it was evidence of openness to a second hearing of Barth and sensitivity to the same needs that were directing nonevangelicals to him as well. Moreover, there was a growing feeling among many of these evangelicals that if Barth himself was not an evangelical he was closer to the evangelical gospel than he had been given credit for in earlier days. At the same time, orthodox scholars who had helped create the strong resistance to Barth remained firm in opposing attempts to picture him as anything other than the father of a theology irreconcilable with true biblical doctrine. The result was confusion. One "expert" had his say only to be refuted by the next. Thus as evangelicalism moved toward the 1980s the role of Karl Barth was one more uncertainty in a situation where evangelicals struggled with a wavering initiative.

This is where evangelicalism stands today. The name of Karl Barth invites a variety of emotional as well as intellectual responses. The past must be searched carefully to understand why evangelicals hold the opinions about Barth that they do. An attempt will be made here to trace the history of the evangelical response to Barth before looking again at the man and his theology.

## The Advent of Neo-orthodoxy

The advent of Barth's theology in the United States during the late 1920s was heralded as the arrival of a new mood known as "neo-orthodoxy." In itself, this term carries no pejorative connotations. It simply means "new orthodoxy." Historically the term describes those theologians who after World War 1, turned away from liberalism and back toward orthodoxy. Their orthodoxy was called "new" because it represented an attempt to extend orthodox thought. While clinging to many orthodox affirmations it refused to release some liberal convictions.

As Colin Brown has noted, however, neo-orthodoxy is "a loose term" and "is generally used by those who would not identify themselves with such a theology, either because it seems to deviate too much from the orthodoxy of the Reformation theologians ... or because it is too narrowly orthodox."[8] Van A. Harvey, who prefers the term "neo-Reformed," questions whether the designation has any clear meaning.[9] Bernard Ramm has commented that "in some instances a neo-orthodox theologian is but an orthodox theologian with a neo-orthodox corrective, and in another instance it is a liberal theologian with a neo-orthodox corrective."[10]

That ambiguity stems from the application of the term to a diverse group of thinkers. Barth is thereby linked with Tillich, the Niebuhrs, Bultmann and others. Narrowed to a historical designation for a movement of significant dimension but brief duration, *neo-orthodoxy* has a more specific meaning. It is likely, however, that its use as an expression to describe a third theological alternative between liberalism and orthodoxy will continue confusing the issues.

Evangelicals must face the facts and make some clear decisions. William Fletcher saw the situation accurately when he wrote: "It seems to me that precisely because his thought runs so close to the position of mainstream Christianity, Barth represents the most formidable threat to the Church today. Or else he is no threat at all, but marks the much needed turning point in the history of modern theology."[11]

The historical transiency of neo-orthodoxy proved the difficulty of existence in the theological void between liberalism and evangelicalism. Trained in liberal theology, the neo-orthodox theologians adopted an evangelical vision:

> The fear that a Christianity dominated by the thought-forms of a disintegrating culture could not survive, and, even more, that a "culture religion" could have no message of hope to a society that despaired of its powers, was the driving force in this creative effort to reestablish Christian Faith on the foundations of God's revelation in scripture rather than on the foundations of Western scientific, political or social thought.[12]

In the course of time, however, the concerns that had brought these theologians together were supplanted by the individual interpretations each held of theology's nature and task in a modern world. Not surprisingly, then, the movement became steadily less uniform as the members moved to the right or the left of the theological spectrum. By the time the movement appeared in the United States it resembled a somewhat chastened and corrected liberalism.

But what of Barth? Did he move progressively to the right, assuming an ever more orthodox orientation in his theology? Or did he remain firmly, albeit subtly, in the camp of liberalism? Barth's own position has troubled evangelicals and nonevangelicals alike.

## Roadblocks to Understanding

Several roadblocks along the way to understanding often shaped response to Barth and conditioned its outcome for individuals and groups. The label *neo-orthodox* is one such roadblock. There are others. The most common, and the one most responsible for some misinterpretations of Barth, is a fixation on his early thought. Such fixation is usually accompanied by ignorance of Barth's *Church Dogmatics*. As one American theologian put it, "Just a few were willing to consider the possibility that Barth's theology might have undergone some change."[13]

Another barrier is that of geography. Barth lived and worked in

Germany and Switzerland. To know that he was a Swiss trained in German theology is some help. But just as Oregon is different from Texas in climate and cultural perspectives, so Basel is different from Zürich, where Brunner held sway. Barth was influenced by his surroundings. Failing to consider that, some have approached Barth as if he were an American writing directly to American churches, or at least thinking like an American when he wrote. Ludicrous misunderstandings have resulted. Others have "charitably concluded that Barth was simply too European for the American mind."[14]

Those out of touch with the Reformed tradition in theology also have a problem; whether or not Barth is considered a true follower of Calvin, it is simply impossible to understand him apart from Reformed theology. Those who disagree with Barth because he claimed to follow Calvin, and not Wesley, merely focus on a valid issue in an irrelevant manner.

Another potential blind spot for Americans is the situation of the church. The believing community of Barth's time and place was not like that in America either past or present. Barth did not speak from a context of denominationalism. The sectarianism of American life was not a prominent or desirable facet for the life of the church as Barth envisioned it. Accordingly, Americans who try to understand Barth without first setting aside their ecclesiastical provincialism are liable to misjudgments and false pronouncements.

A further hindrance has been, and no doubt will continue to be, the propagation of caricatures. Caricatures are attractive because they make black or white what to others is murky gray. But an inaccurate label and false description can border on slander. Such irresponsibility and low regard for the truth drastically threatens the maturing of the church.

Finally, a fundamental structural difference between Barth's theologizing and that of many others has led to problems in interpretation. Barth was creative. He dialogued with tradition. Those who have completely forsaken Christian tradition, or been content merely to recite it, have faced immeasurable difficulties with Barth's use of it. They cannot fully understand or appreciate his attempt to advance and better that tradition. This is especially a problem for many evangelicals. G. W. Bromiley, himself an evangelical, posed the problem this way: "Barth deliberately seeks a new language in which to state the Gospel and to fashion its proclamation in the modern age. This may be sound in principle, but it raises its own problems. The language is often difficult. It makes old truths sound strange. Does it also make them different?"[15]

The above factors coupled with a failure to understand the historical background of Barth and his role in history have produced a muddled and uncertain picture of him. Whatever the reason, "he was not well understood and he could complain, with considerable justification, that in most American interpretations of his theology he 'could hardly recognize in them anything else than my own ghost!' "[16]

# 6

# Early Response to Barth

Evangelical response to Barth has had its share of ghost images, but it has also produced some interpretations of him based on careful study. The judgment that he was a modernist in disguise has been challenged. It has also been defended. But it is no longer the monolithic block it once was. Church historian Sydney Ahlstrom has identified some of the reasons behind that judgment. Evangelicals, he reported, believed that Barth had cut himself loose from religious experience, natural theology, philosophic rationalism and the view of biblical revelation in propositional statements, and was therefore so far from orthodoxy as to be a dangerous proponent of modernism.[1] Others pointed to different facets and contended that given a complete picture one would see a man and theology much closer to the evangelical understanding than commonly believed. Intelligent, reasonable individuals have aligned themselves with both sides.

## Rolston: Guarded Enthusiasm

Evangelical assessment began in 1933 with the publication of Holmes Rolston's *A Conservative Looks to Barth and Brunner*. Appearing five years after the first translation of a work by Barth into English *(The Word of God and the Word of Man)* and only two years after Pauck's important study *(Karl Barth, Prophet of a New Christianity?)*, Rolston's book was the first solid attempt to discuss "Barthianism" from a conservative standpoint. Rolston first heard of Barth in the spring of 1928 while at Union Seminary in Virginia.[2] His interest grew when, in 1929, he spent time studying at Edinburgh and learned of the impact of Barth on students in Germany.[3] He read the "rapidly growing Barthian literature" and wrote in his preface: "As I have read, I have become convinced that God, by the medium of the Scripture and Spirit, is speaking to our generation through the new Swiss theologians. I have sought to humble myself, to be still, and to hear the Word that is being spoken through them."[4]

The result was a careful, enthusiastic presentation of the early theology of Barth and Brunner. Rolston believed that "in general . . . the claim of the Barthians to have gone back to the Reformers can be sustained."[5] In fact, if they differ from orthodoxy it is not without a purpose: "If Barth and Brunner had flamed forth with a message that was identical with the message of orthodoxy, they would not have caught the attention of the world. Their message would have been too familiar to be arresting."[6] Rolston warned, however, "the break with orthodoxy flows from deep conviction, not from expediency."[7]

The character of Barthian theology and its profound impact on modern theology had awakened the interest of conservatives, who wondered whether it signaled the return of orthodoxy to the theological summit or corrupted orthodoxy more dangerously than it appeared to on the surface. Rolston wrote: "In conservative circles, special demand is found for a study of the relation of the Barthian thought to the more orthodox position. To what extent are they in agreement? Wherein do they differ? Are the differences deep-seated and fundamental or are they on the surface? Can the two be harmonized or must a man ultimately choose between them? These and similar questions are being constantly asked."[8]

Regrettably, Rolston's book did little to answer those questions. Despite a fine exposition of the new theology in an easy-to-read style, his study suffered from a lack of comparative analysis with orthodox thought. Nevertheless, the study did provide a good introduction to Barth and Brunner, highlighting certain factors that later played a crucial role in further conservative analyses.

First, and perhaps so obvious it is often passed by, Rolston cautioned that "the Barthian theology is too profound a system to be grasped without effort."[9] He believed that "to those who are willing to pay the price that always goes with mental attainment, the Barthian school will give a message that will richly reward their labor."[10] But he also warned, "it will always be without meaning to those who are not willing to pay the price of serious study."[11]

Second, Rolston was sensitive both to the incomplete character of the young theology and to its self-designated nature as a movement, not a closed system.[12] He noted that "the Barth of today is not identical with the Barth who published the first edition of the commentary on Romans. He has changed his positions in many things."[13] That observation is noteworthy in light of the fact that Rolston published his book before Barth had entered fully into the period of his *Dogmatics*. Even before that change Rolston had seen movement. Further, Rolston predicted, "he is probably destined to revise his positions many times before his final work is done."[14]

Third, in an excellent exposition of "the Barthian doctrine of the Word of God,"[15] Rolston identified the point of sharpest dispute between Barthianism and orthodoxy. Although he found Barth's doctrines in harmony with orthodox thought on Scripture in several respects, he discerned a "break with orthodoxy in their admission of the possibility of error in the testimony of the prophet to the Word."[16] The Barthian move toward orthodoxy was not "a return to the fundamentalist position of an inerrant word."[17]

Fourth, Rolston anticipated what eventually became a main evangelical objection to Barth, that is, his use, or misuse, of the ancient creeds pertaining to Christ.[18] That objection had already been raised by Pauck and rebutted by others.[19] The criticism of Barth was that he changed the creeds "by giving to them a meaning which they did not have in the thought of the ancient Church."[20] Rolston's own conclusion was that "in general the Barthians in their reconstruction of the Person of Christ are moving along lines that are substantially the same as those laid down by the ancient church and reaffirmed in the creative period of the Reformation."[21]

Finally, in his concluding chapter, Rolston spent time in a

careful study of the Barthian view of history, another crucial area of dispute by evangelicals.[22] Rolston was of the opinion that "the general principle on which the Barthians move seems to be established."[23] Rolston explained his understanding of the Barthian conception of the relation between revelation and history in simple terms:

> In every act of revelation there is a certain outer form which all men can apprehend. There is an inner meaning which is opened to the eye of faith. We are now prepared to understand what Barth means when he says that revelation is historical and that it is not historical. It is historical in the sense that it is a movement from God to man that enters the field of history and produces effects that are visible to all. It is not historical in that it moves on a plane that cannot be apprehended by the historian simply as a historian. It must be apprehended by faith.[24]

Accordingly, "when Barth says that the resurrection is not historical, he does not mean that it never happened. He is using the word *historical* with the distinctive meaning which it carries in his thought."[25] Thus, the resurrection "is *in* history but it is not *of* history."[26] In the same way Barthian theology also establishes its epistemology in regard to history. Rolston applauded the fact that "Barth and Brunner have called men from the mockery of trying to enter into the truth of God from the standpoint of the spectator. God opens his truth to those who surrender to him."[27]

Although Rolston set forth the main areas where a more vigorous conflict later arose, he did not champion an evangelical crusade against Barth. That came later. It was not until 1946 that a well-known and influential conservative scholar brought forth a major attack against what that author called "the new modernism."

## Van Til: Frankly Polemical

Cornelius Van Til, professor of apologetics at Westminster Theological Seminary in Philadelphia, had been a colleague of J. G. Machen at Princeton but left that institution to follow Machen to Westminster. In 1946 he set forth his appraisal of the theology of Barth and Brunner in a book entitled *The New Modernism*. Under the influence of Van Til and various other evangelical colleagues the work of Barth was declared off limits to a generation of evangelicals. Van Til's general conclusions, as well as many of his specific criticisms, became the primary response of the American conservative community to Karl Barth.

Van Til began his investigation with the conviction that it was "imperative to go into the question of the philosophical background of both Barth and Brunner."[28] He confessed he was "deeply aware of the fact that to discuss a system of theology in relation to its deepest philosophical bases is a hazardous undertaking."[29] Van Til thus offered his hope "that others may carry on the work and make the necessary corrections and supplementations."[30] His own role he conceived as "setting the Theology of Crisis in the light of the broadest possible philosophical background."[31] But that task was not undertaken out of detached observation.

If this analysis is correct it follows that the Theology of Crisis cannot legitimately be called a Reformed Theology. In fact if the main contention of the present investigation has been established, the Theology of Crisis may expect to find its bitterest foes in the adherents of the classical Reformed Faith. It is this classical or traditional Reformed Faith that has, more than any other form of orthodox theology, stressed the fundamental significance of the ontological trinity and the self-contained counsel of God. And this brings with it a matter of great apologetic significance. Assuming the correctness of the claim just made, it appears that the primary responsibility of calling men back from this new form of Modernism rests with those who have most closely followed Calvin in his adoration of the self-contained God. Having borne the brunt of the attack, they must lead in the process of liberation.[32]

"Our purpose then," Van Til wrote, "is frankly polemical. We would rally the forces of the Reformed Faith and behind them those of evangelical Christianity against this new enemy. This enemy comes in the guise of a friend; he is all the more dangerous for that."[33] A few pages further on he writes, "It will be our contention that the Theology of Crisis is to be classified with modern theology rather than with orthodoxy in its choice of fundamental distinctions."[34] Then, near the conclusion, he says, "If the late J. Gresham Machen spoke of the necessity of making a choice between liberalism and Christianity, we should be doing scant justice to his memory if we did less today with respect to the new modernism and Christianity."[35]

Van Til based his conclusions on what he believed was a rigorous and systematic pressing of Barth's and Brunner's presuppositions to their logical ends. He tried to uncover alien meanings he found inherent in their use of orthodox terms. Through a review of history he attempted to establish clear ties between the Theology of Crisis and the critical philosophy stemming from Kant. At every point he highlighted what appeared to him to be the utter opposition of the dialectical theologians to Protestant orthodoxy. His conclusions thus constituted a grave warning to conservatives.

In the first place, thought Van Til, it could be proved that Barth and Brunner shared the assumptions of the critical theology that also stood behind every form of modernism. Van Til discovered that from the first "Barth apparently shares with Kant the skeptical attitude toward the possibility of anything resembling the old metaphysic."[36] But that was not just a part of Barth's liberal phase, for even at the time of *Die Christliche Dogmatik im Entwurf* (1927) it was obvious that "Barth's whole argument ... is anti-metaphysical in character."[37] This anti-metaphysical root exists because "criticism wants to be activistic";[38] or, to put it all together, "the combination of irrationalism and rationalism that meets us in Criticism may accordingly be called *activistic*. All being is said to be becoming, all reality is said to be method, and all the facts are *fieri*. The same position may also be called *positivistic* or *anti-metaphysical*."[39]

Barth's theology also relies on a philosophy of dialecticism. Thus, following Hegel and Kierkegaard, "he has become known as a champion of the irrational in theology. But to be such he must also be a champion of rationalism."[40] "The two together, when kept in balance with one another, produce phenomenalism."[41] However, "Barth does not employ the principle of rationality otherwise than as a limiting concept to the idea of pure irrationality."[42]

In Van Til's view the Theology of Crisis ... has shown itself in all fundamental respects to be the same as the Modernism of Schleiermacher and his school.... Barth and Brunner have what is, basically, the same sort of view of reality and of knowledge as marks the work of Schleiermacher and Ritschl. Fundamental to everything they say about individual doctrines is the fact that they have, throughout and with vigor, cast away as a filthy garment that on which everything in the field of historic Christianity rests, the notion of the self-contained or absolute God.[43]

An unbroken line can be traced from Barth and Brunner back to Kant by way of Kierkegaard, Hegel and Fichte as well as Ritschl and Schleiermacher, Overbeck and Feuerbach.[44] The result, according to Van Til, is that "we are compelled to speak of the Theology of Crisis as more anti-metaphysical and more activistic, and therefore more phenomenalistic, than classic Modernism."[45]

That theology's threat to orthodoxy, Van Til argued, is increased by its seeming acceptance of orthodox doctrine: "Barth believes in verbal inspiration, in a finished canon, in the necessity, sufficiency, authority and perspicuity of Scripture. He believes in them as he believes in the supralapsarian conception of election. He pours new and radically different meaning into all these ideas by means of his critical epistemology."[46] That remains true, Van Til continued, even though one may wish to speak of an "early" and "later" Barth, and identify some movement in his thought. "If... we are to speak of the recent tendency of Dialecticism, we cannot say that it shows any signs... of a turn in the direction of orthodoxy."[47] Indeed the reverse is true because both Barth and Brunner "distinguished their positions more clearly than ever from traditional Christianity."[48] "The only foe against whom Barth really militates is orthodox historic theology. For him, Christian theism is really the 'Satan of religion.' "[49] Thus, "nothing could be more untrue to history than to say that the theology of Barth and Brunner is basically similar to that of Luther and Calvin. Dialecticism is a basic reconstruction of the whole of Reformation theology along critical lines."[50]

Van Til's final conclusion that "the Theology of Crisis is a friend of Modernism and a foe of historic Christianity"[51] became widely accepted in evangelical circles despite the fierce rejection it received in many scholarly reviews. E. T. Ramsdell, writing in *The Christian Century,* complained, "If Dr. Van Til were as critical with respect to his own presuppositions as he seeks to be with Barth and Brunner, his book would have a good deal more of scholarly interest."[52] Peter H. Monsma, himself an author of a

book on Barth and quoted by Van Til,[53] observed about Van Til's
work that "it does not always distinguish clearly between the expressed views of Barth and Brunner and the author's own interpretations and deductions, and thus prevents the uninformed from
evaluating the pertinence of the criticism advanced."[54] Monsma
found other indiscretions as well. On page 338, "an important
passage from Barth is freely translated with the result that statements are ascribed to him far different from those he actually
made."[55] On the whole, thought Monsma, "it seems to attach too
much importance to statements or conceptions Barth himself has
discarded, while it fails to take account of important influences
Barth himself recognizes."[56] Thus, he concluded, "one wonders
how carefully Dr. Van Til has read Barth and Brunner."[57]

Eventually evangelical criticism began to make itself felt. E. J.
Carnell responded to Van Til in strong terms: "I am utterly
ashamed of the manner in which extreme fundamentalists in
America continue to attack Barth. I felt actual physical pain when
I read in *Time* magazine that Cornelius Van Til, one of my former
professors, had said that Barthianism is more hostile to the Re-
formers than is Roman Catholicism. I propose that Van Til ask
God to forgive him for such an irresponsible judgement."[58] John
Warwick Montgomery, however, in an answer to Carnell warned,
"We should perhaps not be too quick to condemn Van Til's evalua-
tion of Barth. Perhaps he has seen more clearly than others the
implications of Barth's separation of history and theology."[59]

But the criticisms continued. G. W. Bromiley, who with T. F.
Torrance served as translator and editor of the *Church Dogmatics,*
called Van Til's study "strained."[60] Colin Brown, author of *Karl
Barth and the Christian Message,* observed that Van Til's critique
"often appears to take much for granted, not least what Barth
actually says and also the biblical exegesis which Van Til claims
to underlie his own thought."[61] Torrance claimed that turning the
method used in *The New Modernism* on Van Til himself would
prove Van Til as much a "heretic" as Barth.[62]

Hans Urs von Balthasar, the Catholic theologian who authored
the highly acclaimed study on Barth entitled *Karl Barth, Dars-
tellung und Deutung seiner Theologie,* found it ridiculous that
in the late 1930s so many had insisted on interpreting Barth's
later thought by his earlier work. He went on to remark: "The

situation is even more ridiculous ten years later (1947), when Cornelius Van Til... tries to explain the whole theology of Barth and Brunner on the basis of their earlier positions and in terms of the philosophical principles that are supposedly at the root of their system."[63] T. L. Haitjema and M. P. Van Dijk were also critical.[64] So too was Barth himself. He complained that Van Til's study bordered on a willful caricature of his theology.[65]

Nevertheless, Bernard Ramm tried to sound a balancing note between the unqualified praises and total rejection that had mounted in the wake of Van Til's work. Ramm advised:

Van Til's mass of anti-Barthian materials is not to be bypassed because one thinks he systematically misinterprets Barth. Barth's great passion is to make the wall of time that separates the witness of Holy Scripture of God's action in the past from the present fall down or become so transparent that that very Word of God is heard by modern man. The danger in such retranslation is that the new concept is not a faithful version of the older one but its betrayal. This is Van Til's major concern, and therefore before any assent is given to a neo-orthodox version of a doctrine, one must ask if the original biblical substance is retained.[66]

Undismayed by the criticism, Van Til continued to raise the call against Barth. In a 1954 article entitled "Has Karl Barth Become Orthodox?" Van Til reaffirmed his stand: "It is, we believe, to do Barth injustice, and to do the church irreparable harm, when orthodox theologians, for whatever reasons, fail to make plain that dialectical theology is basically subversive of the gospel."[67] In a 1960 article, "Karl Barth on Chalcedon," Van Til concluded:

With Dr. Berkouwer we would therefore say that Barth's theology is destructive of the Reformation principle. This principle starts from the idea that Christ has clearly and directly spoken to men in the Scriptures. A theology derived by simple exegesis of the Scriptures as the direct revelation of God is, Barth himself being witness, a wholly different sort of theology from a theology derived from speculation apart from Scripture. To be sure Barth also exegetes Scripture. And no one need deny that Scripture has had its influence on him. But he interprets Scripture in terms of a Christ derived from pure speculation. His Christ is not the Christ of the Scriptures; it is the projection of the moral and spiritual ideals of modern man as he casts them up for himself into the void.[68]

The final, massive answer to Barth from Van Til was his *Christianity and Barthianism* (1962). In it Van Til concentrated on Barth's ties to the past, his activistic views of a *Geschichte* Christ and his push to move beyond the Reformers.[69] In those respects, as in Van Til's concluding philosophical analysis, the book served to update *The New Modernism*. In addition Van Til devoted a substantial section to criticisms advanced by other Reformed theologians and philosophers with regard to Barth.[70] But the conclusion was familiar: "Speaking as objectively as we can, we must say . . . Barthianism, using the language of Reformation theology, is still only a higher humanism."[71]

*Christianity and Barthianism* was, like *The New Modernism,* immediately subjected to harsh reviews. Carl Henry, writing in *Christianity Today,* noted that for Van Til "Barth's modifications of his positions are considered quite inconsequential."[72] Comparing *Christianity and Barthianism* with Van Til's earlier work, Henry observed that "the appraisal tends still to read Barth in terms of the consistent outcome of his presuppositions even where Barth vulnerably prefers inconsistency."[73] Beyond that, however, Henry took issue with Van Til's conclusion:

> Now if one wishes—as Dr. Van Til apparently does—to take liberties with the definition of humanism (so as to include some advocates of supernaturalism, special revelation and redemption, and a unique divine incarnation in Christ), that is perhaps his prerogative. But those who have switched theological sympathies to Barthianism (whatever its serious defects) seem to us rather to be in revolt against humanism and liberalism (in the generally understood sense of those terms).[74]

James Daane, writing in the *Reformed Journal,* also noted the line of continuity in the criticism by Van Til put forward in his books on Barth but saw that "Van Til's analysis and evaluation of Barth through the years has been almost exclusively philosophical rather than Biblical and Theological."[75] More serious, though, and objectionable, was the manner in which Van Til "used" other scholars to voice his own thoughts and reinforce his own points. That, said Daane, was particularly noticeable in Van Til's treatment of G. C. Berkouwer:

Professor Berkouwer is used generously, even avidly, by Van Til to support his own evaluation of Barth; but Berkouwer's criticisms of Van Til's evaluation of Barth are ignored, leaving an impression that their evaluations of Barth are essentially the same. This is less than fair to Berkouwer, who will doubtless feel that he has been used rather than theologically engaged.[76]

## Berkouwer: Restrained Critique

G. C. Berkouwer, like Van Til a Reformed theologian, nevertheless represented a different evangelical response to Barth. In 1956 his *De Triomf der Genade in de Theologie van Karl Barth* appeared in English translation as *The Triumph of Grace in the Theology of Karl Barth*. Barth was pleased to acknowledge that the book caused him to withdraw "the fierce attack which I made on Dutch Neo-Calvinists *in globo*" earlier in his *Church Dogmatics*.[77] Barth referred to Berkouwer's work as "the great book on myself... written with such care and goodwill and Christian *aequitas*."[78]

Berkouwer was far from a general acceptance of Van Til's conclusions. In fact, an appendix on "The Problem of Interpretation"[79] was affixed to present a summary of Berkouwer's criticisms of Van Til in the footnotes of the Dutch edition of the book.[80] To reject Van Til's analysis in whole or part, Berkouwer pointed out, "does not in the least imply an acceptance of Barth's theology, but constitutes only a criticism of an unsound analysis which draws conclusions which Barth himself draws least of all, conclusions, in fact, *which he himself has more than once and at great length opposed*."[81] Berkouwer stated: "My main objection to Van Til's interpretation is not that he criticizes Barth. I criticize Barth also, and in this very book, but Van Til's analysis does not correspond to the deepest intents of Barth's theology. Hence it does not surprise me that Barth says in *amazement* that he *cannot recognize himself at all* in *The New Modernism*."[82]

*Triumph of Grace* combined exposition and critical analysis. Berkouwer came to his study of Barth convinced that "the search for the basic motif of his colossal dogmatic structure remains vitally relevant."[83] Through his study Berkouwer found that "Barth wishes to emphasize above all the triumph of God's

grace."[84] Having identified that as the dominant theme of Barth's
theology, Berkouwer proceeded to unravel the whole of that theology into such basic constituent parts as the doctrines of creation,
election, reconciliation and eschatology.[85] He also paid particular
attention to the relation of Barth's theology "in its antithesis to
Rome,"[86] and the important question of the degree and nature of
any development in Barth's thought.[87] With regard to the latter
issue Berkouwer commented: "To a certain extent we can agree . . .
that in the first phase of Barth's theological development the
emphasis falls on grace *in the judgment* while the later development showed that he was more concerned to manifest *grace* in the
judgment. It would be improper, however, to speak of an essential
modification."[88]

In a chapter midway through his book Berkouwer took time to
review what he called "ambiguous triumphs of grace in the history
of theology."[89] He called attention to his own justification for
studying Barth and the strictures he had placed upon himself in
the course of evaluation:

> We wish finally to point out that the need of testing Barth's
> emphasis on the triumph of grace flows forth from the fact that
> the history of theological thought has seen more than one tri-
> umph-of-grace theology of which it can only be said that in spite
> of the appearance of honoring the motif of grace, the riches
> and totality of the gospel were obscured. In saying this we do
> not mean at all to make the a priori suggestion that the same
> is true of Barth. This will have to be determined on the basis
> of Barth's own conception of the triumph of grace.[90]

After raising a series of crucial questions to bear in mind, Berkouwer concluded the chapter with the notation, "However we
may have to judge of Barth's theology, one thing is certain: a
judgment made in terms of Reformation theology may detract
nothing from the decisive 'sola gratis.' "[91]

Following his exposition of the basics of Barth's theology,
Berkouwer devoted the remaining chapters to a discussion of various problems and questions. These he likewise grouped under the
broad areas of creation, election, reconciliation and eschatology.[92]
With regard to creation, Berkouwer desired "to point out that
Barth's revised supralapsarianism blocks the way to ascribing
*decisive* significance to history."[93] Barth's relation of the Fall

to creation is a preference made necessary by his doctrine of sin.[94] Together his doctrine of sin and the relative closeness between creation and redemption implicit in his revised supralapsarianism obscured the vital transition from wrath to grace.[95] "For this reason Barth's conception of the nature of the triumph raises the problem of the place of man in this triumph."[96] Thus ultimately it must be asked if man's decision of faith is "of any significance in the triumph of grace."[97]

The conception of the nature of the triumph of grace which Berkouwer found in Barth had far-reaching effects. It meant, said Berkouwer, that "the tension in Barth's doctrine of election arises from the relationship between *universal election* and *human decision.*"[98]

> At this point Barth stands at a cross-roads in his thinking. He can move to the right or to the left, not in terms of the demands of a logical system, but in terms of centrally religious considerations. The one way that is open is that of the apokatastasis in which the reality of the divine decision which has been taken is without qualification declared to be identical with the universality of reconciliation.
>
> The other way is that of *renewed* reflection on the seriousness of the human decision which, according to the overwhelming testimony of Scripture, is associated with the kerugma that goes out to the world....
>
> Probably no one will wish to venture a prophecy as to the direction in which Barth will further develop his thought. It is quite possible, however, to state in a nutshell his central thesis. This is that the triumph of election means, centrally and determinatively, the a priori divine decision of the election of *all* in the election of Christ.[99]

But "the criticism that Barth accentuates grace *too much* is a senseless criticism."[100] Rather, the problem was Barth's faulty hearing of the Scriptures with regard to such critical matters as an understanding of sin. His theology had established an a priori triumph for grace and obscured the history of redemption. "The problem posed by this 'necessary' a priori character of the triumph became *the* problem of Barth's theology."[101]

Berkouwer's book was well received. Eberhard Busch, Barth's assistant during his last few years, wrote that the book gave Barth "a great deal to think about because of its acute analysis and the questions it raised."[102] On 30 December 1954, Barth wrote Berkouwer:

> I'm a bit startled at the title, *The Triumph*.... Of course I used the word and still do. But it makes the whole thing seem so finished, which it isn't for me. *The Freedom* ... would have been better. And then instead of ... *Grace* I would much have preferred ... *Jesus Christ*. My intention, at any rate, has been that all my systematic theology should be as exact a development as possible of the significance of this "name" (in the biblical sense of the term) and to that extent should be the telling of a *story* which develops through individual events.[103]

The response from other evangelicals was also favorable. William A. Mueller[104] of Southern Baptist Theological Seminary called Berkouwer's work "one of the finest and most informing books on Karl Barth ever published ... a classic in theological interpretation."[105] Gordon H. Clark, another conservative Reformed scholar, wrote in his review in *Christianity Today* that as Berkouwer's exposition "is marked with great care, so too his criticism is scrupulously honest and restrained."[106] Colin Brown listed *Triumph of Grace* as one of the two best general introductions to Barth and commended Berkouwer for "a full and fair critique, written from a conservative evangelical standpoint."[107]

Evangelical criticism of Barth, both negative and positive, did not cease with Van Til and Berkouwer. Many evangelicals joined the train of Van Til in assessing Barth's theology as generally inimical to the gospel. Many others, however, followed in Berkouwer's steps, prepared neither to adopt nor to condemn Barth wholesale, but seeking to discern and preserve what was of value in his work. These "negative" and "positive" critics are the subject of the next two chapters.

# 7

# Barth as Foe

Critics who find in Barth a foe of evangelical faith tend to share a common apologetic outlook, with a rigid adherence to inerrancy, a strong predilection for apologetics and a preference for Christian rationalism. In faulting Barth they usually zero in on his doctrine of Scripture and accuse him of fideism, irrationalism and subjectivism. Among them we will in this chapter take up Gordon Clark, John Gerstner, R. C. Sproul, Norman Geisler, Clark Pinnock, Charles Ryrie, Francis Schaeffer, Harold O. J. Brown and John Warwick Montgomery.

## Clark: A Question of Method
Gordon Clark's *Karl Barth's Theological Method* was a heralded study when it appeared in 1963. Although Clark did not approve of Van Til's analysis—and found Berkouwer's "particularly successful"[1]—he nevertheless stood closer to Van Til's eventual conclusions than to Berkouwer's final openness to Barth. Clark began with the concern that "so far insufficient notice has been taken of Barth's theological method."[2] Clark undertook the task of correcting that deficiency.

Clark acknowledged that Barth's theology "may be described, negatively but very aptly, as a total rejection of modernism."[3]

Further, he found that "on the one hand there are clear and strong assertions of rationality and logic; but sometimes there are hesitations that lead the reader to suspect a sort of irrationalism."[4] In fact Clark decided that "Barth's unbiblical epistemology—for who will defend the thesis that Aristotelian abstraction and imagination are proclaimed by the prophets and apostles?—forces him into most embarrassing arguments."[5] A strand of skepticism runs through this epistemology.[6] But did Barth find a way out through his view of revelation? No, said Clark, his "'revelation' fails of intelligible definition."[7] Barth's failure to equate the Bible with propositional revelation, his rejection of "the infallible authority of the Scriptures," left him in a difficult position.

This position is the acceptance, as a norm or canon, of something or other external to the Bible. . . . Since this external norm cannot give us the necessary information, it must be secular science, history, or anthropology. Of course, this is what Barth had vehemently objected to in his attack on modernism. A norm or canon other than Scripture is something Barth does not want at all. But the construction of his system has not enabled him to escape it. The result is that Barth's theology is self-contradictory. He operates on the basis of incompatible axioms, and against his hopes and aims arrives at an untenable irrational position.[8]

## Gerstner, Sproul and Geisler: Theological Irrationalism

John H. Gerstner, a Reformed theologian, concurred with this opinion and went one step further: "It was Kierkegaard who, in theology, tried to say the irrational is the real; while Barth, in spite of his opposition to system, has tried to systematize this theological irrationalism."[9] Unlike Clark, however, who recognized a movement away from Kierkegaard by Barth,[10] Gerstner maintained that still "for Barth, supernatural revelation was known only as a leap of faith and natural revelation as a correlation of gratuitous assumption."[11] Gerstner also took issue with Barth's views on Scripture. Nor was he entirely pleased with fellow evangelical Klaas Runia's response to Barth on that issue. "Klaas Runia," claimed Gerstner, "manifestly prefers Warfield's doctrine of Scripture to Barth's but equally favors Barth's epistemological approach to Scripture to Warfield's."[12] A committed apologist, Gerstner rested his own hopes on a historical apologetic in behalf of biblical inspiration.[13]

R. C. Sproul particularly opposed Barth's stand on errancy.[14] He also linked G. C. Berkouwer with fideism—a charge commonly leveled at Barth.[15] In that, however, both Barth and Berkouwer were in good company. The same charge had been made by Barth's critics against Van Til, Clark, Bavinck, Kuyper and even John Calvin.[16] Here too Barth was alleged to have followed Kierkegaard's course.

Norman Geisler felt justified in writing, "Karl Barth is rightly viewed as the father of Neo-orthodoxy, although he borrowed much from Søren Kierkegaard who might be considered the grandfather of the movement."[17] Eight years later he wrote, "Despite Barth's repudiation and modification of his earlier and more extreme Kierkegaardian existentialism, he remained strongly fideistic in his apologetic."[18] As Geisler was quick to point out, "fideism is not limited to nonevangelicals. Cornelius Van Til speaks from a strong Reformed, Biblical perspective theologically and yet in an absolute revelational presuppositionalism apologetically. As we shall see, this position may be viewed as methodological fideism."[19] Geisler found an "antirationalistic emphasis" in fideism related to its claim that truth in religion rests solely on faith, not reason.[20] Thus in fideism "neither evidence nor reason is the basis for one's commitment to God."[21] Against this, Geisler maintained that "there is no reason, in contrast to Kierkegaard and Barth, that God's revelation cannot be both personal and propositional."[22]

## Pinnock: Epistemological Disaster

Clark H. Pinnock also supported the claim of fideism against Barth: "Barth is the great fideist of the twentieth century, and allergic to Christian evidences, even as Kant and Kierkegaard, his mentors were before him."[23] For Barth, "faith is a closed circle without bridges to the public areas of human knowledge and truth."[24] Thus his position "spells only mysticism and chaotic subjectivity."[25] It is "a less strident form of . . . neognosticism."[26]

However, said Pinnock, "Karl Barth deserves our praise for his insistence against much opposition that the Bible is the only authoritative witness to revelation."[27] "He deserves great credit

for defending the sole authority of Scripture as witness *in* and
*to* the church. Criticism of Barth must not muffle the gratitude we
feel."[28] But Barth must be criticized, declared Pinnock, because
he arrived at his view of Scripture "out of his view of revelation."[29] "Karl Barth is the primary spokesman for this transcen-
dental, personalist view of revelation and Scripture."[30]

In Pinnock's judgment, "neo-orthodoxy must be judged an
epistemological disaster. It offers no help whatsoever to the person who, bothered by nagging doubts about the validity of Christianity, wants to have the matter settled in his mind."[31] The
problem was, as Pinnock saw it, that "neo-orthodoxy sought to
cope with the challenge of positivistic science by disengaging
theological reality from all contact with empirical reality."[32]
Thus "theology became a matter of sheer and unsupported kerygmatic proclamation."[33] In Barth's theology "historical verity
counts for very little."[34] Pinnock concluded:

> Although Barth holds unambiguously to God's entering into
> human history in its concrete actuality in Christ, he holds
> that these salvation events are beyond substantiation and
> authentication by ordinary historical inquiry. We hold that
> unverifiable events are not very different from mythical ones.
> ... Existential subjectivity in Barth's theology is that which
> hampers the outworking of his incarnational theology in the
> field of Christian proclamation.[35]

## Ryrie: Theological Hoax

For Charles Caldwell Ryrie, contemporary theologian of American dispensationalism, "Barthianism" was a "theological
hoax."[36] Ryrie pressed two major criticisms at the neo-orthodoxy
of Barth, Brunner and Reinhold Niebuhr. First, "Barthianism is
most inconsistent and illogical."[37] This is because "it is both
illogical and impossible to accept the 'findings' of destructive
criticism and preach and speak in orthodox terms."[38] Second,
Barthianism is dangerously deceptive. "The chief characteristic
of neo-orthodoxy is its call to the Word of God as the authority,
but the Word of God is not synonymous with the Bible, and this is
the point of deception."[39] Together, inconsistency and deception
constituted the Barthian system:

> More often than not neo-orthodox practice is inconsistent with

the system in coming closer to conservatives' preaching rather than that of the liberals. Herein lies the greatest danger of deception, for this breeds among evangelicals a dangerous tolerance of Barthianism. Conservatives become so interested in the fact that men are being called back to the Word and even to the Bible that they forget what the Word means in neo-orthodoxy and what kind of Bible the Barthians have. Evangelicals must never forget that neo-orthodoxy has just as openly taken its stand against what it considers the errors of conservatism as it has against the errors of liberalism. It is just as sure that conservatives have misconstrued the Bible as it is that the liberals have. It is not neo-orthodoxy but pseudo-orthodoxy.[40]

## Schaeffer: Religious Existentialism

The man probably most responsible for popularizing the Van Til stance on Barth is Francis A. Schaeffer. Where Van Til's philosophic and theological analyses were heavy and hard to read, those of Schaeffer were brief, clear and pointed. Perhaps more evangelicals became acquainted with Barth through the writings of Francis Schaeffer than through any other single evangelical source.

In *The God Who Is There* Schaeffer traced religious existentialism back through Barth to Kierkegaard.[41] Far from representing a radical break with liberalism, Barth was a part of the modern line of thought extending down through Kant, Hegel and Kierkegaard. Schaeffer explained:

So it was not so much neo-orthodoxy which destroyed the older form of liberalism, even though Karl Barth's teaching might have been the final earthquake which shook down the tottering edifice; rather it had already been destroyed from within. To say it in another way—if Barth had spoken fifty years before, it is doubtful if any would have listened.[42]

As it was, "Karl Barth was the doorway in theology into the line of despair.... Karl Barth opened the door to the existentialistic leap in theology. As in other disciplines, the basic issue is the shift in epistemology."[43] Elsewhere Schaeffer argued, "In his *Dogmatics,* II, it is plain that Karl Barth is existentialist as far as epistemology is concerned."[44]

To put it simply, he tried the impossible feat of producing an authority while accepting the results and techniques of higher criticism. To Karl Barth and his followers a statement in the Bible can be historically false and yet religiously true. It was a very simple step but entirely revolutionary. With it theology stepped from the solid earth of rationality into a land where anything can happen.[45]

For Schaeffer, that step removed Barth from any true evangelicalism. In *The Church at the End of the 20th Century,* as elsewhere in his writings, Schaeffer warned of evangelicals who praise Barth. He added, "You may try LSD, you can try the modern theology. It makes no difference—both are trips, separated from all reason."[46] In *The God Who Is There* Schaeffer warned, "The new theology has given up hope of finding a unified field of knowledge. Hence, in contrast to biblical and Reformation theology, it is an anti-theology."[47] "On their presuppositions the Bible contains historical and scientific errors and thus dichotomy, a divided concept of truth, is necessarily central in their concept of 'religious truth.'"[48] In *How Should We Then Live?* Schaeffer observed:

Karl Barth held until the end of his life the "higher critical" views of the Bible which the nineteenth-century liberal theologians held, and thus he viewed the Bible as having many mistakes. But he then taught that a religious "word" breaks through from it. This was the theological form of existentialism and the dichotomy. In other words, the existential methodology was applied to theology. This meant that theology had now been added to all the other things which had been put into the arena of non-reason.[49]

What about the alleged changes in Barth's views? Did Barth become orthodox? Shortly before Barth's death, Schaeffer wrote:

In recent years it is often said that Karl Barth has changed his views. If this is so then all could be easily cared for by his writing one more book amongst his many books and, while he is yet living, making it known that his views of Scripture, his lack of a space-time Fall and his implicit universalism have been publicly repudiated. In the light of his crucial influence as the originator of the new theology and his wide publication, it would seem difficult to think that anything less could meet his responsibility before God and men. If he did this many of us would truly rejoice.[50]

Thus, although "we must have a profound admiration for Karl Barth in that he, as a Swiss teaching in Germany, made a public stand against Nazism in the Barmen Declaration of 1934,"[51] there can still be no bending to his theology. "We may not play with the new theology however much we may think we can turn it to our advantage. This means, for example, that we must beware of cooperation in evangelistic enterprises in which we are forced into a position of accepting the new theology as Christian."[52]

## Brown: Inaccessible God

Harold O. Brown, who in his *Protest of a Troubled Protestant* acknowledged Schaeffer's "marked influence" on him,[53] gives clear evidence of that influence in his critique of Barth: "Barth believed that man has no right to question God or ask him to authenticate those challenging texts which claim to be his voice speaking to man.... But a God who will not let us ask him to show us that he is really there and is really God is a God who will not let man be man. If that is the God of dialectical theology, it is not the God of the Bible."[54]

Perhaps in 1919 what Barth had to say was necessary. But one must step carefully. Brown cautioned:

It is obvious that the figure of Barth, with his profound sense of awe before the majesty of God, and his deep reverence for Christ, is much more appealing than those of the arrogant modern theologians who correct Jesus and dismiss God. But we must be aware that Barth too, despite his attractiveness, contains no real solution, but gives us another version of an inaccessible God whom we may fear but can only trust irrationally, and thus inhumanly and falsely.[55]

Brown acknowledged Barth's position as a critic of the modern theologians, and his doctrinal conservatism, but believed that Barth had not fully escaped the modern tendency "to remove God from history, from anything with which we can have direct contact, by making him the 'totally other.' "[56] Brown found that

Karl Barth is a hard man to analyse. He is frequently attacked as a hopeless conservative by modern theologians, and his monumental writings often lie unread. Yet... Barth has more in common with modern theology than he likes to admit. The problem is this: a man who believes as Barth believes may be a sound Christian in his own life, but he is incapable of communicating the truth of historic Christianity to the next generation.[57]

## Montgomery: Wholly Unverifiable

John Warwick Montgomery, a sophisticated Lutheran theologian, was not afraid to defend Van Til's attention to "the implications of Barth's separation of history and theology."[58] Montgomery agreed with Clark about Barth's faulty relationship to science, his low view of inspiration, his arguments for scriptural errancy and his irrationalism.[59] Like many others Montgomery tied Barth to Kierkegaard. But unlike most others he also extended the historical line from Barth to specific representatives of modern theology in the sixties.

For example, Montgomery argued that "like the other death-of-God theologians, van Buren began his reflecting as a Barthian."[60] How then did he end by proclaiming God's "death"? It was the logical outcome of the Barthian notion of God. Barth and Rudolph Otto, said Montgomery, "provided a God who is wholly transcendent—who cannot be adequately represented by any human idea."[61] If that view of divine transcendence was true, it of course implied radical theological outworkings.

Montgomery saw the "Kierkegaardian-Barthian concept of faith as a 'blind leap' without objective justification."[62]

And why does the Kierkegaardian-Barthian theology operate as a "closed circle"? Because of its basic premise that, as MacIntyre succinctly puts it, "The Word of God cannot be identified with *any* frail human attempts to comprehend it." Since the logical consequences of such a principle are a fallible Scripture and a kenotically limited Jesus, the Bible appears to secular man as no different qualitatively from other human writings, and the Incarnate Christ becomes indistinguishable from other men. The believer thus moves in a closed circle of irrational commitment which the unbeliever finds impossible to accept. The God of such an irrational faith has no recourse but to become a transcendent Wholly Other, and when analytical philosophy poses the obvious verification question as to the ontological existence of the transcendent, no answer is possible.[63]

This whole arena of verification concerned Montgomery with regard to Barth's theology and the Christian faith. He found that "Barth's concession that the Bible was an erroneous book and that Christ's miraculous work was untestable removed all ground for accepting its Gospel message. . . . Barth's flight to a transcendent Gospel put him in a realm of unverifiability."[64] Thus, while Montgomery could commend Barth for noting that the virgin birth demonstrates God the Father in a unique entrance into history,[65] he still found it true that "to a greater or lesser degree the central figure of the Christian faith is disassociated from the realm of historical verifiability resulting in his exemption from historical testability and consequent dependence on blind fideism."[66]

Montgomery discovered that both God and man in Barth's thought had problems with history: "Barth's *Church Dogmatics* shows a remarkable indifference to man's over-all temporal experience."[67] "In concentrating attention on the biblical affirmation of man's radical need before God, Barth lost interest in general history and in God's creative and preserving work outside the sphere of *Heilsgeschichte*."[68] "Karl Barth attempts to find God in the realm of *Geschichte* ('supra-history') rather than *Historie* (ordinary history), and as a result he gets exactly nowhere."[69] "Thus Barth's view of total history as 'all-conquering monotony' relates to what critics have well called his 'unitarianism of the Second Person'—his absorption of all theology into Christology."[70]

Part of this Christology is Jesus Christ as the "revealed Word." But revelation has an aspect of hiddenness. About that Montgomery remarked, "The Barthian concentration on 'hiddenness', with its resultant dualism, stems, I believe, from fear—fear of intellectual attack from the steadily growing 'post-Christian' forces of our day."[71] That fear had drastic consequences.

Barth's fear of being unable to defend the Christian revelation historically has thus led him to the point where . . . he ignores the existence of unbelief and denies the ontological existence of evil. To be sure, Barth has removed the Christian faith from criticism and from the necessity of apologia—but at a frightful cost—at the cost of the Incarnation which lies at its very center, at the cost of any meaningful attempt to relate the gospel to general human history. He has turned the historic Christian faith into a timeless, unsupportable religion of the order of Buddhism, Hinduism, and their theosophical counterparts.[72] Barth's subjectivity was also impressed upon Montgomery in 1962 during Barth's lectures at the University of Chicago. Montgomery observed: "Perceptive non-Christian seekers after truth in the academic audience at Chicago could not help concluding that ultimately it is Barth's personal preferences that determine theological truth for him—and thus that they had every right to consider 'his' theology as but one option among the numerous conflicting claims of our time."[73] Accordingly, concluded Montgomery, "evangelicals have a holy responsibility to lead present-day historiography out of its naturalistic blind alley."[74]

# 8

# Barth as Friend

Not all evangelicals are willing to consign Barth to the outer reaches of liberalism. Some find in Barth not a foe but a potential friend. Unwilling to set Barth either wholly outside or wholly inside the evangelical fold, these "positive" critics seek to identify the valuable evangelical elements in Barth and to profit from them. They are concerned to establish meaningful lines of communication and understanding with others like Barth who seem to stand with one foot in orthodoxy and the other somewhere else. These critics usually focus on resolving problem areas in Barth while accentuating evangelical emphases. As a group they favor less rigidity in determining evangelical boundaries than do the "negative" critics. They also show less reliance on apologetics and more on proclamation. But they are no less emphatic in affirming historic evangelical beliefs. Among such critics are E. J. Carnell, Colin Brown, James Daane, Bernard Ramm, Klaas Runia, G. W. Bromiley, J. I. Packer, George Ladd, Carl F. H. Henry, F. F. Bruce and Klaus Bockmuehl, whose assessments are the focus of this chapter.

## Carnell, Brown and Daane: Much to Be Learned
Edward John Carnell, theologian, apologist and at one time a

student of Van Til, was, like Montgomery, present in Chicago during Barth's visit there. The effect of that time, however, was far different on Carnell than it had been on Montgomery. Carnell had been invited to the University of Chicago as a member of a panel putting questions to Barth. Carnell later summed up his impressions for *The Christian Century* in an article titled "Barth as Inconsistent Evangelical." Although unable to say that his dialog with Barth "left nothing wanting," Carnell concluded, "I am convinced that Barth is an inconsistent evangelical rather than an inconsistent liberal."[1]

The inconsistency, in Carnell's opinion, was a lack by Barth of *doctrinal* consistency. Carnell questioned Barth's hermeneutic and wondered if his theology was as safe from the threat of subjectivity as it might be. But what impressed Carnell, even more than the greatness or weakness of various doctrines, was the person of Barth himself. Carnell commented, "There was nothing affected about him; it seemed obvious that he lives by the grace that he preaches."[2]

Colin Brown's *Karl Barth and the Christian Message* attempted "to try to get inside Barth's mind; to see the main issues as he sees them; to try to bring into critical focus Barth's approach to the Christian message."[3] He desired "neither to whitewash nor to condemn wholesale."[4] Brown believed that a careful study of Barth would be profitable if for no other reason than because "Barth sees issues in breadth and depth. Above all, he brings to bear on them a profound and penetrating understanding of the Bible."[5] But he advised:

> I have tried to point out Barth's relevance, his strengths and weaknesses. From time to time I have tried to take bearings on the older, classical Protestant and Catholic positions in order to bring out points of contrast and also to try to see which comes closer to the truth. Above all I have tried to assess Barth's ideas in the light of the criterion which Barth himself insists is the ultimate criterion of all our ideas of God and man—Holy Scripture.
>
> To those who want me to come clean and say where I stand I would simply repeat that there is much that we can learn from Barth.[6]

James Daane, a Reformed scholar, felt the same pull as Carnell and Brown to heed closely Karl Barth the man and the theologian. "Barth is a man of uncommon dimension," wrote Daane. "He is a theologian's theologian."[7] Daane's approach to Barth was cautious:

> I know of no distinctive doctrinal formulation of Barth which Reformed theology ought to accept as a substitute for its own. I cannot recommend that any particular Reformed doctrine be discarded and replaced by one taken over from Barth. This is not the way to learn from Barth.
>
> Perhaps it were better not to ask whether we can learn from Barth, but instead to ask whether by the study of Barth we can learn some things for ourselves. Can a study of Barth help us to discover the weak, soft spots, the undeveloped areas in Reformed theological thought? Can he arouse us to the inadequacies of our long, embittered, and fruitless theological controversies? Can a study of his thought help us to help ourselves to put an end to our long season of theological quest and advance?
>
> I think a study of Barth *can* help us to help ourselves. . . . As for me, I am not willing simply to swap doctrines with Barth. But I do believe that a study of his thought may jab us awake and give us that new and much needed theological vigor and excitement necessary to look again and learn from our theological history and to thrust out in new avenues of approach so that our theology may again be on the move. Enriched and deepened, it may again be a name in the world and a force to be reckoned with.[8]

### Bloesch: Invaluable Ally and Useful Foil

Donald G. Bloesch, one of the issuers of the Chicago Call,[9] has also shown an interest in Barth. In his book *The Evangelical Renaissance* Bloesch pointed out that among his other efforts "I have also sought to reassess the contribution of Karl Barth, showing how it is possible to learn from his theology even while not embracing it as the answer for our times."[10] Bloesch wrote:

> While openly questioning much of what Barth says, we think that it is possible to appreciate some of his novel and daring formulations of the age-old truths of the Bible. Even though not wishing to be known as Barthian or neo-Barthian, we believe

that Barth must be taken with the utmost seriousness by any theologian of evangelical or Reformed persuasion.... First of all it should be said that Karl Barth is himself an evangelical theologian.[11]

Evangelicals, continued Bloesch, can stand with Barth on several points. They should applaud Barth's call for a theology of revelation, his affirmation of the wrath of God and divine holiness as well as God's love, and his "ardent espousal of the substitutionary atonement of Christ."[12]

Barth's defense of the Virgin Birth of Christ and His bodily resurrection likewise marks him as an evangelical.... His brilliant exposition of the doctrine of the Trinity should also be appreciated by those of an orthodox persuasion.... Finally Barth's understanding of prayer as being primarily and essentially heartfelt supplication before a holy and merciful God can surely be recognized as biblical and evangelical.[13]

Bloesch also had some reservations, however: "Although Barth can be considered for the most part to be an evangelical theologian, this is not to gainsay that there are nonbiblical and even philosophical elements in his theology."[14] Bloesch had difficulty with Barth over a natural knowledge of God, universalism in salvation, the existence of evil, Christian belief and various lesser problems stemming from these.[15] Bloesch concluded

We regard him as a brother within the evangelical and Reformed family but one who perhaps at times has sought to be too inclusive, too open to the world....

In my estimation one has the right to criticize Barth only when one sees the errors that he warns against and seeks to counteract. Barth's contribution to the contemporary theological discussion must be taken seriously. This great theologian cannot be dismissed, for too much of what he says rings true. Even those who find themselves in serious disagreement with him would benefit from wrestling with his works.[16]

In a later book, *Jesus Is Victor! Karl Barth's Doctrine of Salvation,* Bloesch began by stating, "I have been led to write this book partly in order to counteract popular misunderstandings of Karl Barth's theology and also partly to show how authentically modern Barth really is.... It is also my purpose to demonstrate that Barth falls short of constructing a theology that is both fully evangelical and catholic, though he has made great strides toward it."[17] Further on he said:

I must admit that when I first began this project I was more averse to Barth's doctrine of salvation than when I ended. I became more positively disposed toward Barth as I continued my research, though I expect I shall never be a bona fide Barthian. His influence is definitely perceptible in many of my earlier writings. For some time his theological method has elicited my admiration and support. I have nevertheless always sought to maintain a critical stance, which may disconcert some thoroughgoing Barthians. In some areas of theology Barth has been an invaluable ally and in other areas a useful foil.[18]

In this same book Bloesch devoted a chapter to a discussion of Barth's "continuing relevance."[19] He identified scholars "who have treated Barth sympathetically though not uncritically," and those among Barth's "more negative critics."[20] Bloesch pointed out that "lately, with the rise of a theology of interpersonal relations in evangelical circles, there have been signs of a reaction in favor of more objectivity in theology, and Barth's position is now being entertained as a viable option."[21] But, wrote Bloesch, "Karl Barth's theology just as it stands cannot be the answer for the church of tomorrow, since it is too one-sided in its emphasis on the rational over the mystical and sacramental."[22] Nevertheless, the church cannot ignore Barth in the future any more than it can in the present because "the battles that he fought and won will have to be recognized and appreciated by any new theology that seeks to be at the same time evangelical and catholic."[23]

### Ramm and Runia: Running the Risk

Bernard Ramm, who like Bloesch had done graduate study in Basel under Barth, was in favor of a "dialectical" reading of Barth. In his book *The Evangelical Heritage* Ramm provided a short section on "the evangelical response to neo-orthodoxy."[24] He noted three responses. The first, based on the fundamentalists' assumption that all Protestant theologies were either liberal or evangelical, was to call the neo-orthodox "neo-liberals."[25] This group was represented by Van Til. Second, "the opposite of Van Til's assessment would be to urge that in the truest and most historic sense of the word Barth is orthodox."[26] This conclusion was reached by Helmut Gollwitzer, Otto Weber, Arthur Cochrane, and Thomas F. Torrance.[27] The third possible response, and the one Ramm espoused, was to read Barth dialectically:

> To react uncritically with a theologian is to accept every line he writes as gospel truth. To react negatively to a theologian is to attempt to shred everything the man writes. To react dialectically is to read a theologian and assess, evaluate, judge, weigh, criticize, approve, and so on. . . .
>
> The evangelical who reads Barth dialectically is just as ready to grant Barth one point as to criticize him at another. This means being very hard on Barth when he clearly drifts away from historical evangelical positions but applauding him when he scores a point. Obviously, each evangelical who reads Barth dialectically differs enormously in what he accepts and what he criticizes.[28]

Others representative of this response, Ramm said, include Gordon H. Clark, G. W. Bromiley, Klaas Runia, and G. C. Berkouwer.[29] Utilizing this approach in his next section, Ramm identified various elements of value an evangelical could acquire.[30] These included an appreciation for the attacks mounted against liberalism, the renewed summons to Scripture as the source and authority of theology, the return to the Reformers and the interaction with the whole history of theology.[31] But what of the risks encountered in studying a Barth or Brunner? Ramm answered:

> The fear of many evangelicals and fundamentalists is that this is a risk. How can a person read these men without being converted to their theology or being pulled out of the evangelical orbit? The plain truth is that there is no education without risk. If a school indoctrinates, it does not educate. Furthermore, carefully controlled indoctrinated teaching may create radical rebellion rather than conformity. Furthermore, the student not exposed to nonevangelical options in an evangelical atmosphere is an easy prey to a nonevangelical option offered in other circumstances. Play the game any way you want. You cannot eliminate risk. Yes, there is risk in the serious study of Barth and Brunner. But serious risk in any discipline is the price of real scholarship, so if we want the scholarship we have to run the risk.[32]

Klaas Runia "ran the risk" in producing his major study, *Karl Barth's Doctrine of Holy Scripture*. Runia, a Dutch Reformed theologian, followed Berkouwer in his approach and basic conclusions. While applauding Barth's starting point[33] as well as various points Barth brought forward, Runia did not hesitate to criticize where he found faults. The result of Runia's labors was what G. W. Bromiley hailed "a valuable work which deserves to be widely studied and which should serve as a model for similar investigations into the many detailed themes of the *Dogmatics*."[34]

### Bromiley, Packer and Ladd: Worthy of Respect

Bromiley, translator and general editor of the *Church Dogmatics*, found in Barth qualities "which we cannot fail to respect, which we may seek to emulate even in our criticisms and which we should covet earnestly for all theological endeavor."[35] Bromiley also sounded a warning concerning the problems in evaluating Barth:

Barth covers so wide a field in his *Church Dogmatics*, and his material is so closely interrelated, that evaluation is extremely difficult. In the last analysis, it is necessary to work through the exegetical and historical matter in detail before there can be confident judgment on his statements. A thorough knowledge of the whole *Dogmatics* is also required, for the various themes may appear in different connections and there is even an element of emendation or retraction. To try to proceed only in terms of broader points of censure or commendation is to run a high risk of facile and misleading generalization.

There is also a problem of approach. Some men's works are so obviously biblical or unbiblical in the orthodox sense that a clear-cut position may be taken regarding them. Barth, however, attempts a biblical and evangelical dogmatics which cuts across established orthodoxy at many points. This makes a definite attitude more difficult. Almost all readers will find things they approve and things they suspect or condemn. But how is a final assessment to be made? Is the good to be interpreted in terms of the bad and discounted? Is the bad to be exculpated by reason of the good? Even in an objective statement of defects and qualities much may depend upon the emphasis. A semi-Pelagian may be the same, but not sound the

same, as a semi-Augustinian. The stress and even the order may
be enough to tip the scales.[36]

Bromiley decided, "This opens the way to the only possible conclusion. Without some measure of improper partisanship, it is
difficult to strike a balance between the more dubious and the
more solid aspects. It is possible, however, to bring out certain
more general features ... which are commendable and exem-
plary."[37]

J. I. Packer commended Barth for his quest for unitive theological exegesis, but added, "If we think that his venture was not
wholly a success, it behooves us not to dismiss his objective, but to
take the task in hand ourselves and try to do better."[38] Although
Packer accused Barth of "an inadequate grasp of God's sovereignty
over all His world,"[39] and found Barth's view of history his most
fundamental weakness, there nevertheless was in Barth something in which to rejoice. As Packer had expressed it earlier, Barth
represented "a recognizable recovery ... of a Christ-centered,
redemption-rooted faith in the living God."[40]

George Ladd, in contrast to Packer, had earlier expressed appreciation of Barth's perspective on history:

> The basic problem for the modern theologian is this, Shall we
> insist upon a definition of history broad enough to include such
> suprahistorical events as the resurrection; or shall we accept
> the modern view of history as a working method but insist that
> there is a dimension within history which transcends historical
> control? The latter is the method of Karl Barth; and it appears
> to be the only adequate explanation which satisfies the data of
> redemptive history.[41]

## Henry: A Way to Fruitful Interchange

Carl F. H. Henry could well serve as a model of the kind of dialectical reading of Barth recommended by Ramm. Henry did not hesitate to disagree sharply with Barth on some points and uphold him
on others. In 1948 Henry commended Barth's protest against the
usual practice of Protestant dogmatics to treat first the attributes
of God and then append a discussion of his triune nature.[42] But
Henry also felt that "one of the major weaknesses in the Barthian
position is that of objective authority, in view of the lessened
centrality given the Bible in Barth's view of revelation."[43] In

another 1948 publication, *The Protestant Dilemma,* Henry wondered if Barth had "fully escaped the influence of Rationalism."[44] Following Van Til's general analysis, Henry traced Barth and Brunner back through Bergson and Kierkegaard to Kant.[45] He accused Barth of an "over-simplified reductionism" in equating Jesus as the Word of God.[46]

By 1957 Henry showed greater reliance on the work of Berkouwer than on that of Van Til. He agreed with Berkouwer that "Barth's basic theme is triumphant grace in Christ."[47] Now Henry could say of Barth: "Doubtless he raised long-neglected evangelical doctrines to a position of earnest theological importance and study. On the other hand, his present theological position revolts against elements in both Reformation and biblical theology."[48] Henry found that "nowhere is the Barth-Brunner theology more disappointing than in . . . exalting Schleiermacher's objectionable definition of revelation."[49] However, the concepts of the Trinity, of redemption and of atonement as treated by Barth represent a positive move in modern theology. "From the standpoint of a vagabond liberalism, such concepts reflect an evangelically oriented framework toward which contemporary theology is being propelled."[50] Yet "the dialectical approach accomplishes only a limited return to biblical theology and provides only a relative opposition to liberal theology."[51] Therefore, "only with caution . . . may the evangelical speak of a debt to Barth."[52]

Following Schleiermacher's understanding of revelation, Barth refused to identify the Bible directly with the revealed Word of God, and his "return" to the Bible was thus hindered. Henry commented, "Beneath this halting return to the Bible lurks a dialectical prejudice that imparts an anti-intellectual turn to the neo-orthodox view of divine self-disclosure and hence to its definitions of revelation and inspiration."[53] Barth failed "to acknowledge the inspiration or 'inspiredness' which the New Testament ascribes to Scripture (II Tim. 3:16), and on which evangelical theology therefore insists."[54] Despite this, Henry discovered that "even with respect to Scripture as the norm of Christian doctrine, Barth has given us many statements which, as far as they go, have an evangelical ring and rigor."[55]

In *Christian Personal Ethics,* also published in 1957, Henry again linked Barth with Kierkegaard under the banner of "revelational existentialism."[56] While it seemed to Henry that Barth was "not as antithetical as many writers assume,"[57] this fact must be understood rightly. "It is necessary to show that the ethical perspectives of Kierkegaard, Barth, and Brunner are rooted fundamentally in a philosophical perspective rather than in any special Divine revelation."[58]

In 1960, in a *Christianity Today* editorial entitled "Barth Among the Mind-Changers: Some Unresolved Issues," Henry commented:

> Not a few evangelical writers feel that, while he may not subjectivize the Gospel as Bultmann finally does, he sets it in a sphere of transcendence which breaks its contact with true history and thus deprives it of genuine objectivity. If this is true, the *Dogmatics* is vitiated from the outset and must finally be adjudged a liberal work in spite of its express intention and the apparently good points or passages to be found in it. On the other hand, some contend that there is an intrinsic improbability in this reading in view of Barth's explicit aim and the fact that Barth himself dismisses as misconceived caricatures the various representations of this kind, usually drawn for the most part from his earlier writings.[59]

Later in 1960, in a news feature for *Christianity Today,* Henry wrote:

> Whatever its inadequacies, Barth's theology must be credited with a remarkable influence on Swiss church life.... Barth provoked many of the clergy to a searching of the Bible in quest of its unique message. Before his impact, week-night Bible meetings were scorned as an activity of "narrow-minded pietists," Sunday School classes and youth guilds were to be found only outside the "regular" churches, which administered the Lord's Supper only four times a year. Today a congregation... is considered abnormal if it lacks a Bible meeting, Sunday School classes and youth guild, and many churches are introducing a monthly communion service.[60]

In 1964, in his *Frontiers in Modern Theology,* Henry explored the "differences which have increased markedly with the years" between Barth and Bultmann so that "the contrariety of their positions cannot be denied."[61] However, Henry complained, "while a dialectical theologian like Barth deplores the vagaries of Bultmann's existentialism, his own strongly asserted 'objectifying elements' remain inaccessible to objective reason and historical research."[62] In fact, for Henry, Barth's objectification in theology left Barth open to the charge of subjective tampering since these so-called objective elements appeared to remain closed to scrutiny.

Henry was especially sharp in his criticism of the manner in which Barth handled history: "Karl Barth absorbed history into the decrees of God and emptied it of revelation-content by locating justification in creation and by viewing all men as elect in the man-Jesus."[63] "Barth ... by distinguishing *Geschichte* from *Historie* obscured Christianity's historical foundations."[64] Thus Barth too was ultimately threatened by subjectivity.

In an earlier piece of writing Henry had identified this problem as a basic issue in assessing Barth. Henry asked "whether Barth's claim that faith seeks understanding—that is, genuine knowledge of the Religious Object—is worked out by Barth so as to assure knowledge that is universally valid apart from subjective decision."[65] Yet, as Henry also pointed out, in *Frontiers in Modern Theology,* Barth did seek to avoid an empty subjectivism. Henry noted that "in later writings Barth affirms that God is an object of knowledge: God's revelation in Christ provides a basis for genuine ontological statements."[66]

Henry's *Faith at the Frontiers,* published in 1969, still worried that Barth compressed divine revelation into "a christomonistic reduction of ontological knowledge."[67] But, as he had seen earlier, "because there is little else, the dogmatics of Barth and Brunner, appropriated critically, serve as the main theological supply of many conservative students."[68] Henry wrote, "It is important ... that the evangelical ... response be concerned with ... genuine rather than perhaps illusory defects and qualities."[69] Proper response, concluded Henry, would open the way "to fruitful interchange which may lead, not merely to clearing up misunderstandings, but to putting right the defects and harnessing significant emphases to the service of biblical truth and evangelical witness."[70] In another work he adds: "It remains for evangelical theology, however, to reinforce the still inadequate positions to which Barth and Brunner have lifted much of the prevailing theological outlook by setting forth the basis and content of sturdier biblical claims."[71]

## Bruce and Bockmuehl: In the Reformation Tradition

F. F. Bruce was quite succinct in his appraisal of Barth. A printed dialog with Bruce speaks clearly:

Q. I am considerably perplexed by the variety of opinions I hear expressed about the orthodoxy of Karl Barth. According to some evangelical leaders, he was the pioneer in a return to truly biblical theology; according to others, he was a dangerous neo-modernist, all the more dangerous because of his use of orthodox terminology. Where does the truth lie?

A. It lies much more with the former representation than with the latter. Barth stood squarely within the Reformation tradition. . . . There is no point in continuing to criticize him on the basis of writings which he later considered himself to have outgrown as belonging to his "egg-shell" stage.[72]

Klaus Bockmuehl wrote of Barth that "faith was real to him, and his letters show a cheerful spirituality that not all theologians call their own. . . . Barth in his later years turned more and more to the Scriptures as the only source of theology, refusing domination by philosophies."[73] He warned though that "Barth's theology needs to be tested, and not a little of it contested. . . . Barth was 'a man with his contradictions.' But he was also a father in Christ, a man of God, and we see him drawing always nearer to the authority of God's Word."[74]

## Neo-modernist or Neo-evangelical?

Was Karl Barth a dangerous neo-modernist, or was he a pilgrim on a journey that brought him ever closer to evangelical faith? Can the matter be decided, or is it a matter of simply casting ballots? Helmut Thielicke has observed: "In every theological controversy . . . a point is reached where one has to say to the other side that the thrust of your thinking seems to point in a specific direction. . . . You may mount all kinds of rear-guard or flanking movements with the help of massive arguments, but my assessment cannot be shaken."[75] Otherwise, "a purely intellectual encounter in question and answer form can go on forever and never reach a decision."[76]

The evangelical response to Barth has seen the alignment of scholars along two lines. Both sides have formulated their decision with regard to Barth. The one side—"negative" in that it cannot accept Barth except as an example of what must be avoided, resisted and overcome—points to the data confidently in the expectation that it will again and again show a neo-modernist. The other side—"positive" in that it welcomes evangelical elements in Barth while still finding his theology a "mixed bag"—warns of finding in Barth "what is not there" and insists that the data substantiates its claims.

Which side is right? Together, the two lines of response have created an evangelical impasse. Each side has seen the thrust of the other and still argued that "my assessment cannot be shaken." Yet the question of Karl Barth's potential as a resource for evangelicalism transcends purely intellectual encounters between the two sides. It strikes to the heart of the current dilemma.

Karl Barth presents to evangelicalism a crucial decision. To accept the man as an example and his theology as a positive resource means to answer the question of evangelical identity in a much different manner than that advocated by Barth's "negative" critics. Barth's acceptance also raises afresh the question of evangelical unity. Will those who grapple with Barth be the victims or perpetrators of division? Can evangelicals risk redeeming Barth's theology, or is such a task even necessary? Finally, the issue of Barth's eventual acceptance or rejection must reflect to some degree on the validity of maintaining a substantially unchanged orthodoxy in the modern world.

The thesis of this study is that the "positive" critics are nearer the truth in regard to Barth, that Barth did move progressively closer to the older orthodoxy, and that he can teach evangelicals much of great value. As has been seen, this conclusion is disputed. Obviously, therefore, it is necessary to review the data, even though this can be done here only in part. The discussion in part three is admittedly sympathetic, in that many characteristic criticisms are omitted. The goal is exposition rather than criticism.

# Part III

## Barth's Theology

# 9

# Barth's Method

A ny effort to understand Barth's theology must take into account the context of his upbringing, education and early experiences as a pastor. This is particularly true because of the pronounced changes he underwent. Failure to take into account his personal pilgrimage and the marked changes in his perspective has served to lead many of his interpreters and critics astray.

## A Pilgrim Theology
Karl Barth, born in 1886, was the son of Fritz Barth, a conservative Reformed pastor and theologian. This simple fact, the "existential given," has been too little considered. Yet the influences of his early training and the context in which it occurred played a more instrumental role in Karl Barth's development than has usually been thought. It has often been forgotten that Barth's theological training was until 1906 conducted principally under conservative scholarship. In the light of new understanding provided by the social and behavioral sciences it is no longer permissible to ignore these early influences.[1]

Nevertheless it remains true that during the period 1908-15, Barth, under the influence of Harnack, Gunkel and above all Hermann, became an uneasy convert to liberalism. Ritschlian *manity of God* appeared. Comprising three essays, it provided a clear glimpse into Barth's maturing theology and also showed some of the great breadth of Barth's expertise. The first essay was historical, the second, autobiographical and dogmatic; and the third, ethical. In these essays Barth revealed his growing concern to speak in ever more biblical terms about God. This, he declared, meant realizing more fully that "who God is and what He is in His deity He proves and reveals not in a vacuum as a divine being-for-Himself, but precisely and authentically in the fact that He exists, speaks and acts as the *partner* of man, though of course as the absolutely superior partner. He who does *that* is the living God. And the freedom in which He does *that* is His deity."[10]

Not long afterward Barth was faced with retirement. Rather than introduce yet another part of his *Church Dogmatics,* he chose to lecture on what, as he put it, "I have basically sought, learned, and represented from among all the paths and detours in the field of evangelical theology."[11] Barth, however, did not wish to do this in the form of a final summary of his theology. Nor did he desire to reiterate what had been said before. So he chose the form of an introductory presentation on evangelical theology, "that theology which treats of the *God of the Gospel.*"[12]

Typically, publication of *Evangelical Theology: An Introduction* was not regarded by Barth as his final word. An interesting dialog recorded during his 1962 visit to the United States makes that clear:

*Question:* "When you first began writing Dogmatics, you called it 'Christian Dogmatics.' Then you changed it to 'Church Dogmatics.' Now you've given these lectures under the title of 'Evangelical Theology.' Do these changes indicate changes in your thinking about the task or place of theology?"

*Answer:* "Well, let me try to give a thoughtful answer to this question. Here we have a good example of a theologian who is clearly a human being and who lives in time and moves with time. Why not? It would be a dull sort of theology if I had stayed simply in the 'twenties, or in the 'thirties. No, I *must* grow old and so here in this question you have an illustration of the movement through which I have gone as a theologian. From 'Christian Dogmatics' to 'Church Dogmatics' and now 'Evangelical Theology'—I ask you to see this movement as one

towards a less formal, more material, less abstract, more concrete kind of thinking. I don't know whether I will ever find a
fourth way! This certainly is not the last word, but I think for the
moment it is a satisfactory word."[13]
Right up to his death, Karl Barth continued to search and find
better expressions for the truth of God in Jesus Christ. The evening of his last day found him still laboring over the theology of
the church. In fact, he was exploring the future. He challenged the
church to set out, to return and to confess. In his last words it is
still true for Barth that "in Jesus Christ we may take seriously,
and rejoice in what we truly are in him who was and is and will be,
even Jesus Christ, our Lord and Savior."[14]

### Barth's Intent

Although Barth lived a long life, and although he grew as a theologian, certain features of both his life and thought were constant.
Yet it is possible to sketch his diversity even within this unity.
Being and becoming, essence and act, stood inseparably together
in Barth. Thus the pilgrim theologian was never lost when Barth
found his home in Christ. The continuity has at times been over-
emphasized but its existence must be noted.

The developmental aspect of Barth's theology has already been
briefly set forth above. That development bore the character of a
slow but steady maturing. The importance of the changes in
Barth's conclusions cannot be denied. But closer attention must
now be given to Barth's *methodological* development, examining
both his intent and methods at each place along the way.

From the beginning Barth's intent was both prophetic and pastoral. To be more exact, the prophetic nature of Barth's work
stemmed from his pastoral concerns. "It is difficult to understand
Barth without considering that he started as a preacher,"[15] Herzog reminds us. As a young pastor Barth was confronted by the
peculiar pastoral problem of the sermon. When liberal theology
proved inadequate he turned to the Bible. What he found there he
expressed in his preface to the first edition of *The Epistle to the
Romans*. Barth then believed that "if we rightly understand ourselves, our problems are the problems of Paul; and if we be en-
lightened by the brightness of his answers, those answers must be
ours."[16]

In the preface to the second edition, as Barth sorted out the criticisms to the first edition and responded to them, he indicted liberal theology for its bankruptcy in preparing men for the pastoral ministry. He charged:

> I myself know what it means year in year out to mount the steps of the pulpit, conscious of the responsibility to understand and to interpret and longing to fulfill it; and yet, utterly incapable, because at the University I had never been brought beyond that well-known "Awe in the presence of History" which means in the end no more than that all hope of engaging in the dignity of understanding and interpretation has been surrendered.[17]

Barth's sense of urgency in his ministry demanded more than historical and literary criticism could deliver. He was aware that each Sunday morning "there is in the air an *expectancy* that something great, crucial, and even momentous is to *happen*."[18] It was at this point that Barth said, "If then I have not only a *view*point, but something also of a *stand*point, it is simply the familiar standpoint of the man in the pulpit. Before him lies the Bible, full of mystery: and before him are seated his more or less numerous hearers, also full of mystery—and what indeed is more so? *What now?* asks the minister."[19]

To answer that question Barth examined the content of the pastoral task and its difficulty. He found that all ministers were placed in a common situation to which they must respond. He characterized this by the following formulations: *"As ministers we ought to speak of God. We are human, however, and so cannot speak of God. We ought therefore to recognize both* our obligation and our inability *and by that very recognition give God the glory.* This is our perplexity."[20]

At that point it seemed to Barth that all he could say was "the word of God is at once the necessary and impossible task of the minister."[21] The paradox in which the minister found himself, however, could not remain for Barth the final word. Although he continued to speak with dialectical language, he sought to move beyond crisis to resolution. Fully aware of the immensity of saying anything at all, he was still convinced of the absolute necessity of having something said. What he wanted to hear was God's Word.

In the midst of his search to find a way out of the dilemma, Barth read Anselm. Soon he could say of Anselm, "My view is . . .

we are confronted by a very pronounced rejection of speculation that does not respect the incomprehensibility of the reality of the object of faith, by a recognition of the indirectness of all knowledge of God, and . . . by the reference to the Pattern of faith which is the basis of everything."[22]

Barth could say that not only of Anselm but of himself as well. Philosophical speculation could not speak of God or say anything meaningful for Christian faith. Christian theology, on the other hand, could give God the glory through its affirmations. Thus, deep into his work on his *Church Dogmatics,* Barth could say, "Several are seeking to track down the secret of the real or ostensible change of direction which I am supposed to have made sometime between 1932 and 1938, or rather later according to some scholars. From my own standpoint, the comparatively simple truth is that, although I still enjoy debate, I have gradually acquired more and more feeling for the affirmations by and with which we can live and die."[23]

As Barth concentrated on these affirmations he discovered two things about himself and his theological vocation. The first related to his twelve years in the pastorate. He recalled, "It was extremely fruitful for me . . . to be compelled to engage myself much more earnestly than ever before with the Bible as the root of all Christian thinking and teaching."[24] This led him to his second discovery, the conviction that theological training must orient itself to Scripture if it would serve the church and prepare the pastor. Thus he stated, "The aim of teaching systematic theology, as I see it, consists in the student's learning to orientate his thought as rigorously as possible within the message entrusted to the Church, a practice which is indispensable for his future work as pastor of a church as for any academic occupation which may fall to him later on."[25]

As student, pastor and teacher, Barth was mindful not only of the centrality of the gospel but of its nature as well: "Its content is message, *kerygma,* proclamation. Indeed it is message of a special kind, namely, the message which brings and is calculated to awaken joy."[26] Because he had to say something as a pastor, that something could only be God's Word. Hence he was also a prophet. It was not the latter leading to the former. Rather, one was a prophet because the pastoral task must always be "to say that *God* becomes *man,* but to say it as God's word, as God *himself* says it."[27]

Pastoral proclamation has a note of authority. The prophetic voice, speaking God's Word, is the voice of power and authority. And Barth certainly spoke with authority. Critics were sometimes moved to complain that Barth wrote "as though he were sitting in the lap of God and laying bare the very heart of the Almighty, telling the seeking world just what God has to say about all sorts of things."[28] Such criticism misses the point. Hans Urs von Balthasar was much nearer the truth:

> The whole pageant of Barthian theology, from its earliest days on, was dominated by the same single-minded preoccupation. Barth was consumed with a passion for God. His outlook and terminology may change, but he resolutely refused to move one inch away from the center where Revelation, biblical man, and the upright believer reside. Not for one moment did he forget that the purpose of creation is to give glory to God. His aim was to spell out this glory, to show his love for it, and to reveal its grandeur. Rarely in Christian circles has love for God echoed so forcefully through a man's lifetime work.[29]

## The Method and Message from Romans through Anselm

To extol God was Barth's aim, and to proclaim the Word of God was his means to that end. Simply put, the message of the church is, for Barth, the gospel—and the good news is Jesus Christ, the glory of God. The pastor must preach, and from the beginning Barth sought to answer questions surrounding the sermon. As Herzog comments, "The well-known situation of the pastor working at two desks in his study, the historical-critical and the practical, was deplored by many, but Barth made a constructive effort to make one desk out of the two. Herein we may find the strongest impetus which led Karl Barth to put his hand to the plow in an unusually determined way."[30]

In *The Epistle to the Romans* (first edition) Barth determined "to see through and beyond history into the spirit of the Bible, which is the Eternal Spirit."[31] But that did not, as far as he could see, mean having to choose between the historical-critical method of investigation and the doctrine of inspiration. Although he confessed that if driven to choose between the two he would "without hesitation" adopt the latter, he was able also to say, "I am not compelled to choose between the two."[32]

Putting his two desks together produced a startling result. The distillation of the first edition provided by Hans Urs von Balthasar is enlightening:

> The theme is dynamic eschatology, the irreversible movement from a doomed temporal order to a new living order ruled by God, the total restoration *(apokatastasis)* of the original, ideal creation in God. This movement of a doomed world, which still knows its true origin but cannot get back to it on its own, is due solely to God, who shows his mercy in Christ. In Christ he implants life in the dead cosmos. In Christ he implants a seed which will sprout and spread overpoweringly until everything is transformed back into its original splendor. All this will not take place in plain view but will work itself out eschatologically.[33]

Barth's enthusiastic vision was met by mixed reviews. His own growth, aided by the critics, convinced him to rewrite the commentary. In the second edition Barth confessed:

> I know that I have laid myself open to the charge of imposing a meaning upon the text rather than extracting its meaning from it, and that my method implies this. My reply is that, if I have a system, it is limited to a recognition of what Kierkegaard called the 'infinite qualitative distinction' between time and eternity, and to my regarding this as possessing negative as well as positive significance: 'God is in heaven, and thou art on earth.'[34]

By so voicing this conviction Barth understood himself to be a descendant of the theological line running back through Kierkegaard, Luther, Calvin, the apostle Paul and the prophet Jeremiah. That line, however, did not include Schleiermacher in Barth's estimation, because Schleiermacher had an inadequate view of human need and because "one can *not* speak of God simply by speaking of man in a loud voice."[35] Barth was sensitive to what Paul had to say; what Paul said was entirely about an awesome, transcendent God. Despite the distance of the call from God to humankind, the content of the message was very good news indeed.

In *The Epistle to the Romans,* both editions, Barth was concerned with exegesis. As late as 1932 he was still pressed by criticism to reassert that "my sole aim was to interpret Scripture."[36] Yet intentional or not, a *theology* emerged from the commentary unlike any other theology of the time. The minister suddenly found himself preaching to a great many people. Barth, the village pastor, was directed to the task of theologizing. Torrance comments, "It is because he is a preacher that the preacher has forced upon him the critical task of theology, but because he is a preacher he must also go on to take up the positive task of theology, in seeking to unfold and develop the content of the Church's message by the rigorous control of exegesis and under the guidance of the historic confessions of the Church."[37]

The theological method that Barth took up in the period of 1921-31 was dialectical. In the necessity and impossibility of speaking about God, Barth discerned three directions that might be taken in trying to solve the problem. Dogmatism and self-criticism, the first two, have merit in many dimensions but cannot allow a person to speak truly about God. Neither can the third alternative, dialectics, although "it is the way of Paul and the Reformers, and intrinsically it is by far the best."[38]

Dialectics, to Barth, was the way of witness. "The word dialectic ... refers to a process of setting one word against another ... in order to point out a direction or find a way through this unavoidable vis-à-vis."[39] Thus, for example, the term *Yes* might be set over against the term *No* in order to say what neither term alone is able to convey. By using dialectics, Barth felt he was best able to preserve the hiddenness of God while, at the same time, doing justice to his revelation. In that regard it is the function of dialectics to "defend the divine quality of Revelation."[40] So the pastor who may not speak about God is able to give God the glory by pointing to him.

As Hans Urs von Balthasar has pointed out, Barth adopted dialectics because "theology needs dialectics to serve as a continuing *warning sign* and *corrective*."[41] Torrance is correct in seeing how much Barth's dialectical thinking owed to Kierkegaard and how for both, communication through dialectics "all hinges upon the concrete historical reality of God in Jesus Christ."[42] Both Von Balthasar and Torrance have pointed out that in his dialectical thinking Barth was engaged in a struggle. He had to reckon with the problems of theological and philosophical language.

When he had fought through to a resolution of these, he could drop the dialectical form and move to an even more positive manner of theology. That shift was from dialectics to analogy.[43] Torrance has identified several dominant concerns that emerged during Barth's dialectical period.

First, Barth questioned the pervasive immanentism, reductionism and anthropocentrism of liberal Protestantism. Against it he brought at least two principal charges. To begin with, liberal theology had forsaken its proper task. Its identification with culture by its subjection to culture ultimately rendered it an anachronism. Further, liberal theology had forsaken the object and content of faith. It had focused instead on faith itself and had displaced God with religious self-awareness.

Second, in Barth's teaching a profound and realistic conception of sin became evident. Luther, Kierkegaard, J. Müller, Dostoyevsky, Kähler and above all the apostle Paul heavily influenced him. Several concepts were stressed by Barth in his doctrine of sin. First, sin is dominant in the world; all human existence is conditioned by it. Second, death clearly reveals the negative, broken relationship between God and human beings. Third, human sin is bounded and limited by the judgment of God. In other words, sin must also be seen from God's side. Seen from man's side, sin in its loftiest form is religion; it expresses man's utmost possibility, yet also his limitation. At the point of confrontation between man and God, man steps forward in rebellion. Contrasted to this is grace, which is God's claim on and over humankind. Grace is the divine possibility for human beings that establishes the positive truth of religion, the law and ethics.

Third, Barth made eschatology a dominant motif. In this he was influenced principally by Blumhardt, Overbeck and Johannes Weiss. To a lesser extent Bengel and Schweitzer were also influential. Barth gave up a timeless eschatology to rethink the doctrine Christologically. He began to view eschatology as focused not on *eschaton,* but on *Eschatos,* that is, on Christ who is both the First and the Last.

Fourth, Barth's dialectical thinking was so notorious that his theology became identified with it during that period. That way of thinking stresses that God speaks, man hears and only then does man speak in obedience what he has heard. Dialectical theology came about as a new attempt to do justice to the witness of the Bible to the revelation of God. Barth's dialectic was vastly different from that of Hegel in that no synthesis was sought. Rather, both the *Yes* and the *No* of God's Word to man were allowed to stand and to speak through each other.

Fifth, Barth became vitally interested in the church. Early on, Barth saw the church's theological relevance in its character as a negative counterpart to the kingdom of God. Somewhat later he corrected that notion. He then saw the church to be the place where the God/man relationship in grace takes place. With its source and ground in God's grace, and arising from election and revelation, the church is the vehicle of God's revelation and grace into human time and history. The church, however, is not itself God's revelation nor is its history God's revelation. It is and remains under the judgment of God's grace as it awaits Christ's return.[44]

The climax of Barth's dialectical period came when his *Christliche Dogmatik* was published in 1927. Unlike *The Epistle to the Romans,* the new book did not contain the same total rejection of "religion." Though still viewed as the archenemy of revelation, religion, too, was seen as open to God's redemption. "Nevertheless, certain themes and motifs from *Romans* crop up in the *Prolegomena;* their presence eventually forced Barth to reject his new formulation and to start from scratch once again."[45]

In the summer of 1930 Barth began to study Anselm. When the publication of his results appeared in 1931, it represented "the decisive turning-point in his thinking, for it marks the final point in his advance from dialectical thinking to Church dogmatics."[46] Among Barth's findings at least six should be identified. First, faith's essential nature is *fides quaerens intellectum,* that is, "faith seeking understanding." Second, God is seen as *que mains cogitari nequit,* that is, "that which no greater can be conceived." This reaffirmed Barth's own thought of the exalted, ultimate objectivity of God. Third, true knowledge of the object in its objectivity requires penetration into its inner rationality. Fourth, the rational nature of knowledge demands a relation of likeness, or resemblance, between it and the object it approaches. That relation is not, as regards God, a natural point of contact in man. Instead, it arises from God's revelation, his self-communicating. Fifth, the rational nature of theological knowledge implies a correspondence between itself and the object. In other words, theological knowledge works with what is given to it by its object. When God is the object, faith is the specific mode of rationality, for it is only this that the object allows for the establishment and verification of knowledge. To insist on any other approach is the height of irrationality. Sixth, knowledge of the truth in relation to God moves from the ground given it by the object. That is, knowledge of God moves from actuality outward; it is *a posteriori*, after experience. Theology does not posit the possibility of God but proceeds from God's actuality.[47]

At last Barth was prepared to move on to the task of constructive theology. In 1932 he began publishing his *Church Dogmatics*. All that had gone on before now stood him in good stead. Divorcing himself from philosophy and discarding his strong dialectical form, Barth put to work his new insights. His steady focus on Christology became even more prominent. So, too, did his hermeneutics.

### Barth's Hermeneutics

As Bernard Ramm notes, "Karl Barth ushered in a new era in Biblical interpretation when he published his *Romerbrief* at the end of World War I."[48] But the methods by which Barth interpreted Romans brought a storm of criticism. Those who supported him became members of a vocal school for a new theology. That early hermeneutic, however, was not exactly defined and, in time, each crisis theologian moved it in his own particular direction. For Barth this meant an increasingly Christological concentration.

Barth's hermeneutical movement can be traced in two directions. First, as Herzog points out, *"he deepened the historical-critical method and supplemented it with a concern for wholeness encompassing text and subject-matter."*[49] By so doing, Barth found God's Word in the words of the Bible. Second, Barth not only went beyond strict historical criticism, but he also sought *"to correct Biblicism and the theory of verbal inspiration."*[50] He was concerned to stress the wholeness of the words and to take them with greater seriousness than either liberalism or biblicism had shown.

Barth faced the hermeneutical problem squarely and formulated a new response to it. That problem, which might be expressed in various ways, can be seen in the form of two questions. First, is there any continuity of experience in a world where change appears the only constant? Second, and more particularly, is there any continuity between the biblical world view and ours? These questions constitute the problem "to which Karl Barth addressed himself by pointing to *die Sache* which remains the same, notwithstanding the variety of its linguistic expressions."[51]

In pointing to *die Sache,* the substance of the biblical text, Barth found relevance for modern men and women. "The concentration on the subject matter (God, Jesus, grace, etc.) bridges the gap between the centuries, and it does so since they cannot but be the same."[52] That is why Barth found Paul speaking so forcefully. The issues that Paul addressed, and the answers he put forward, speak as eloquently to modern persons as to those of the first century. This is true because God stands above human history.

Barth elevated Christology to an exalted position in his hermeneutic. In doing so, he placed himself squarely in the middle of the Reformation tradition. As Brevard Childs has noted:

Calvin's interpretation of the Old Testament has been frequently misunderstood by modern scholars. On the one hand, Calvin inveighed against the fourfold use of Scripture that had been practiced by the fathers because it destroyed the certainty and clarity of Scripture.... He renounced allegory and demanded that the literal sense of Scripture *(sensus literalis)* be normative. Yet on the other hand, his own interpretation of the Old Testament frequently spoke of Jesus Christ and the life of the church. The usual explanation of this dual aspect as a sign of Calvin's inconsistency completely misses the point. For Calvin the literal sense of the Old Testament spoke of Jesus Christ. Once the term "literal sense" became identified with the historical sense, which happened in the eighteenth century, Calvin's position became unintelligible. To use another terminology, Calvin's literal sense refers to the plain sense of the text, but when interpreted within the canonical context of the church.[53]

For twentieth-century biblical scholarship an exalted Christology was both sensational and revolutionary. "Christological exegesis such as practiced by Luther and Calvin, among the Reformers, or by Barth, Bonhoeffer, or Vischer, among contemporaries, was almost universally eschewed."[54] But Barth brought a fresh vigor to theology with this starting point and sparked the biblical theology movement of the last few decades. Characteristically, however, Barth did not come to be closely identified with that movement. As Childs comments:

> Again, one of the curious things about the whole Biblical Theology Movement was its misunderstanding of Karl Barth's exegesis. . . . Usually it was dismissed by the Biblical theologians as well as by the older Liberals as 'precritical,' and at best tolerated as an unfortunate reaction against his past. Yet amazingly enough, Barth remained invulnerable to the weaknesses that beset the Biblical Theology Movement.[55]

As might be expected, Barth's understanding of hermeneutics came out of his pastoral concerns. By the time he had come to constructing the *Church Dogmatics* his thinking had vastly matured. When he addressed himself to the pastoral and ecclesiastical task of proclamation, Barth would not consider the use of any language within the church that was separated from Scripture. Such an isolated language would be arbitrary religious language. Rather, the proclamation of the church "must be language controlled and guided in the form of homily, that is, the exposition of Scripture."[56]

Accordingly, principles of interpretation must be not only sound but relevant. Dogmatics and preaching are intimately related. Theology does not operate in a vacuum but in the church. Proclamation cannot be empty but must be the content of Scripture. Thus, as has been noted by David Mueller, "In addition to the renaissance of exegesis and biblical theology which Barth's theology helped precipitate, one must recall that from first to last he intended his theology to undergird the preaching of the church. . . . This interest is also evident in the *Church Dogmatics*—a veritable treasure of biblical exegesis and exposition."[57]

Three fundamental hermeneutical principles supply the foundation for the exegesis found in the *Church Dogmatics*. First, and determinative for *Christian* theology, is the Christological principle. It is obvious that "in Barth's over-all strategy the Christological principle reigns supreme, namely, that Jesus Christ is the clarity of Scripture and the clarity of every doctrine of Scripture."[58] Every text of Scripture stands to bear witness to Jesus Christ. Perhaps to call that a principle, though, is to miss the point. Certainly Barth himself would not allow such an abstraction any conscious role in his theology.

Barth was keenly aware that "God's thoughts in His Word do not come to us *in abstracto* but *in concreto* in the form of the human word of prophets and apostles."[59] Moreover, as Barth realized, "the divine Word itself meets us right in the thick of that fog of our own intellectual life, as having taken the same form as our own ideas, thoughts and convictions."[60] It is no mere principle of interpretation that bids the exegete to relate a matter to and through Jesus Christ. It is the presence of Christ himself, as he is concretely witnessed to in the Scriptures, who beckons every person to hear and receive the Word of God.

So in a sense it is misleading to refer to a Christological principle. Rather, the presence of Christ necessitates the "principle of literal sense" as utilized by the Reformers. The *sensus literalis* always stands in the presence of Jesus Christ. The exegete, then, must aim at the meaning of the text. Barth comments:

> We might glance at this point at the excellent definition which Polanus has given of biblical interpretation:*Interpretatio sacrae Scripturae est explicatio veri sensus et usus illius, verbis perspicuis instituta ad gloriam Dei et aedificationem ecclesiae.* [The interpretation of Holy Scripture is the explication of the true sense and its practice; from clearly examined words interpretation has been established to the glory of God and the building up of the church.] ... From this we see that it is a question of (1) the *verus sensus* and (2) the *verus usus* of Scripture. Both remain obviously clear in and by themselves. Yet both need *explicatio;* hence there is a need of interpretation and application. The region of the *verba,* lying between the two, is problematical. Here there is a need, and there arises a responsibility. It is a question of the *verba perspicua* in regard both to the *sensus* and also the *usus* of Scripture. That the necessary work of communication should be done: *ad gloriam Dei et aedificationem ecclesiae,* is the task of *interpretation,* and therefore a matter of the responsibility laid upon members of the Church.[61]

This, in a nutshell, was Barth's perspective. He utilized observation, reflection and appropriation. These three stages included the work of historical and literary criticism, the interpretation and absorption of meaning, and a self-identification with the witness of Scripture.[62] In other words, Barth did not engage in a naive exegesis. Nor was his hermeneutic "pre-critical." Most especially was it not "spiritual" exegesis.

The second fundamental principle of hermeneutics discernible in the *Church Dogmatics* is the totality principle. "Barth has consistently worked from an avowed theological context, namely, from the context of the Christian canon."[63] The Scripture is the witness to the church of the Word of God. But it is not a witness in either abstraction or part. Just as it is a concrete witness, so it is a whole witness. Here, however, rises the question of canon. What constitutes the canon? Is every part of the Bible also a part of the canon? Is the canon closed? "Barth's own method of interpreting Scripture by Scripture throughout the whole of the *Church Dogmatics* is the best indication of his approach to the question of canon."[64]

With the context of canon, the context of any verse is the entire Scripture. Bernard Ramm has noted:

Barth defends some of his odd interpretations, especially in the Old Testament, by claiming that he has a right to bring the entire contents of Scripture to bear upon any particular passage. This is a principle difficult to manage, but it does say procedurally or programmatically that the "universe of discourse," the "locale," the "habitat" of any passage of Scripture is the total Scripture. It sets the general mood, gives the general perspective, governs the fundamental assumptions, or sets the possible limits of meaning for the interpreter of Holy Scripture.[65]

The third fundamental principle of hermeneutics is the faith principle. Both principles of *sensus literalis* and canonical context are implicit in the third. Faith is the hermeneutical principle *sine qua non* for the Church. Hermeneutics itself is a search for understanding. As Barth learned from Anselm, *"Credo ut intelligam* means: It is my very faith itself that summons me to knowledge."[66] *Credo ut intelligam,* that is, "I believe in order that I might understand," stands at the center of Christian hermeneutics and church dogmatics.

Taken together within the bounds of the *Church Dogmatics* these principles resulted in a body of invaluable exegesis. As William Fletcher, a critic of Barth, commented, "He gives a great deal of fresh insight into every area of theology, insight which is valid and Scriptural. And he is an able expositor of the Scriptures, bringing out meanings which other commentators miss time after time. He possesses a vast knowledge of the Bible and he usually lets the Bible speak for itself, letting Scripture interpret Scripture."[67]

Barth's exegesis is an essential foundation of the *Church Dogmatics*. In fact, "a number of the volumes of the *Dogmatics* are little more than huge commentaries accompanied by theological interpretation."[68] Obviously they provide a wealth of aids for a pastor. That is just as Barth intended. They provide more than simply commentary, however: "They are indispensable to a full understanding of the theological expositions preceding them, and anyone who wants to attack the latter will have to examine first whether the biblical exegesis on which they are based is at fault."[69]

# 10

# The Construction of the *Dogmatics*

In the previous chapter we traced the development of Barth's method, particularly his hermeneutical method, from the time of the first edition of *The Epistle to the Romans* up to the beginning of the *Church Dogmatics*. We saw that much of the *Dogmatics* centered in exegesis which was rooted in a Christological principle, a totality principle and a faith principle. As fundamental as exegesis was to Barth in constructing the massive *Church Dogmatics,* many other factors contributed as well. These other factors constitute the focus of this chapter.

## Theology and God's Freedom
In 1956 John Godsey made four general observations about the *Dogmatics*. First, he noted how its theology is bound to the sphere of the church. Second, he identified the role of biblical exegesis. Third, he found the incorporation of ethics in an integral relation to its theology. Fourth, he recognized its completely Trinitarian structure.[1]

Godsey also identified twelve of what he considered the more obvious methodological principles employed by Barth. These are:
1. Dogmatics is a function of the Church.
2. Dogmatic thinking is based on the Word of God alone.

3. The first and last question of dogmatics is the question about God.

4. Dogmatic thinking knows only the God revealed in Jesus Christ.

5. Dogmatic thinking about the God revealed in Christ is automatically Trinitarian thinking.

6. Dogmatic thinking relates every part of dogmatics to its Christological centre.

7. Dogmatic thinking acknowledges its limits and preserves the mystery of God.

8. Dogmatic thinking insists on the freedom of the Gospel from an *a priori* relation to human existence.

9. Dogmatic thinking does not separate ethics from dogmatics.

10. Dogmatic thinking refuses to admit any dualism and so refuses to take evil as seriously as it does grace.

11. Dogmatic thinking moves from action to being, from reality to possibility, from Gospel to Law, from God's "yes" to God's "no."

12. Dogmatic thinking knows that a dogmatics may be both architecturally beautiful and theologically correct.[2]

Barth's principles constitute a good starting point. In a certain sense, as the above list makes plain, each is united with all the others through the enterprise of dogmatic thinking. Barth was no irrationalist. As Godsey insists, "Karl Barth belongs to the very centre of the great European tradition which has sought to give reason its fullest place in exact and careful thinking."[3] Those who have seen strains of irrationalism in Barth have failed to understand both his approach and thought. A careful reading of Barth's *Anselm* could have prevented such misjudgments.

Part of the problem in interpreting Barth's work has stemmed from a common tendency to miss or disregard Barth's own understanding of the history of church thought. Barth found himself in the company of the Reformers in steering a middle course between two equally rigid and anthropocentric forms of thought.

As figure 1 illustrates, Protestantism "fell prey to the absolutism with which the man of that period made himself the centre and measure and goal of all things."[4] That happened long before the full devastation of modern liberalism was felt. By the nineteenth century theologians had come to focus their attention on "man's supposedly innate and essential capacity to 'sense and taste the in-

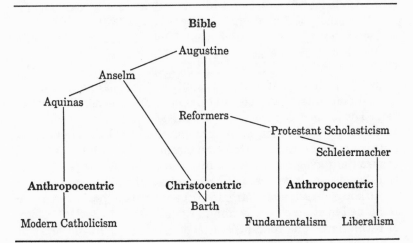

Figure 1

finite' as Schleiermacher said, or the 'religious a priori' as later affirmed by Troeltsch."[5] With man himself its center, that theology could not be one of revelation "in so far as it asks first what is possible in God's freedom, in order afterwards to investigate God's real freedom."[6]

Fundamentalism, more an heir of Protestant scholasticism than of the Reformation, fell prey to the same error with regard to its view of the Bible. Protestant scholasticism insisted that every word of the Bible was supernaturally inspired, not only as to style but even down to punctuation. The freedom of the Reformers was exchanged for a rigidity that could be seen as denying the Bible not only its vitality but also its authority. Scripture's authority, removed from its proper source in God and his revelation, was placed in the hands of human beings. The true sense of the Scripture's authority, said Barth, "is not the 'fundamentalist' one, which would have it that the sacred text as such is the proper and final basis of knowledge."[7] The Bible's authority rests in its relation to God's revelation, not in its existence as the final revelation itself. Barth warned:

> But we should be fools—real fools in the biblical sense of the word—if either to ourselves or others we pretended to be the expert bearers of revelation, appealing for our authorisation ... to

a knowledge of revelation which is either transmitted to us institutionally or infused personally, like the Roman Catholic to the authority of his Church, the "Fundamentalist" to the biblical texts, and the sectarian to his inner voice.[8]

On the other side, Catholicism has centered revelation in the Pope.[9] Tradition's authority, apostolic succession and Mariology are all elements of a circle that denies God's freedom in revelation. The focus is the *analogia entis,* the analogy of being. Here a point of contact in man is the ground of natural theology and a natural apprehension of God's revelation. Of this Barth said, "I regard the *analogia entis* as the invention of Antichrist, and think that because of it one cannot become Catholic."[10]

Although Barth later retreated from such strong statements, he remained in staunch opposition to Roman Catholicism's theology of revelation. "The concept 'truths of revelation,' in the sense of Latin propositions given and sealed once for all by divine authority in wording and meaning, is theologically impossible."[11] Such a concept, which severs revelation from its freedom in Christ Jesus, is theologically impossible because "revelation has its truth in the free decision of God, made once for all in Jesus Christ."[12]

Barth's center in Christ necessitated full respect for the function of humanity as witness to God's revelation but never its bearer. He returned to the Reformers and to Anselm for an actualism that moved from the reality of God and his revelation downward to humankind. He respected the freedom of God's grace. In all this, Barth claimed to represent a truly evangelical theology.

## Theology and the Church

In contrast with God's freedom is that activity of the church called dogmatics. Between 1927 and 1932, between publication of *Christliche Dogmatik* and the first part of the *Church Dogmatics,* Barth decided on a significant change for the title of his systematic theology. Barth himself explained the change from "Christian" to "Church" dogmatics: "Dogmatics is not a 'free' science, but one bound to the sphere of the Church, where and where alone it is possible and sensible."[13] Beyond that, however, Barth was now sure of his purposes. Freed from bondage to existential philosophy, he could speak not only as an individual but for the church as well. Thus he could claim, "The communion, in and for which I have written this book, is the communion of the Church."[14]

Dogmatics is not a "free science." It is bound to the church. But it is a real "science" and its subject is the Christian church. Again the contribution of Anselm shines through in Barth's justification of dogmatics as a science: "The subject of a science can only be one in which the object and sphere of activity in question are present and familiar."[15] Dogmatics works with evidence, the proclamation of the church. Dogmatics is a critical science. It measures, evaluates and corrects the proclamation of the church by the standards of the Holy Scriptures and the confessions of the believing community.

The exercise of dogmatics in the Christian church is one of faith. This is true because "in faith self-testing is necessary in view of responsibility before God."[16] Apart from faith, dogmatics could be only idle speculation. By faith it is human action related to the reconciling action of God. Because it is the work of faith, dogmatics stands in close relation to prayer. In fact, prayer is "the attitude apart from which dogmatic work is impossible."[17]

Dogmatics, however, is dogmatic thinking. As a rational operation of and within the church, dogmatics must incorporate within itself an epistemology. Barth had seen that "the only *intelligere* that concerns Anselm is that 'desired' by faith."[18] Barth was in agreement with this. Like Anselm he understood that "fundamentally, the *quaerere intellectum* is really immanent in *fides*. Therefore it is not a question of faith 'requiring' the 'proof' or the 'joy.' There is absolutely no question at all of a requirement of faith. Anselm wants 'proof' and 'joy' because he wants *intelligere* and he wants *intelligere* because he believes."[19]

Faith seeks understanding because understanding is characteristic of its very nature. But a problem is present. One must move from the moment of faith to that expression of understanding called theology. A theologian must adopt a stance toward this problem. Barth admitted, "I believe I learned the fundamental attitude to the problem of knowledge and existence of God ... at the feet of Anselm of Canterbury."[20]

The epistemological process that Barth adapted from Anselm bridged the gap from faith to theology through God's revelation. For Barth, "Christian faith is the illumination of the reason in which men become free to live in the truth of Jesus Christ and

thereby to become sure of their own existence and of the ground
and goal of all that happens."[21] Does this imply salvation by
knowledge? Not at all, for as Barth also explains, "Christian faith
is the gift of the meeting in which men become free to hear the
word of grace which God has spoken in Jesus Christ in such a way
that, in spite of all that contradicts it, they may once for all, exclusively and entirely, hold to His promise and guidance."[22]

In other words, faith is dependent on revelation for its existence but, once present, faith seeks an understanding of the revelation which is the ground of its existence. Inasmuch as the revelation of God is not static, or present in mere propositions, but alive
in the person and history of Jesus Christ, the knowledge sought
by faith is also active. In Jesus Christ, God's Word to humankind,
there is "the mediation and establishment of a specific knowledge,
namely, the knowledge whose subject and content is neither directly nor indirectly the man who knows, but He Himself, who also
mediates and establishes it."[23] The word of man must be separated
and kept distinct from the Word of God. Man is to *listen* to God's
Word, not *speculate* on it. Barth warned:

> We cannot impress upon ourselves too strongly that, in the lan-
> guage of the Bible, knowledge *(yada, gignōskein)* does not
> mean the acquisition of neutral information, which can be ex-
> pressed in statements, principles and systems, concerning a
> being which confronts man, nor does it mean the entry into pas-
> sive contemplation of a being which exists beyond the phenom-
> enal world. What it really means is the process or history
> in which man, certainly observing and thinking, using his
> senses, intelligence and imagination, but also his will, action
> and "heart," and therefore as whole man, becomes aware of
> another history which in the first instance encounters him as
> an alien history from without, and becomes aware of it in such a
> compelling way that he cannot be neutral towards it, but finds
> himself summoned to disclose and give himself to it in return, to
> direct himself according to the law which he encounters in it,
> to be taken up into its movement, in short, to demonstrate the
> acquaintance which he has been given with this other history in
> a corresponding alteration of his own being, action and conduct.
> We can and should say even more emphatically that knowledge
> in the biblical sense is the process in which the distant "object"

dissolves as it were, overcoming both its distance and its objectivity and coming to man as acting Subject, entering into the man who knows and subjecting him to this transformation.[24] This is knowledge. It is a knowing effected by God's claim on human beings and received through faith. This total knowledge is instrumental in the transformation of the individual reconciled to God. Accordingly, it is to faith that epistemology in the church is related. "But it is the Word, it is Christ, to whom faith is related, because He gives Himself as object to it, who makes faith into faith, into real experience."[25]

## Sources of Misunderstanding

Much of the confusion about Barth's theology is centered in the language he used to express his ideas. A simple illustration is provided by the interpretations of Bernard Ramm and Gordon Clark. As Ramm evaluated Barth's epistemology and message he discerned that "Barth's way of writing theology closely parallels the contemporary analytic program in philosophy."[26] Ramm identified five points demonstrating this relation. First, a theological statement is meaningful if it can be referred to the Word of God. Second, a theological statement is meaningful if it refers to Jesus Christ. Third, a statement is meaningful if it speaks to the God-and-man covenantal relationship. Fourth, a theological statement is verifiable within the structures determined by God. Fifth, theological statements are verified within the revealedness of the Holy Spirit.[27] Ramm's summation is as follows:

> Barth recognizes the peculiar logical character of theological statements. They are behests *(Befehle)*, not straight factual assertions, and cannot be verified by ordinary empirical methods. They have a content which presumes the faith of the person and the revealedness of the Holy Spirit. . . . A behest grips us as the truth of God as we grasp it in faith and as the Spirit illuminates it in his witnessing power. To speak of verification apart from such a context is therefore meaninglessness.[28]

Clark has an entirely different perspective. He accused Barth of having adopted "a theory of images and a process of abstraction that is more Aristotelian than Biblical."[29] After citing portions from the first part of volume two of the *Church Dogmatics,* Clark concluded that "the same section contains broader epistemological statements to the effect that knowledge is based on images."[30] In fact, said Clark, the observer should "note here the representational theory of truth: we do not directly perceive the object of knowledge; we perceive it only in an image."[31] Clark was of the opinion that Barth had created an epistemological problem in regard to the knowledge of God from which successful extrication was highly doubtful.

As is evident, two variant understandings of Barth's language, both claiming support from the *Church Dogmatics,* have led to vastly different interpretations of Barth's message. In this particular instance, it is difficult to say that either Ramm or Clark is wholly right or wrong. Ramm's analysis, however, does attempt to keep in mind those epistemological guidelines set down by Barth himself. On the other hand, while citing evidence to support his case, Clark seems to force a scheme of thought on Barth that Barth never acknowledged. Thus, although Clark introduces a few good observations, his conclusions lack force because of failure to understand fully the inner dynamic of Barth's epistemology.

Problems of interpretation are not confined to Barth's language. It would be impossible to discuss the problems at every point of exposition. One source of the many problems is the immense length of the *Church Dogmatics,* over eight thousand pages. The following introduction to Barth's style is also helpful:

The style of the *Church Dogmatics* is impressive and difficult. It expects its reader to have some knowledge of five languages, and presupposes a considerable background in theology and its history. The format of the work is not an easy one at first; it follows a very loose logical sequence, and repeats its subject matter over and over again from different aspects. Every page or two there is a lengthy insert in fine print, giving a detailed study into a specific, allied problem. Thus it takes some getting used to. But the further one digs into the work, the easier it becomes. Barth's strange style is not unsuited to his thinking, and the more one becomes accustomed to Barth, the more he appreciates it, for it is designed to help the reader cover the ground as rapidly or as carefully as he wishes to. The language, for all its learning, is easy, dramatic, and powerful. It alternates between rigid, scholarly analysis and eloquent preaching, with the preaching element far the dominant one.[32]

It should be obvious that studying Barth is no easy task. But it is immensely rewarding. Barth had the rare capacity to cause human beings to think *and* give God the glory. His work is rich in thought and praise to God. The problems must be faced, but they must not be allowed to stand in the way of a thorough appreciation and appropriation of the insights Barth put forward. Yet to gain an accurate and relatively complete picture of the *Church Dogmatics* demands not only an awareness of Barth's hermeneutics, his view of church history, his epistemology, language and style, but also the distinctive methodological features that attend them.

## Distinctive Methodological Features
*Positivistic Ground.* The first of these features has often been referred to as Barth's positivism. Ordinarily that term refers to a way of thinking that limits acceptable verification of truth statements to verification established solely on the empirical evidence of the physical world. When applied to a theological system it refers to any system built immediately on some theological foundation and not having any substantial or dependent connection with metaphysical or philosophical foundations. In this sense, Barth was a positivist when he built his theology on God's revelation given in Jesus Christ. Yet Barth was not the first to be positivistic in his approach. "Reformation theology also was positivistic in the sense that it renounced the scholastic method of the Roman Catholic theologians and taught the self-credibility *(autopistia)* of the Christian Scriptures."[33]

Regrettably, through the influential interpretation of Dietrich Bonhoeffer, the concept gained so much popularity that it became a convenient label by which to put Barth in a theological corner. Worse, the manner of Bonhoeffer's interpretation, especially as adapted by the secular theologians of the sixties, caused many to dismiss Barth as irrelevant. Bonhoeffer wrote: "Barth was the first theologian to begin the criticism of religion—and that remains his really great merit—but he set in its place the positivist doctrine of revelation which says in effect, 'Take it or leave it': Virgin Birth, Trinity or anything else, everything which is an equally significant and necessary part of the whole, which latter has to be swallowed as a whole or not at all."[34]

Bonhoeffer saw in this an unhealthy separation of the church from the world. He believed Barth was leaving the world to its own devices.[35] But Barth found this a strange accusation. The so-called positivism of revelation, "which Barth, in a letter to Eberhard Bethge, Bonhoeffer's biographer, describes as incomprehensible,"[36] is not a matter of stone tablets fallen from heaven. "Revelation, he contends, is not a rigid codex but an appeal to all men and, above all, a story, the story that God has acted, is acting, and will act among men."[37]

Theological positivism is necessitated by the Word of God. Barth noted that "in dogmatic systems the pre-supposed basic view acquires inevitably the position and function which . . . can be ascribed only to the Word of God."[38] Revelation, however, while indeed the truth, is not a truth fixed and limited in a view, idea or principle. It can only be reported concretely.[39] As that given by God, revelation alone, in and of itself, is the sole acceptable foundation of theology.

*Scientific Thrust.* A far less controversial feature of the *Church Dogmatics* is its appearance as a *scientific* theology. The essence of science is the inductive method of proceeding from particulars of datum to general statements. In a strict sense this meant for Barth the movement from the concrete reality of God and his revelation outward. In a less strict sense Barth saw this as the approach utilized by Schleiermacher in his concept of theology regulated by one principle consistently followed. The Reformers also operated in this manner, only not thoroughly enough:

It was, of course, said that Holy Scripture is the Word of God to the extent that it presents Christ. But the programme of Reformation theology did not allow for any radical consideration of the meaning, importance and function of Christology in relation to all Christian knowledge. For that reason this theology was in many spheres . . . able to think and argue from Christology only very indirectly and implicitly, or not at all.[40]

A variety of terms illustrate Barth's own scientific thrust. It is characterized by *objectivism*. This foundation is the recognition of a reality independent from man and totally noncontingent. Barth's dogmatic theology is also characterized by *in concreto* theologizing. Rather than by a process of abstraction, Barth's theology is shaped by the reality of the self-revealing triune God. Given an objective reality outside man, theology can and must proceed on the basis of that reality, in its "given-ness." Thus, there is a focus on *actuality* as over against possibility. Actuality is descriptive of a movement in thought from reality, from what is given in revelation, and not from philosophical speculation. All of this leads to the *in actu* character of ontology. In other words, Barth's ontology is one of *actualism,* that is, acting and being cannot be separated. For this reason Barth includes ethics in the doctrine of God.[41]

*Historie, Geschichte and Heilsgeschichte.* Another somewhat controversial feature of Barth's *Church Dogmatics* is his treatment of history. Evangelicals in the United States, in particular, have been confused and troubled at this point. The German terms *Historie, Geschichte* and *Heilsgeschichte,* all referring to history, are sometimes not clear to them. Occasionally an English translation fails to bring out a clear distinction of what in the German original is designated by more than one term. *Historie* has in view past events as these events are subject to the objective measures of accepted historical research. *Historie* is thus an objectified, reportable history where events are external and verifiable. *Geschichte,* on the other hand, views history in an interior manner where real events are discussed in terms of their significance to those who report the historical acts. That is not to imply that *Geschichte* is unknown history. Rather, it is in a sense existential history. The two German adjectives *geschichtlich* and *historisch* have as English counterparts the terms *historic* and *historical,* respectively. *Heilsgeschichte,* or "salvation history," is a term popularized by Oscar Cullmann and is used with reference to the history of the Bible. It is "holy history" because it records the acts of God.

Part of the problem in regard to Barth's view of history stems from identifying his understanding of *Heilsgeschichte* with that of either Cullmann or Rudolph Bultmann. Bultmann's thoroughgoing historicism excludes *Heilsgeschichte* and *Geschichte* from the realm of actual events in time. Acts like the resurrection are admittedly nonverifiable to Bultmann and thereby also nonactual in space and time. They are relegated by him to the psychological reality of a believing community. In contradistinction Barth insists that nonverifiable events are nonetheless actual events, objective in space and time, but only rightly reportable as significant acts of God.

Barth's view is substantially different from Cullmann's. Nevertheless, though many evangelicals have likened Barth's understanding to that of Bultmann, in truth Barth is much closer to Cullmann. Yet in his classic *Christ and Time* Cullmann repeatedly separates himself from Barth at crucial points. To be sure, there is a fundamental unity in their approach as well. Yet Cullmann believed he found in Barth "the last traces of a philosophical and non-Biblical statement of the relation between time and eternity."[42] In this regard, Herbert Hartwell's treatment of Barth on this subject is deficient, although what he has said about Barth's view of *Heilsgeschichte* is good as far as it goes.[43] Hartwell is not alone, however, in passing over the distinction between Barth's view and Cullmann's, and the protests of Cullmann have by and large gone unheard.

Brevard Childs is a notable exception. He has stated that "Barth's own concept of *Bundesgeschichte* should not be identified with the classic *Heilsgeschichte*."[44] That is *Bundesgeschichte*, the "covenant history," is determinative for *Heilsgeschichte*. With this understanding, Barth's view becomes much clearer:

> The history of salvation is *the* history, the true history which encloses all other history and to which in some way all other history belongs to the extent that it reflects and illustrates the history of salvation. . . . No other history can have any independent theme in relation to this history, let alone be a general and true history in the context of which the history of salvation can only be one among others. The covenant of grace is *the* theme of history. The history of salvation is *the* history.[45]

*Bundesgeschichte* differs from Cullmann's *Heilsgeschichte* in its conception of time. For Cullmann, *Heilsgeschichte* is *Offenbarungsgeschichte*, that is, the "history of revelation." Time is linear and the biblical time line consists of a succession of individual saving-events. Eternity is simply the line extended so that time is unending, or it is an infinite series of ages.[46]

On the other hand, for Barth, *Offenbarungsgeschichte* is within *Bundesgeschichte*. The stress is not on the *history* of revelation but on *revelation* history. "Revelation is never a predicate of history; on the contrary, history is a predicate of revelation."[47] The event of revelation in time means God has time for man. Time and eternity, however, are qualitatively different. Eternity is related to time as pretemporality, supratemporality and posttemporality.[48]

God's covenant is seen in history. Specifically, it is displayed in time, and time is marked by creation as the first among God's works. "All the things distinct from God begin with it."[49] The Bible witnesses to this act of God. To this most American evangelicals can readily agree. But Barth has taken one further step that appears suspicious.

"In accordance . . . with the unique nature of its theme, the biblical history of creation is pure saga."[50] At once questions are raised. Does the term *saga* denote something that is false? Is *saga* history? What is really meant by *saga*? How does it differ from myth? To each of these questions Barth had an answer.

First, the concept of *saga* must be distinguished from *history*. This does not mean that saga describes an imaginary event. According to Barth, "A saga is a poetically designed picture of a concrete once-for-all pre-historical 'Geschichtswirklichkeit' (historical reality), subject to temporal-spatial limitations."[51] Klaas Runia has examined this definition closely and put forward some observations clarifying the relation of saga to history.

Runia notes first that in a more general definition the "pre-" on the word "historical" would be omitted. It appears here in connection with the creation event and story which are, at least in human terms pre-history. The definition embraces two elements. In the first place, sagas deal with events that did happen. Creation, for example, did happen. But, in the second place, sagas deal with events which cannot be expressed by ordinary human language. Runia explains: "They are 'geschichtliche' (historical) reality and belong to the succession of time-filling events. But they are not 'historische Geschichte' (historical history), i.e., they are outside the reach of all historical observation and record. They cannot be described in our ordinary words and concept."[52]

Second, the concept of *saga* must be distinguished from *myth*. That Barth carefully distinguished the two can be seen from his definition of myth:

> The customary definition that myth is the story of the gods is only superficial. In myth both the gods and the story are not the real point at issue, but only point to it. The real object and content of myth are the essential principles of the general reali-

ties and relationships of the natural and spiritual cosmos which, in distinction from concrete history, are not confined to definite times and places. The clothing of their dialectic and cyclical movement in stories of the gods is the form of myth. The fairy tale, which is more interested in details than in the whole (as are legend and anecdote in relation to saga), and which inclines not to concrete history but to all kinds of general phenomena, truths or even riddles of existence, is a degenerate form of myth as are legend and anecdote of saga.[53]

Obviously, then, saga is a literary term used to describe various portions of the biblical material. It does not denote something false. It describes events that actually happened. It is not the same as myth. Yet, despite this, questions still remain in the minds of many. Why? First, the term *saga* has misleading connotations for many people, scholarly and unschooled alike. They think of Norse mythology or some other kind of subhistorical, fictionalized account when they hear the term. Second, the general tenor of Barth's language is unusual enough to keep many cautious minds wary and suspicious, especially when Barth talks about such crucial events as the resurrection. Since Barth's understanding of the resurrection is suspect to some, we will look at it carefully.

William Hordern has noted that "Barth's whole system was built upon the historical nature of the revelation, that it was an event that happened—that Jesus Christ was born of a virgin and raised from the dead."[54] But on an issue so crucial it is important to see what Barth himself has to say.

In an exegetical study of Matthew 28:11-20, Barth made two significant observations about what he termed 'the *fact* of Easter':

1. We must be quite clear that these accounts relate a *real event* in space and time, and not just some thought or idea....

2. These texts speak of an "historically" inconceivable event, but do not mean that this event was subsequently interpreted or construed, much less invented by the faith and piety of the Church.[55]

These remarks are sufficiently unambiguous to make clear what Barth meant. In the same context Barth went on to say, "To speak here of a 'myth' would be to confuse categories. Easter is an absolutely *unique* event."[56] However, Barth continued, "These narratives are recounted not in the style of history but, like the story of creation, in the style of historical saga."[57]

One cannot read the *Church Dogmatics* (or anything else by Barth) without quickly coming to the realization that, as far as Barth is concerned, everything in theology begins, ends and continues solely on the objective actuality of God's self-disclosure in Jesus Christ, who as the Son of God and Son of man was born, lived, died and *resurrected* in the framework of history. Saga does not deny history. Yet some persist in reading a subjective twist in Barth because, as Carl Henry expressed it, "the objectifying elements Barth introduced into his system are not really objects of historical research."[58] This criticism was met by Hordern who first asserted that history as the investigation of what has happened in the past was indispensable to Barth in his whole system. History in that sense is present in the witness of the Scripture. "But," Hordern went on to add,

> If by history you mean what so many people mean today, that which can be verified by modern historical method (and when that in turn means that by definition any miracle cannot have been historical), then it seems to me that Barth is forced to say that historical criticism cannot help the Christian faith, or that it cannot produce anything other than a non-biblical Jesus. *By definition* it cannot, if this is what one means by historical method, and this is what is widely meant. That is why Barth, speaking of the resurrection, can say, Of course this is not historical if by history (I am not quoting him verbatim) you have the concept that miracles are not historical by definition. But, he says (and I can imagine the twinkle in his eye), that doesn't mean it didn't happen. In other words, Barth is arguing that more has happened objectively ... than what would be discovered by historical method.[59]

There is no radical discontinuity between Barth's view of history and the view espoused by some evangelicals. His language may have been different but his central conviction was thoroughly orthodox.

*The Rejection of Natural Theology.* Another feature of Barth's *Church Dogmatics* has seemed very unorthodox indeed; namely, his rejection of natural theology and, in particular, the concept of *analogia entis,* the "analogy of being." As already noted, Barth rejected the *analogia entis* as coming from the antichrist. He considered it the single sufficient reason for separation from Roman Catholicism. Moreover, it was the issue of natural theology that caused the sharp break between Barth and Brunner in 1934. Barth rejected natural theology on theological, logical and biblical grounds.

Theologically, natural theology is opposed to God's freedom in revelation. Barth had acquired from Anselm the understanding of theological knowledge as that rational operation induced by faith, conducted through faith, but dependent on faith's source, that is, on grace. In other words, theological knowledge is rational and scientific only insofar as it is limited to what its object of inquiry yields to it. Natural theology abrogates God's revelation in Christ because it denies that this revelation stands alone, not as one revelation—albeit the greatest—among many. Natural theology is not truly theology, that which proceeds from God, but anthropology, that which proceeds from man.[60]

Logically, natural theology leads first to the perversion of the gospel and then to its setting aside. This is so because natural theology means more than just a natural knowledge of God. When Barth used the term he included, among other things, "all doctrines concerning man and all moral doctrines which lay claim to defining a relationship to God independent of Christian Revelation."[61] From the possibility of theological knowledge outside God's revelation in Christ it is but a very small step to the restructuring of Christianity. "Natural theology is the doctrine of a union of man with God existing outside God's revelation in Jesus Christ."[62] Such a theology can have devastating consequences.

To see such consequences, one need only to look to history. Robert McAfee Brown, in the introduction to his translation of Casalis's *Portrait of Karl Barth,* has done that:

All of Barth's fears about what happens when men reason from themselves to God were confirmed by what happened in Germany in the thirties. The "German Christians" found it possible to start with natural theology and move easily and comfortably to an acceptance of Adolph Hitler and the Nazi party as expressing God's will in their own day, since they had no criterion drawn from revelation by which to judge the rightness or wrongness of their assessment of Hitler. It was clear to Barth that when one judged all of God's work in the light of his revelation

in Jesus Christ, no peace could be made with Hitler.[63]
Although this instance might be protested as unique, and certainly not a necessary corollary of natural theology, it nonetheless serves to support Barth's essential contention. German national socialism was fully compatible with a natural theology; God's revelation in Jesus Christ, however, precludes the possibility of a "German Christian" church. How, then, can natural theology not only be present in the church but be considered vital? Berkouwer says, "The only answer he [Barth] can find to this question is that man resists living *exclusively* in terms of *grace*."[64]

The insidious character of natural theology is masked by its pretense of Christian innocence. "By the very fact that it grants a place to and admits the preeminence of revelation, it absorbs revelation and domesticates it; instead of a question which confronts man, revelation becomes an answer which man gives."[65] This again is the vitality of natural theology; "the vitality ... is the vitality of man as such."[66] But, of course, its vitality is also the ground of its illegitimacy. Natural theology is an illusion, but a deadly illusion, one that perverts revelation by its modest identity with revelation.[67]

Biblically, natural theology is untenable. From the start Barth had declared, "Our thesis, that the knowability of God is to be equated with His grace and mercy in the revelation of His Word and Spirit, is based on the witness of Holy Scripture."[68] Qualifying this, Barth continued, "At this point, too, it is best for us to begin with an open concession. There are not only individual passages, but a whole strand running through Scripture, in face of which we can certainly raise the question whether we are not invited and summoned to natural theology by Holy Scripture itself. Indeed, we must raise it in order that we may give it a correct answer."[69]

Accordingly, Barth undertook the exegetical task and brought to bear the canonical witness on each text commonly put forward as supportive of natural theology. He gave special attention to the celebrated text in the first chapter of Romans. Of all Barth's particular textual studies his exegesis of Romans 1:18-32 is too important to this discussion to pass by without some attention.

The exposition of this text is given in two complementary passages of the *Church Dogmatics*. In the second part of volume one (pages 306-7) Barth's treatment is in the context of his discussion of religion as unbelief. In the first part of volume two (pages 119-21) the exposition is included in a discussion on the knowability of God. When carefully harmonized and brought together, the two passages produce one exposition. In vastly reduced form that exposition can be outlined as follows:

Q. Does Paul actually stand in this first chapter within the development of the theme announced in 1:17?

1. We must bear in mind that the very words which are so often regarded as an opening or summons to every possible kind of natural theology are in reality a constituent part of the apostolic kerygma....

2. The passage is the formulation of an accusation....

3. If Rom. 1:18-21 existed for us on its own... we should hardly have any other choice than to acknowledge that it says that man in the cosmos in himself and as such is an independent witness of the truth of God. But as a matter of plain fact, it stands in a quite definite context in Paul's Epistle to the Romans. In this context it does not say this, and what is more, it cannot say it....

4. It is a Christian statement presupposing... the event which took place between God and man in Christ that... [causes Paul to say] that the knowledge which the Gentiles have of God from the works of creation is the instrument to make them inexcusable and therefore to bring them like the Jews under the judgment and therefore under the grace of God....

5. It is, therefore, not the case that Paul was in a position to appeal to the Gentiles' possession of a knowledge of the invisible nature of God as manifested from creation.... In his proclamation of Jesus Christ he could not let it appear even momentarily that he was speaking of things which were already familiar by virtue of that "primal revelation."...

6. He is not, then, speaking of man in the cosmos in himself and in general. The Jews and the heathen of whom he speaks are very definitely characterized as Jews and heathen objectively confronted with the divine *apokalupsis* in the Gospel (1:16-18).... There can be no doubt that Paul meant by this the revelation of the grace of God in Jesus Christ....

7. Now that revelation has come and its light has fallen on

heathendom, heathen religion is shown to be the very opposite
of revelation: a false religion of unbelief.[70]
The crux of the issue in rightly determining the meaning of this
text is in correctly answering the question about Paul: "Does he
speak in this chapter too as the apostle of Jesus Christ, or does
he, between 1:18 and 3:20, speak anthropologically, as a religious
and historical philosopher?"[71] Of course, what this question implies is the necessity of a decision about a basic hermeneutical
issue: the delimiting of context. The question, and indeed Barth's
whole exposition, again moves toward reconsidering exegesis as a
work undertaken in the context of the Christian canon. If, as Barth
argues, it is true that the whole canon is the proper context and
true that the canon's theme is the revelation of God in Jesus
Christ, then it must be true that each text be seen in light of the
theme of the entire canon.

Thus far, then, Barth had set forth theological, logical and
biblical reasons for rejecting natural theology. Yet, he said, all this
evidence must not be used to attack natural theology. The lines of
argument are not eristic or apologetic at all. Rather, the grounds
for rejecting natural theology rest in, and only in, the perspective
provided by grace. There natural theology is seen to be an illusion,
but the knowledge of its illusory character cannot be turned
against it. To attempt such is to fall victim to it. "To strive against
this . . . as such is meaningless. In this sphere it is inevitable."[72]

Finally, then, natural theology must remain outside the church
but not outside the church's interest. So long as pagan man exists,
the church must be ready to persuade and convince him that truth
is other than he thinks. However, to do that, the church must be
free of natural theology's snare. It must stand free in God's gracious revelation. When this happens the profound contrast between the church and the world is once more evident. Outside the
church, "natural theology is the only comfort of the natural man
in life and death."[73] But within the church "we have . . . complete
comfort for the whole man."[74] Jesus Christ is that comfort.

Barth was not content to let the matter rest at that point. In an
exercise of constructive theology he proceeded to present an understanding that frees the church from natural theology and renders
the *analogia entis* an unnecessary explanation for man's knowledge of God and relation to him. As Barth developed his counter-

proposal he was subjected to intense criticism and strange interpretations. Hans Urs von Balthasar perceived in Barth's proposal, amazingly enough, a move, not away from, but actually toward an acceptance of the analogy of being.[75] Berkouwer criticized Von Balthasar's analysis, pointing out that such a move was inconceivable within the framework of the *Church Dogmatics*. Rather, Berkouwer saw both Barth's rejection of the *analogia entis* and his alternative as steps in the consistent defense of God's triumph of grace.[76] Hans Küng, like Von Balthasar an astute Catholic observer of Barth's theology, believed "Barth's fundamental objection to Catholic teaching can be rejected as unjust and untenable."[77]

What occasioned the debate was Barth's introduction of the *analogia fidei*, the analogy of faith. Barth had by no means denied the concept of analogy. Rather, taking his cue from Romans 12:6, he described the analogy of faith as "the correspondence of the thing known with the knowing, of the object with the thought, of the Word of God with the word of man in thought and in speech."[78] The *analogia fidei* explains Paul's turning human knowledge of God into man's being known by God. The *analogia entis* shifts the emphasis on the knowledge of God to an innate capacity within man; the *analogia fidei* restores the emphasis to man's being known by God.[79]

Barth was intent on preserving an appreciation for the freedom of God. In fact, the concept of freedom is one of the most distinctive features of the *Church Dogmatics*. Until recently, this feature has often been set aside unexamined.

In his essay *Der Theologe Karl Barth*, carrying the striking subtitle *Zeugnis vom freien Gott und freien Menschen* (Witness to the Free God and Free Man), Jürgen Fangmeier, pointing out that Barth never understood how his theology could be reduced (by his critics) to the formula 'God is everything and man is nothing,' rightly states that God's freedom for man and man's freedom for God is one of the main concepts of Barth's theology.[80]

The concept of freedom is probably the dominant expression of Barth's "actualism" to be found in the *Church Dogmatics*. In fact, Barth, in another work, said: "The words 'free grace' by their very juxtaposition indicate first and last nothing other than the nature of Him whom Holy Scripture calls 'God.' "[81] The revelation of God is an expression of that free grace. It is God's freedom in Jesus Christ that is at work in election. God is free for humanity in Christ. But humanity is called to be free toward God in Jesus Christ too. In fact, human beings are free only as they are free toward God.[82]

Part of God's freedom is that implicit in the Trinity. The whole theological focus of the *Church Dogmatics* is on God's freedom within a Trinitarian framework. One of the amazing and distinctive features of the work as a whole is its Trinitarian ground. "Barth's doctrine of the Trinity represents the most imposing attempt in modern times to restate the orthodox doctrine of the Trinity. Above all, it is grounded upon God's revelation of Himself in Christ."[83]

"In Christ": the words reverberate like the triumphant theme in the gospel of God's grace. Is this Barth's theme? "For all Barth's works want only to point to Him, the Alpha and Omega."[84] All who have read Barth carefully realize that God's revelation in Jesus Christ was Karl Barth's all-consuming passion. Christ is the Alpha and Omega, the beginning and the end, in Barth's theology. Yet its statement in a single theme has eluded even some excellent scholars. Berkouwer's understanding of the theme as "the triumph of grace" has merit but is more abstract than Barth intended. So too with many other "themes" that might be put forward for consideration. The person and work of Jesus Christ stand at the center of every part and of the whole of Barth's theology. The "primary *theologia crucis* ... is wholly and exclusively that of the cross of Jesus."[85]

# 11

# The Message of the *Dogmatics*

The several thousand pages of the *Church Dogmatics* develop in a powerfully consistent manner all the distinctive features of its varied parts and massive whole into one resounding message centered and united in the person of Jesus Christ. Its size notwithstanding,[1] the *Church Dogmatics* has its own kind of simplicity. Daniel Williams, for example, has reduced Barth's efforts to the single declaration that "the task of theology is to expound the Bible correctly."[2] Although Williams's characterization is certainly true, it is also true that in the service of that task Barth brought into his work a keen interaction with others both inside and outside the church. Barth was a superb historian of the church.[3] He was also an exegete, historian, dogmatician and, above all, preacher.

The *Church Dogmatics* must be understood as a part of Barth himself. He was, as H. Richard Niebuhr said, "the theologian who does not disappear in his theology."[4] Barth was a pastor claimed by the Word for a lifetime work of proclamation. His proclamation unfolds in four major volumes, although originally Barth had intended five. In addition to his prolegomena and treatment of the doctrine of the Word of God, Barth planned that "the second volume should contain the doctrine of God, the third the doctrine of

Creation, the fourth the doctrine of Reconciliation, the fifth the doctrine of Redemption."[5] But the years passed too quickly, and Barth never attempted the last volume.

Despite or perhaps because of Barth's personality, the *Church Dogmatics* has a ring of authority resulting from close correspondence to the gospel. Barth is always there, but as prophet and preacher. He is never so powerful a figure that he obscures the person of Christ, but because of Christ Barth is never so powerful as when he preaches loudly. Nevertheless (a very great *nevertheless*), Barth was also *simul iustus et peccator*, "at the same time justified and still a sinner." Barth never forgot that. Nor did his critics—nor can anyone who studies him. The *Church Dogmatics* is a flawed work. Thus, although a steadfast witness to the glory of God, the work, as the man himself, must be viewed in God's grace.

With such thoughts in mind, the following brief expositions of the four volumes of the *Church Dogmatics* are presented. Only incidental comments about the praise and criticism addressed to them by others can be included. The purpose here again is not to criticize but to expound. Of course, what follows should not be substituted for a reading of the original sources.

## The Doctrine of the Word of God

The first volume, published in two parts under the title *The Doctrine of the Word of God*, comprises four chapters. It is "an exposition that occupies all of fifteen hundred pages and is definitive for everything that follows."[6] Beginning with a prolegomena discussing the nature of theology, the bulk of the volume is a development of the basis of true theology, the Word of God in its three forms: the Word of God as preached, the written Word of God, the revealed Word of God.

*The Word Preached.* The Word as preached is likened to the sacrament of the Last Supper. It is God's vehicle through which he speaks to human beings today. As with the sacrament, proclamation does not make human words divine but allows the divine Word to be heard. There are four decisive connections between the Word of God and proclamation. First, proclamation rests on what God has given, namely, the Word of God. In this sense, the Word is a commission—in fact, *the* commission. Second, the Word is the object of proclamation. Only so long as the Word is the object is proclamation real proclamation. Third, proclamation is judged by the Word of God. Proclamation is real proclamation only when it stands submitted to that judgment and reveals itself as true language that rightly demands obedience. Fourth, "the Word of God —and here at last we utter the decisive word—is the event itself, in which proclamation is subject to the canon."[7] As Barth explained:

> By recognising the existence of a canon, the Church declares that particularly in her proclamation she is aware of not being left alone, that the commission on the basis of which she proclaims, the object which she proclaims, the judgment to which her proclamation is liable, the nature of real proclamation as an event must come from another source, from without, and concretely from without, in the complete externality of her concrete canon—as an imperative, categorical yet utterly historical, becoming articulate in time. And by acknowledging that this canon is actually identical with the Bible of the Old and New Testaments, with the Word of the prophets and apostles, she declares that this connection of her proclamation with something concrete and external is not a general principle or a mere determination of form, the content of which might be this or even a totally different one, but that this connection is completely determined in content, that it is an order received, an obligation imposed, that this bit of past happening composed of definite texts is her directions for work, her marching orders, with which not only her preaching but she herself stands or falls.[8]

*The Written Word.* The content of the Bible can be summed up in the declaration: "the prophetic apostolic Word is the word, the witness, the proclamation and the preaching of Jesus Christ."[9] Like proclamation, the Bible has an "event" character. "In this event the Bible is the Word of God, i.e., in this word the human word of prophets and apostles represents the Word of God Himself."[10] But what does this mean? Does it mean that the Bible *becomes* the Word of God?

"For me the Word of God is a *happening,* not a thing. Therefore the Bible must *become* the Word of God, and it does this through the work of the Spirit."[11] This candid admission by Barth has caused a great deal of unnecessary worry and unevangelical reaction on the part of conservatives. They have tried to understand Barth on the basis of incomplete evidence. Some have accused him of saying there is a divine Word which must be separated from the human words by human judgment. Others have accused Barth of saying that the Bible is only the Word of God to the degree that persons so accept it, and then only in those parts where they decide for themselves that they hear God. But these are inadequate assessments. They bear slight resemblance to what Barth actually said.

"This very fact of the language of God Himself becoming an event in the human word of the Bible is, however, God's business and not ours."[12] Here man is put in his place. "The Bible is God's Word so far as God speaks through it."[13] Here no human decision is required but that of obedience or rebellion. As William Hordern emphasized about Barth: "He very definitely believed—quite apart from man's knowledge of it—that God was in Christ, that the Bible is . . . the Word of God, and that this is true whether or not man recognizes it."[14] Of course, "the statement, 'The Bible is God's Word,' is a confession of faith."[15] Faith sees that the Bible becomes God's Word by the act of revelation. Only now does Barth's celebrated statement become clear: "The Bible therefore becomes God's Word in this event, and it is to its being in this becoming that the tiny word 'is' relates, in the statement that the Bible is God's Word."[16]

Other objections have arisen in relation to Barth's treatment of Holy Scripture. Some object to the description of Scripture as a witness to revelation. Most of the objections stem from misunderstanding. Geoffrey W. Bromiley has justified Barth's usage of the word *witness:*

The word "witness" is a dangerous one if used in its ordinary sense, but if we think of the Bible as a witness in the way in which the Bible itself describes the prophets and apostles as witness—"he that receiveth you, receiveth me"—it is perhaps not quite so objectionable as some critics of Barth suppose. This is at least how Barth himself is thinking of it, and in this sense it has the merit of being a word which the Bible uses even about itself (cf. John 5:39).[17]

Finally, some have accused Barth of a faulty view of Scripture because he said, "The men whom we hear as witnesses speak as fallible, erring men like ourselves."[18] If this is indeed a denial of inerrancy, then where is Scripture's authority? Why did Barth posit such an idea? To answer the latter question attention must be redirected to Barth's central convictions. It must be recalled that the *Church Dogmatics* is rooted in the ground of God's free revelation in his Word, Jesus Christ. The Bible is not, in and of itself, the Word of God. If it were, then it would exist as an independent source of knowledge about God, an independent witness to God's revelation in Jesus Christ. Instead, it is the dependent witness that arises from revelation. In its identity as true witness-proclamation, it is one with the Word of God. In short, the Bible *becomes* the Word. It is a miracle, and miracles are a stumbling block; "that sinful and erring men as such speak the Word of God; that is the miracle of which we speak when we say that the Bible is the Word of God."[19] But the offense of Scripture is grounded in the mercy of God:

> For that reason every time we turn the Word of God into an infallible biblical word of man or the biblical word of man into an infallible Word of God we resist that which we ought never to resist, i.e., the truth of the miracle that there fallible men speak the Word of God in fallible human words—and we therefore resist the sovereignty of grace, in which God Himself became man in Christ, to glorify Himself in His humanity.[20]

This is, as Barth acknowledged, a hard thought to accept. But it is the line of thinking that shows clearly that Scripture has not its own authority but the authority vested in it by God's action. Moreover, it is not man's place to sit in judgment upon the Bible—indeed, he is judged by it. "The Word of God is so powerful that it is not bound by what we think we can discover and value as the divine element, the content, the spirit of the Bible."[21]

Holy Scripture is inspired by God and "the inspiration of the Bible cannot be reduced to our faith in it."[22] Its trustworthiness is always standing before men and women waiting and able to prove itself. Ontologically, it is not infallible—if ontology is all that is being considered. Again Barth's actualism resolves the matter: the Scripture is not an "in-itself, for-itself" entity but exists in the act of God's revelation, for God and for man, as the Word of God to man in the words of man himself. Scripture proves

itself functionally infallible only in the act of God's gracious opening of human eyes to see Christ—and, once opened, human eyes be-
hold the glory of God in the earthen vessel of human words. Thus
one understands the inspiration of Scripture. Thus Barth concludes: "Scripture is recognized as the Word of God by the fact that
it *is* the Word of God. This is what we are told by the doctrine of
the witness of the Holy Spirit. . . . When we say 'by the Holy Spirit'
we say that in the doctrine of Holy Scripture we are content to give
the glory to God and not to ourselves."[23]

But another objection has been raised. Klaas Runia, sympathetic to Barth's viewpoint in many regards, nevertheless separates from him on the issue of the Bible's fallibility. Runia is no
alarmist. He, as well as Barth, speaks from a Reformed position.
He is appreciative of Barth's attention to the human element in
the composition of Scripture. But on this point he says:

> Here we strongly disagree with Barth. In our opinion Barth is
> guilty of a leap of thought which has no adequate grounding.
> Humanity and fallibility may indeed coincide on the purely
> human level, as we all experience daily, but this gives us no
> right to draw the same conclusion with regard to the Bible. For
> —and this is the decisive point—we are not on a *purely* human
> level here. We have to do with the inspired Word of God, i.e.,
> with the Word that came into being not by human activity only,
> but in and through this human activity by the operation of the
> Holy Spirit. There is therefore no ground for such a straight-
> forward identification of humanity and fallibility.[24]

Barth, in response, would argue that the Spirit's work in inspiration need not remove the human authors' capacity for error. The
inspiration by God's Spirit yields a union of human and divine that
retains the integrity of both—the human capacity for error and
God's infallibility. Runia, Barth would argue, brings this union too
close to a fusion. We are not faced with an "either-or" but a "both-
and." Scripture as a divine Word bears God's infallible authority
yet as a human word retains a human capacity for error. Those
who would be quick to judge Barth's position as untenable would
do well to keep in mind two things. First, even if we accept that God
gave us an infallible Bible in the original autographs, God has not
been hindered, even since the first autograph was copied, from
conveying his infallible truth through faulty means.[25] And second,

textual criticism shows clearly that many of the original auto-graphs contained faulty grammar. Yet no one would argue that fallible grammar in any way inhibits the communication of God's infallible truth. The question remains, what kind of document has God given us? Can God, has God, truly worked *with* and through man at the *purely* human level? Must God have superintended in such a way as to present us with an infallible document? Barth's answer is no; for if God needed to raise the human authors of Scripture above their created nature as fallible and dependent images of God to communicate truthfully to humankind, then he likewise would have needed to raise prefallen humanity above *their* fallibility to communicate with them, since they too possessed a capacity for error. But this would deny the significance of the Fall. No, says Barth, God allows humanity to stand as fallible and performs his miracles even there.[26]

*The Revealed Word.* The third form of the Word of God in Barth's understanding is the revealed Word, Jesus Christ. "Revelation in fact does not differ from the Person of Jesus Christ, and again does not differ from the reconciliation that took place in Him. To say revelation is to say, 'The Word became Flesh.' "[27] Paul Schilling suggests that in this regard "for Barth the crucial text in the New Testament is John 1:14."[28]

Jesus Christ, the revealed Word, is the ground of Scripture and proclamation. Scripture attests the past revelation and "to attest means to point in a definite direction beyond oneself to something else."[29] The Bible, in turn, stands between the revelation in Christ and the proclamation of the church; "the promise in proclamation rests upon the attestation in the Bible, the hope of future revelation upon faith in that which happened once for all."[30] The authority of both Scripture and the church's proclamation is located in the revealed Word of God.[31]

This emphasis is disturbing to Gustaf Wingren. He finds an "unexpressed presupposition" in Barth's doctrine of the Word of God. That presupposition is Barth's anthropology which, Wingren claims, "is in reality definitive for Barth's theology. We could express this in another way by saying that his anthropology determines his hermeneutics."[32] Wingren admits the strangeness of his accusation.[33] He stands by it, however, and maintains that it is at root the cause for the distortion of the gospel that he finds in Barth.

Wingren complains, "Barth has a tendency to shift the emphasis in the gospel of Christ from the death and resurrection to the incarnation, the birth, the miracle of Christmas. When the death and resurrection stand in the center—as they do in all the four gospels and in the rest of the New Testament—the gospel has the character of a struggle."[34]

For Wingren, this shift undermines the gospel message. It forces a reinterpretation that minimizes the sense of conflict in the New Testament, sets the death and resurrection of Jesus to one side and makes the problem of the knowledge of God pre-eminent. Above all, Barth's view of sin seems to Wingren to represent an unbiblical position. It arises from his unhealthy emphasis on the Incarnation and contributes to his lack of any sense of the conflict that appears in Scripture.[35]

Wingren's criticism highlights a significant possibility of danger in Barth's position. It is possible to lose sight of sin's power, to exalt the triumph of God's grace at the expense of forgetting how much it did indeed cost God. It is possible, and undesirable, to start with the Incarnation and never do justice to the crucifixion and resurrection. Did Barth, however, fall to such temptations? Was he forced by his presuppositions to an unbiblical position?

Wingren's conclusions presuppose an anthropological foundation in Barth that is at odds with Barth's own stated intentions. Of course, Barth could have been blind to his own real assumptions. Have his other critics likewise been blind? Although Wingren's analysis stands alone in this criticism, his claims are not necessarily invalid.[36] Yet it must be said that Barth sees Jesus Christ as the one who unifies Incarnation, crucifixion and resurrection so that no one of these acts assumes a pre-eminence against or apart from the others. If Barth's theology is anthropologically based, it is on the anthropology of Jesus Christ. The "humanity of God" certainly begins with the Incarnation, but it climaxes in the death and resurrection of the One who centers all conflict in himself, but does so in order to make peace.

Wingren's complaint against Barth that the problem of the knowledge of God is made the central issue of theology may seem reasonable in light of the attention it receives. But the construction of the *Dogmatics* argues more that the epistemological issues are the *first* to be examined, not necessarily the *most important* to be examined. Epistemology is the *sine qua non* prerequisite to all other theological considerations. But, as Barth said often enough, the real concern is with Christ Jesus himself.

*Interrelationships.* Barth neatly summarized the interrelationships between proclamation, Scripture and the revealed Word as follows:

> The revealed Word of God we know only from the Scripture adopted by Church proclamation, or from Church proclamation based on Scripture.
>
> The written Word of God we know only through the revelation which makes proclamation possible, or through the proclamation made possible by revelation.
>
> The proclaimed Word of God we know only by knowing the revelation attested through Scripture, or by knowing the Scripture which attests revelation.[37]

From the exposition of the three forms of the Word of God, Barth moved to his exposition of the doctrine of the Trinity. Even in his earlier discussion the doctrine of the Trinity was present, though unexpressed.[38] In the second chapter of volume one, part one, Barth moved to a full and explicit discussion of this doctrine. In placing it so early in his *Dogmatics* Barth stood common procedure on its head. "Handbooks on Christian doctrine usually begin with an account of their principles of authority and method."[39] But Barth had his reasons for his approach. As G. W. Bromiley noted, "The Word is God Himself in His self-revelation. But the God thus self-revealed is the triune God. Hence the primary theme of Christian dogmatics is the doctrine of the Trinity, to which there correspond the three aspects of revelation as revealer, thing revealed, and act of revelation."[40]

Barth knew that Christian theology is necessarily Trinitarian theology. In fact, in light of the prominence given by Barth to this doctrine, charges of Christomonism appear rather empty. While fully accepting the ancient formulations of Trinitarian doctrine, Barth also realized that they were not the final word on the subject. He offered as his own understanding one that was shaped in the givenness of God's revelation:

> We mean by the doctrine of the Trinity . . . the proposition that He whom the Christian Church calls God and proclaims as God, therefore the God who has revealed Himself according to the

witness of Scripture, is the same in unimpaired unity, yet also
the same in unimpaired variety thrice in a different way. Or, in
the phraseology of the dogma of the Trinity in the Church, the
Father, the Son and the Holy Spirit in the Bible's witness to
revelation are the one God in the unity of their essence, and the
one God in the Bible's witness to revelation is in the variety of
His Persons the Father, the Son, and the Holy Spirit.[41]

In part two of volume one the three forms of the Word of God are
each examined again in greater depth. The revelation of God is
seen in the Incarnation of the Word. "The Word or Son of God became a Man and was called Jesus of Nazareth; therefore this Man
Jesus of Nazareth was God's Word or God's Son."[42] Jesus Christ is
both the *objective* reality and possibility of revelation; the Holy
Spirit is both the *subjective* reality and possibility of revelation.
This means:

> Subjective revelation can consist only in the fact that objective
> revelation, the one truth which cannot be added to or bypassed,
> comes to man and is recognized and acknowledged by man. And
> that is the work of the Holy Spirit. . . . Subjective revelation can
> be only the repetition, the impress, the sealing of objective rev-
> elation upon us; or, from our point of view, our own discovery,
> acknowledgment and affirmation of it.[43]

### The Doctrine of God

Volume two of the *Church Dogmatics* (*The Doctrine of God*, published in two parts) explores the knowledge and reality of God.
The *fides quaerens intellectum* proves decisive to the knowledge
of God and the actualism of the living God to the reality of God.[44]
In the second part of volume two, Barth's important treatment of
election is developed. The volume concludes with the ethical dimensions of everything previously discussed under the doctrine of
God.

Barth's doctrine of election is revolutionary. As Bernard Ramm
contends:

> Karl Barth has attempted to give the doctrine of election an en-
> tirely new formulation. He attempts to find a way that is neither
> orthodox Calvinism with its absolute decree nor watery Armin-
> ianism. His chief objection to the former view is that it makes
> the pre-temporal and therefore secret decree of God more deter-

minative than the open and historical counsel of the death and resurrection of Jesus Christ. Thus the pre-temporal secret decree is in reality the deeper and prior word of God than that word spoken in the death and resurrection of Christ. The complaint against Arminianism is that it fails to do justice to the freedom and grace of God.[45]

In contrast with the past, Barth concentrates on viewing election in full relation to Christ. His high view of election is summed up in the declaration: "The election of grace is the sum of the Gospel—we must put it as pointedly as that. But more, the election of grace is the whole of the Gospel, the Gospel *in nuce*."[46] This is not at all an arbitrary statement. Barth had already explained:

The doctrine of election is the sum of the Gospel because of all words that can be said or heard it is the best: that God elects man; that God is for man too the One who loves in freedom. It is grounded in the knowledge of Jesus Christ because He is both the electing God and elected man in One. It is part of the doctrine of God because originally God's election of man is a predestination not merely of man but of Himself. Its function is to bear basic testimony to eternal, free and unchanging grace as the beginning of all the ways and works of God.[47]

In his review of the classic formulations of this doctrine Barth discovered many elements of value that needed to be retained. The positions of both supralapsarians and infralapsarians, however, needed reconstruction. Polman has identified four suppositions in those positions that Barth discovered and rejected. First, for both positions man, not Christ, is the object of predestination. Second, both positions posit a system of election to which God is bound since he created it. Third, a balance is created where God's mercy is perfectly matched with his judgment, but in a double predestination where some are elected to grace while others are consigned to damnation. Fourth, the notion of a divine absolute decree is set independent of Jesus Christ; "in the background God stands alone and not in Jesus Christ."[48]

Nevertheless, those who have in the past taken the doctrine of election seriously have been united in certain points of agreement. "All serious advocates of this doctrine see God's freedom, God's mystery, and God's righteousness authenticated in election by grace."[49] Christ, however, must be central. God's election is not apart from Christ: "It is the name of Jesus Christ which, according to the divine self-revelation, forms the focus at which the two decisive beams of the truth forced upon us converge and unite; on the one hand the electing God and on the other elected man."[50]

Bromiley notes, "Since God's election of Jesus Christ is His eternal will, a reconstructed supralapsarianism naturally follows."[51] What takes place in election takes place in Christ but is established from before the Fall. With his starting point in Christ, Barth could speak in concrete terms. As Weber enthusiastically observed, "We are not speaking about an abstract God but about God in Christ! And we are not speaking about an abstract man-in-himself, but about the man Jesus Christ!"[52]

God's election in Christ focuses on Jesus Christ as the electing God, the elected man and the rejected man. Barth is quite firm in this matter. Election cannot be separated from the person and work of Jesus Christ. It is useless to look for God's election anywhere else. Barth reaffirms:

> We must not ask concerning any other but Him. ... There is no such thing as a *decretum absolutum*. There is no such thing as a will of God apart from the will of Jesus Christ. Thus Jesus Christ is not only the *manifestatio* and *speculum nostrae praedestinationis*. And He is this not simply in the sense that our election can be known to us and contemplated by us only through His election, as an election which, like His and with His, is made (or not made) by a secret and hidden will of God. On the contrary, Jesus Christ reveals to us our election as an election which is made by Him, by His will which is also the will of God. He tells us that He Himself is the One who elects us.[53]

Barth's key texts here are Ephesians 1:4 (referred to over twelve times) and John 1:1-2 (referred to eight times). In regard to the former text Barth observed that it was a keen reminder "that knowledge of the election is only a distinctive form of the knowledge of Jesus Christ."[54] No one, he maintained, should be surprised at his treatment of this doctrine: "It is not as though we are really making an innovation when we describe the name of Jesus Christ as the basis of the doctrine of election."[55]

But Jesus Christ is not the electing God alone: "He is *the* Rejected, as and because He is *the* Elect."[56] This is good news for elected man. The judge has taken the place of the judged; the elect are fully acquitted. Those whom God elects in his Son are set free, free to be what God has intended for humankind from the beginning:

> In the One in whom they are elected, that is to say, in the death which the Son of God has died for them, they themselves have died as sinners. And that means their radical sanctification, separation and purification for participation in a true creaturely independence, and more than that, for the divine sonship of the creature which is the grace for which from all eternity they are elected in the election of the man Jesus.[57]

There is, however, a shadow side to election. There is a *praedestinatio gemina,* a double predestination. Some still resist the grace of God. Some still try to take upon themselves what Jesus Christ has already borne. These are the individuals who live in the shadow of God's election. Their rejection is the futile self-imposition of a wrath already poured out upon Christ.[58]

Berkouwer is critical of Barth at this point. He complains that "the rejection of man has a place in Barth's doctrine of predestination only in the sense that it is carried, put away and destroyed, by Christ."[59] In particular, Berkouwer argues, Barth here teaches a doctrine of universal election.[60] Colin Brown, who also finds fault with Barth at this point, believes that "it is important to notice how flimsy is the exegetical support for this momentous doctrine."[61] He is not, however, in complete agreement with Berkouwer as to where the doctrine must lead Barth. Brown notes, "If this line of thought brings Barth to the brink of universalism, he hesitates to take the final step."[62]

Barth himself was quite clear in his opposition to universalism. The doctrine of the restoration of all things *(apokatastasis pantōn)* denies the freedom of God's grace. *"Apokatastasis pantōn?* No, for a grace which automatically would ultimately have to embrace each and every one would certainly not be free grace. It surely would not be God's grace."[63] Yet, at the same time, Barth said:

> But would it be God's free grace if we could absolutely deny that it could do that? Has Christ been sacrificed only for our sins? Has He not, according to 1 John 2:2, been sacrificed for the whole world? Strange Christianity, whose most pressing anxiety seems to be that God's grace might prove to be all too free on this side, that hell, instead of being populated with so many

people, might someday prove to be empty![64]
At first glance such a statement certainly seems to open wide the
door to universalism. Actually it cracks open the door just wide
enough to allow God in his freedom to upset even the best human
theologies. Barth would not have any person, including himself,
put God in a box. Weber captures the essence of Barth's thought
when he observes that in Barth's doctrine "God's electing and rejecting bears in itself nothing fixed and static at all, nothing of a
universal law settled in advance. On the contrary, it possesses the
'character of actuality.' "[65] Thus in the final analysis all abstract
ideas about what God could or should have done must be set aside
in preference to what God has done. Arnold B. Come has summarized Barth's theme by a striking warning: "Any attempt to separate election from Jesus Christ allows it to slip into the irrational
darkness of an unknown God."[66]

Barth's concluding portion of volume two examines ethics as
God's commandment. Barth contended that ethics is a task of the
doctrine of God: "As the doctrine of God's command, ethics interprets the Law as the form of the Gospel, i.e., as the sanctification
which comes to man through the electing God."[67] The command is
also God's claim on man: "As God is gracious to us in Jesus Christ,
His command is the claim which, when it is made, has power over
us, demanding that in all we do we admit that what God does is
right, and requiring that we give our free obedience to this demand."[68]

Barth examined God's commandment in three sections. The
first, the commandment as God's claim, stresses his righteous
power in demanding human obedience. The second, the command
as God's decision, emphasizes that "His command is the sovereign,
definite and good decision concerning the character of our actions."[69] The third, the command as God's judgment, means
that "He judges us in order that He may make us free for ever-
lasting life under His lordship."[70] In all three aspects, and in every
aspect of the relation of ethics to the divine command, the covenant
between God and man is presupposed.[71]

## The Doctrine of Creation
Volume three of the *Church Dogmatics (The Doctrine of Creation)*
examines closely the covenant in the context of creation. "The

doctrine of Creation turns our attention for the first time directly to a reality different from the reality of God, the reality of the *world*."[72] Divided into four parts, the discussion of volume three is a comprehensive treatment that takes up more than two thousand pages.[73] The parts explore creation and covenant (III/1), the doctrine of man (III/2), the *nihil* (III/3) and ethics (III/4).

Creation stands first in the order of God's works. "The world is then a reality in itself, a proof of the mercy of God who agrees to the existence of something outside of himself."[74] It marks both the beginning of all that is distinct from God and the beginning of time. About the latter character of creation it must be said: "Since it contains in itself the beginning of time, its historical reality eludes all historical observation and account, and can be expressed in the biblical creation narratives only in the form of pure saga."[75]

Accordingly, a clear distinction must be made between *Historie* and *Geschichte* as well as between saga and myth. If the biblical account is to be taken seriously, and that means honestly, then it is essential that these distinctions be made. Thomas Ogletree notes about *Geschichte* and *Historie:* "In Barth's usage, the former refers to the reality of history christologically understood, history as determined by the sequence of encounters between God and man which has come to a decisive climax in the person of Jesus Christ. The latter designates the notion of history which is characteristic of modern historical thinking—history in the 'historicist' sense."[76]

After distinguishing between creation, history, and "creation history," Barth proceeded to his main subject: "the demonstration of the relationship between creation and covenant."[77] Simply expressed, the relationship is as follows: creation is the external basis of the covenant and covenant is the internal basis of creation.[78] There is only one covenant, that of redemption in Jesus Christ.

"Creation is not itself the covenant."[79] The two must not be equated or in any way blurred; a sharp focus must be kept. It must always be made clear that "the covenant is the goal of creation and creation the way to the covenant."[80] As the external—but only the external—basis of the covenant, creation occupies an indispensable position. Küng comments: "Creation makes the covenant technically possible; it sets aside the spaces and furnishes the subjects for it. It requires the existence of man and world, and love presupposes the existence and reality of the beloved. Barth makes all this clear in a long exegesis of the first creation account (III/1, 97-251)."[81]

The internal basis of creation "consists in the fact that the wisdom and omnipotence of God the Creator was not just any wisdom and omnipotence but that of His free love."[82] God the Father willed a covenant with man through Jesus the Son. That purpose of God is the raison d'être of creation. But man rebelled. Yet God the Creator had said Yes to what he had created. As Barth expressed it: "The work of God the Creator consists particularly in the benefit that in the limits of its creatureliness what He has created may be as it is actualized by Him, and be good as it is justified by Him."[83]

The second part on the doctrine of creation focuses on man. Concerning it, Hartwell comments: "Barth's doctrine of man is the most consistent one of its kind and is revolutionary in content."[84] Not surprisingly, this is because Barth once more started with Jesus Christ. "The nature of the man Jesus alone is the key to the problem of human nature. This man is man."[85] There is again a movement from the particular to the general, giving anthropology a theological and particularly Christological character.[86]

The third part on the doctrine of creation contains three great themes: "the fatherly providence of God, His kingdom on the left hand, and ministry of angels."[87] Where in the previous part Barth explored the relationship between Creator and creature in the light of Jesus Christ, in this part he has turned to the continuation of that relationship under the providence of God. Thus this part begins with an examination of the ground and structure of the doctrine of providence. Barth held that "the simple meaning of the doctrine of providence may ... be summed up in the statement that in the act of creation God the Creator as such has associated Himself with His creature as such as the Lord of its history, and is faithful to it as such."[88]

Once the doctrine has been established and described, it is immediately discussed in detail under the rubric of God the Father as Lord of his creature.[89] However, "there is opposition and resistance to God's world-dominion."[90] That problem is the problem of *das Nichtige,* the nothingness.[91] Yet even *das Nichtige* cannot be known or explained apart from Christ. To comprehend it one "must revert to the source of all Christian knowledge, namely, to the knowledge of Jesus Christ."[92]

Several facts become evident about *das Nichtige*. In the first place, "it is not a creaturely element confronted by others as elements of good."[93] But *das Nichtige* is real. Barth urged that "we cannot argue that because it has nothing in common with God and His creature nothingness is nothing, i.e., it does not exist."[94] On the contrary, *das Nichtige* exists and manifests a definite character in its opposition to the Creator and creature. "The character of nothingness derives from its ontic peculiarity. It is evil."[95] Yet about *das Nichtige* it must finally be said:

What is nothingness? In the knowledge and confession of the Christian faith, i.e., looking retrospectively to the resurrection of Jesus Christ and prospectively to His coming again, there is only one possible answer. Nothingness is the past, the ancient menace, danger and destruction, the ancient non-being which obscured and defaced the divine creation of God but which is consigned to the past in Jesus Christ, in whose death it has received its desert, being destroyed with this consummation of the positive will of God which is as such the end of his non-willing. Because Jesus is Victor, nothingness is routed and extirpated.[96]

This third part of volume three is concluded by a discussion entitled "The Kingdom of Heaven, the Ambassadors of God and Their Opponents."[97] The volume as a whole concludes with a massive fourth part on ethics. An ethic of freedom is developed as first, freedom before God; second, freedom in fellowship; third, freedom for life; and fourth, freedom in limitation.[98]

## The Doctrine of Reconciliation

Volume four of the *Dogmatics* (*The Doctrine of Reconciliation*, also published in four parts) can be summarized in three statements. "The first is that in Jesus Christ we have to do with very God."[99] This statement is elucidated in the remainder of the first part under the thought "Jesus Christ, the Lord as Servant." It is only a part of the picture, however. "The second christological aspect is that in Jesus Christ we have to do with true man."[100] This is the theme of the second part as it is developed under the title "Jesus Christ, the Servant as Lord." But one more statement must yet be made: "The third christological aspect to which we must now turn is at once the simplest and the highest. It is the source of the two first, and it comprehends them both. As the God who humbles Himself and as the One who is very God and very man in this concrete sense, Jesus Christ Himself is one. He is the 'God-man,' that is, the Son of God who as such is this man, this man who as such is the Son of God."[101]

In the doctrine of God's active reconciliation of man, several important things about man come to light. These matters, however, are still known only through Jesus Christ. God's purpose stands firmly prior to man's Fall. The work of reconciliation, therefore, "is the fulfilment of the covenant between God and man."[102] Reconciliation is the manner of covenant fulfillment that God has chosen to meet the problem of human sin. In view of that, Bromiley has noted: "In a preparatory survey of the doctrine Barth then points out: (1) that this divine work is still grace; (2) that it is not part of a higher dialect; (3) that it cannot be deduced; (4) that it is sovereign; and (5) that it is a fact in Jesus Christ."[103]

Jesus Christ is the Mediator between God and man.[104] Through him man is truly known. "The first man was immediately the first sinner."[105] The Fall was man's word to God but a word unknown to man himself. In fact, apart from God there is no knowledge of sin.[106] But "from the particular christological standpoint which is our present norm ... the sin of man is the pride of man."[107]

The answer to the problem of sin is reconciliation. To the doctrine of reconciliation also belongs the doctrine of justification. "Pardon—by God and therefore unconditionally pronounced and unconditionally valid—that is man's justification."[108] On the human side it must be said that man is justified *sola fide,* by faith alone. Faith is "the human action which makes a faithful and authentic and adequate response to the faithfulness of God."[109] In its simple and concrete form, "faith is the humility of obedience."[110]

Justification by faith has a divine promise attached to it. "And the pardon of man, declared in the promise concerning him, the reality of his future already in the present, is no less than this: *totus iustus.*"[111] The promise holds within itself three aspects: the forgiveness of sins, the giving of the rights of a child of God, and the placement of man in a position of hope.[112] "The justification of man begins in his past and it is completed in his future."[113]

Sanctification, the complement to justification, is presented in the second part on the doctrine of reconciliation. Barth explained:

What is meant by sanctification *(sanctificatio)* might just as well be described by the less common biblical term regeneration *(regeneratio)* or renewal *(renovatio)*, or by that of conversion *(conversio)*, or by that of penitence *(poenitentia)* which plays so important a role in both the Old and New Testaments, or comprehensively by that of discipleship which is so outstanding especially in the synoptic Gospels.[114]

The third part of volume four, published in two half-parts, is entitled "Jesus Christ, the True Witness." Here a major section is given over to a discussion on the vocation of man. Barth knew about the elect that "in believing in Him they are acknowledging that when He died and rose again, they too, died and rose again in Him, and that, from now on, their life, in its essentials, can only be a copy and image of His."[115] This means that "the purpose of a man's vocation is that he should become a Christian, a *homo christianus*."[116]

The final part on the doctrine of reconciliation, and the final segment of the *Church Dogmatics,* is no more than a fragment of what Barth had projected. Barth had planned that "the volume was to deal with Christian (human) work as this corresponds to, and thus has its own place in respect of, the divine work of reconciliation."[117] But it was not to be. The hoped-for portions on the various practical aspects of Christian life under the guidance of the Lord's Prayer and the doctrine of the Lord's Supper were left incomplete. Only the fragment on baptism, as baptism with the Holy Spirit and then baptism with water, was included.[118]

Barth never completed his *Church Dogmatics.* A few years before his death he realized that the task would have to remain unfinished. The projected volume on the doctrine of redemption was never attempted. Nonetheless, Barth had left a stunning legacy for the church. The *Church Dogmatics* alone contains a wealth of valuable material to stimulate the thought of scholars for a long time. When Barth's many other works are also considered, an awesome picture emerges. Those who ignore his writings, or are ignorant of his life, remain the poorer.

Neither criticism nor adulation should obscure the importance of Barth as a resource for the Christian church. But the value of this resource resides also in wise, judicious use. This means, first of all, an awareness of the need to which the resource is to be applied. Second, its wise use demands careful attention to the resource itself. Finally, a thoughtful attempt must be made to apply the resource to the need. The resource should neither be substituted for what it purports to help, nor superficially applied as a Band-Aid to cover some visible but unimportant blemish. The process requires a cost from those who pursue it. To dare to think with Barth, to try to follow his reasoning, is a task as frightening as it is exciting. But individuals who have already walked with Barth and been enriched can help those who wish to walk with him. Such is the task before evangelical men and women when they consider Barth: to hear him, walk with him, learn from him —to the benefit of the community of which they are a part.

# Part IV

## Evangelical Theology on the Move

# 12

# Barth
as Guide

Where are evangelicals going in the 1980s? Will they find themselves pushed further along bleak roads to the lonely caves of a wilderness cult in a secular society? Or will they find themselves "born again" through reformation and renewal?

Karl Barth, it seems to me, could provide a measure of inspiration and direction for the healthy renewing and reforming of evangelical theology to move evangelicalism away from the caves toward the warmth of a redemptive society. As we have seen, not all evangelicals would agree. Nevertheless, I have attempted to show that there is good reason to agree with the following assessment of Donald Dayton:

> Evangelical reaction has varied from the early attacks of Cornelius Van Til, for whom Barth's thought was The New Modernism (1946) and perhaps the most dangerous heresy in the history of the Church, to more appreciative but not uncritical evaluations by men such as Donald Bloesch, who devotes a chapter to "A Reassessment of Karl Barth" in *The Evangelical Renaissance* (1973). Surely the truth lies more with Bloesch, and evangelicals ought to welcome a reawakening of interest in Barth's theology as a most potent force for biblical and evangelical renewal in America.[1]

History tells its own story of evangelicalism's effort to take the good news of Jesus Christ to each new generation—to the very ends of the earth. But the evangelical church itself has had to rediscover that good news, and its own reason to exist, every generation. Missionary motive, biblical content and church context have provided an energizing spirit to evangelical reform and renewal. In the face of challenges in every decade to these commitments, an American evangelicalism has emerged at times stronger, at others weaker. Yet in each instance it has remained committed not to any vague motive, content or context, but to the commission of Jesus, to an authoritative Scripture and to the church as the body of Christ.

This generation's evangelical community stands in the ancient line of Christ's challenging command and beneath the wilting exposure of mass media attention. In the current crisis, the issues are at least familiar: Unity—why does evangelicalism exist? Validity—is the Bible valid for twentieth-century human beings, and does evangelical theology reflect that validity? Identity—who is the church? Who are the evangelicals? Responsible answers are demanded in a society that has "come of age" only in its skepticism.

With the examination of evangelical history as a starting point and the study of Barth as a resource, there remains the task of drawing together those particulars that can strengthen evangelicalism. Peeling away the dross should reveal the inner foundation of the gospel of Christ. Close attention to Barth can help recover the essentials of that gospel. Adding certain features from Barth to the ongoing development of evangelical theology may help consummate important elements that have briefly surfaced at various points in evangelical history. The evangelical presentation of the gospel to this society can be enhanced by Karl Barth. The historical use of his work in this generation may vouchsafe to coming generations a brighter heritage.

This process must be an exercise of faith to be called *evangelical*. It must be characterized by positive or *constructive* use of Barth's theology, a bold or *dynamic* approach to problems, and a *dogmatic* insistence that all be conducted under the authority of the Word of God. It must be a glad work, hopeful in the faith that the renewing and reforming of the evangelical church is a washing in the Word by the Lord of the church. The faith to undertake the task is itself the Lord's gracious gift. Shall the church refuse it?

## The Constructive Theologian

Barth was an individual of the church. During his life he was prophet, pilgrim, preacher and pastor. As prophet, he sent forth in his *Epistle to the Romans* a strong word about human sinfulness, the awesome sovereignty of God, and the great gulf separating human beings from God. As pilgrim, Barth adopted the language of dialectics to speak about God while he sought restlessly for a more adequate way. As preacher, Barth wrote his *Church Dogmatics* for the proclamation of the church. As pastor, Barth not only preached but passed the tasks of his Christian vocation on to those of the next generation. At every step along the way Barth was a member of the church, dedicated to the service of the church as service to the Lord.

As a positive theologian, Barth shaped his theology by constructive action, not reaction. That meant a "good confession," a gospel and a Bible undisturbed by the higher criticism. At the same time, however, Barth was not one to retreat and hide. He refused to allow apologetics, in the more traditional sense, any place in his theology for the simple reason that the gospel had no need of it. He would not leave room for Brunner's "eristics" either. Brunner conceded that "Karl Barth's hostility to Apologetics is, however, to this extent justified, because it is true that discussion with non-Christian thought cannot be the basis and the starting-point for dogmatics itself. His opposition to 'eristics' was necessary, so long as this was proclaimed as the 'foundation' of dogmatics."[2]

Because of the power of the gospel and his confidence in it, Barth could risk—in fact, feel compelled—to speak of *legend* (the depiction in saga form of a concrete individual personality) and *saga* to describe certain portions of the Bible. He was seeking an exactness of language for the church's proclamation. Narratives like the creation account seemed to be other than *Historie*, but clearly not "myth." When Barth used either the term *legend* or *saga* he meant by it something unambiguous. This was quickly recognized by other theologians like Brunner who replied: "The word 'myth' is to be preferred (in spite of its ambiguity) to 'legend' (which Barth suggests), because 'legend' refers to historical fact."[3] Barth never challenged the factuality of biblical events by the use of these terms. He distinguished literary genres.

At every turn Barth set forth the gospel of Jesus Christ. H. R. Mackintosh wrote that "Barth's mind is dominated by the thought of God which emerges from the Bible. In the service of that thought he finds perfect freedom."[4] It was unabused freedom. It was the freedom of the Christian mission.

Constructive theology is necessarily mission theology. The most positive message that can be proclaimed is the message of God in Jesus Christ. Mission theology for Barth was necessarily Trinitarian and Christocentric theology. According to Barth, when Jesus was delivered up to Pilate and the Gentiles by the leading representatives of Israel, it was "the event which necessarily transformed the mission to Israel (Mt. 10:1f) into a world-wide mission: 'Go ye therefore, and make disciples of all nations' (Mt. 28:19)."[5] Mission, in essence, is "a reflection of the way which God Himself went from those who have all things to those who have nothing."[6] Here, as everywhere else, the center is Jesus and the message is the gospel.

## The Dynamic Theologian

Barth's constructive efforts were supported by his dynamic outlook. As one member within the body of Christ, he felt he had to be in dialog with others. Barth was adept at dialoguing with Scripture, past theologians and present thinkers—and then challenging future theologians to think through and rethink every issue.

Gabriel Vahanian said Barth was "truly faithful to the intentions and structure of the rediscovery of the gospel that took place in the period of the Reformation."[7] That was because Barth did not canonize the Reformers' conclusions. Like them he was in the process of creating the Christian tradition, not cementing it. Dialog was at the heart of Barth's work. It meant more than just speaking; it meant listening to and learning from others.

## The Dogmatic Theologian

The results of Barth's dialog were expressed in the form of dogmatics. Within the context of the church and by the standards of the Christian canon, Barth reviewed the language of the church in order best to express and fulfill its mission. Was he successful?

Colin Brown has suggested that one of Barth's most significant contributions to the church today has been his bringing of "fundamental questions back into the centre of attention."[8] Barth has focused the issues and, as Brown noted, "He has also raised again key themes of the Bible which are regularly pushed into the background in the church today."[9] As Thomas F. Torrance commented, "Both in its grandeur and in its profundity Barth's massive explication of our knowledge of God has established such contact with reality that it will be a constant source of surprise and discovery for students who may have something of the same awe and humility, the mingled joy and wonder and responsibility, that characterised Karl Barth himself."[10]

Barth's dogmatic theology cannot legitimately be ignored. It represents a constructive theology actively engaged in productive dialog. It demonstrates one way to review, renew and reform the theology, the proclamation and the life of the church. Perhaps Geoffrey W. Bromiley has said it best:

> Here is a dogmatics which seeks its starting-point in faith, which depends for its strength on prayer, which consciously orientates itself to the Lord, and which finds its true climaxes in praise. Reverence is, of course, no substitute for truth; yet the truth is not honored without reverence. Hence these are qualities in Barth's theology which we cannot fail to respect, which we may seek to emulate even in our criticisms and which we should covet earnestly for all theological endeavor.[11]

### Reflections

Norman F. Langford has said that "Barth is above all a theologian for practical preachers and teachers."[12] Those who cannot find time for a complete reading of the *Church Dogmatics* can still draw on that work's excellent resources for classroom and pulpit. The greatest value of Karl Barth as a guide is ultimately much deeper. He has shown the way for evangelical theology to move with the times without capitulating to the current situation of any given moment. Theology is always *theologia viatorum,* theology along the way. It is the proclamation of an eternal message in a moment-by-moment relevancy of expression. God's revelation is neither irrelevant nor ethereal:

> On the contrary, the event of revelation as described for us in Scripture has everywhere a natural, bodily, outward and visible component—from the creation (not only of heaven and also of earth), by way of the concrete existence of the people of Israel in Palestine, the birth of Jesus Christ, His physical miracles, His suffering and death under Pontius Pilate, His physical resurrection, right down to His coming again and the resurrection of the body.[13]

More than twenty years ago Nels Ferré indicated some of the many ways Barth can serve as a guide for the evangelical today:

> We have great need to return to main Christian assumptions. In method Barth puts faith first: the faith of revelation, of the Bible, and of the Church. In doctrine he is a thorough-going supernaturalist of a decisive evangelical faith. His stress on the Bible and Christ magnifies God and refuses to be bound by all narrow limits of history and experience. How mightily he combines the sovereignty of God and his limitless love! In eschatology, although he rightly eschews all human predictions and basis for hope, he announces the final victory of God in clear and unmistakably Christian terms. How can any Christian teacher be thankful enough to Karl Barth![14]

To see how Barth may guide evangelical efforts today, one has only to examine his final message to the church. "It is no accident that Barth in his very last work intended to challenge ... Christians ... to set out, to return, and to confess."[15] Together those challenges comprise a way forward into the future.

The *setting out* of the believing community is, thought Barth, "an affirmation of the Church's future and only then, and because of it, the abandoning of the past."[16] Thus setting out follows a constructive order. First the future is affirmed because of the presence of Christ going on before his church and beckoning her to follow. Then the past is "abandoned," but neither recklessly nor regrettingly. The church cannot simply criticize or venerate the past. Neither protest nor contempt, neither praise nor glorification are acceptable alternatives. The past is abandoned to the future so that the past may be truly past but never lost.

Today's evangelical community appears uncertain as to how it should relate to its past. Contemporary prophets do not hold forth a promising future. Evangelical generation gaps emerge as some advocate regenerating the past while others protest. A consensus indicates a setting out is needed, but the direction is unclear. Few of those who urge a moving ahead are confident enough to openly affirm the future.

There is great need today to rediscover that the affirmation of the future is possible because Christ insures the inevitability of a future worth affirming. Barth insisted that "the setting out of the Church is genuine and right if the Church envisages as the New, and therefore as its future, the unambiguous and definite Promise given to the Church by Jesus Christ."[17] If, as Barth said, "the genuine and right setting out of the Church must be performed in orderly fashion,"[18] then the first step forward for today's evangelical community must be to take heart and be of good cheer, in light of a future certainly determined by the promise of Christ.

Barth suggested that the setting out of the church meant a "both-and" for the past and future. The Church need not choose one at the expense of the other. Neither need be compromised. But the past must be given up for the future, and the future can only be found through *returning* to the past. Barth advised: "The movement of the Church is, secondly, a vigorous returning to what has taken place at the beginning."[19] The setting out is thus guided by the past. It is, in fact, a return to the past. But the return is not to any other point in the past than the very beginning. Barth specified that "the crucified and risen Jesus Christ is both the Old and the New to whom the Church must turn in that it returns."[20]

Evangelicals are often plagued by not returning far enough. Wesleyans return to Wesley, Arminians to Arminius, Lutherans to Luther and Calvinists to Calvin. Where scholastic thought once believed the task of theology was to think God's thoughts after him, today's evangelical often only rethinks Puritan theology or one of a great number of other conservative alternatives. This is not wrong in itself. We are doing the same thing in studying Barth. But we must not return just to Barth any more than we simply return to Wesley or Calvin or Augustine.

The right returning of the Church to any point in its past is only in using that point as a concrete resource for being rightly turned to Christ. By this endeavor all historical differences can be bridged in the unifying task of relating properly to the one living Lord of the church. Those distinctions that today threaten evangelicalism can become resources for a vital missionary unity.

Thus the third aspect of the one movement of the Church is necessarily its *confessing*. In every work undertaken by the church in the present confession should be characteristic. The polemics within the community that must go on must also be harnessed to the fruitful effort of sharpening the proclamation of the church. The setting out of the church is a confident confession of the surety of the promise and the faithfulness of the Promiser. The returning of the church to its past is the confession of those who are teachable, of those who build upon the solid labors of others. At every turn the confessing of the church is the preaching of the gospel.

This last aspect was not developed in written form by Barth. The evening of these final thoughts was the last evening in his life. But, as Hartwell noted, in Barth's outline "the last key-word 'Fröhlich ernstnehmen' (let us take seriously and rejoice) is a comforting legacy to future generations. It could be the epitaph to the life and work of Barth himself, who once described himself as 'God's joyful partisan.' "21

In the final word, the movement of the church must be taken seriously but with joyfulness. The resources provided by Karl Barth's life and work remain ready for profitable use by evangelicals in their own movement. Those who dialog with Barth have already taken a first step toward creating a more positive presentation of evangelical theology. It is not necessary to accept every, or even any, thought of Barth without revision or qualification. But it is necessary to hear him, to learn from him and with him to point to Jesus Christ.

# 13

# Responding to the Current Crisis

The orderly *setting out* of the evangelical church is dependent on its grateful affirmation of God's purpose in Christ and its hopeful faith in his promise that Christ shall return in power. Setting out demands looking forward in anticipation to the fulfillment of God's work. What God has already done in the church and world is affirmed as the church steadfastly refuses to be bound to the past but abandons it for God's promise: Christ shall return to the church that has been kept safe and made ready for him.

Abandoning the past frees the church for *returning* through the past to its point of origin. By not holding to the past the church is free to be guided by its wisdom. Refusing bondage to what has happened allows the church to see the future and the past in the light of Christ—the Alpha and the Omega.

Thus the *confessing* of the church assumes a continuing contemporaneity in which freedom to change the expression of that confession is guided by the past but open to the future. The authority of Scripture is thus seen as active and relevant not only to the church in the past but in the future as well. God's promise still before the church finds its constant witness in the Bible no less than God's already fulfilled promises have.

Accordingly, the missionary motive impelling the evangelical to *set out* is accompanied by a continual *return* to the Scriptures and to the Christ they declare. The evangelical *confession* is of the Christ of Scripture, the One who was, who is, and who shall be. But this confession is in the church—it is the church's confession —because it is in the church that past and future are joined under the lordship of Jesus Christ.

The American evangelical church has always been in movement. The setting out, returning and confessing of the church is not unique to today. Evangelicalism has always been involved in one or another of these three. In what manner, though, can Karl Barth's vision of appropriate movement address the current evangelical crisis of unity, validity and identity? It seems to me that his vision suggests three theses:

1. Evangelicals must be unified, but on the right issues and in the right way.

2. Evangelicals must validate their evangelicalism, not by appeals to unanswerable—and unproven—hypotheses, but by faithful proclamation of the gospel.

3. Evangelicals must both broaden and sharpen their community identity.

### Unity

Evangelical unity is fundamentally related to the missionary motive that gives evangelicalism its name and only proper existence. The evangelical church is the community of "communion between God and man, informed by the gospel of Jesus Christ as heard in Holy Scripture."[1] It is a self-extending community under the direction of the Holy Spirit and by the authority of Christ's command (Mt. 28:19). The missionary nature of the evangelical church is rooted in the command of Jesus as received through the text of Scripture.

Barth's most specific work on the biblical basis for the Christian mission was his *"Auslegung von Matthäus 28, 16-20,"* translated by Thomas Wieser as "An Exegetical Study of Matthew 28:16-20."[2] His argument runs as follows.

The *fact* of Easter is the unveiled revelation of the resurrected Jesus, "a *real event* in space and time," that marks the presence of the *eschaton*. This is all revealed to the disciples when Jesus appears to them. Moreover, "He appeared to them not in order to continue his ministry of teaching and healing . . . but to disclose the hitherto hidden purpose of his life and death to his followers and to give them the charge of proclaiming his Lordship and the kingdom now manifest before their eyes." Easter is thus the essential preliminary to the commission that follows.

The import of Easter is clearly displayed when at the appearance of the Lord both worship (17a) and doubt appear; "worship and doubt have a common cause; the servant figure of the man Jesus was garbed in the glory of God. Revelation always has a *terminus a quo* and a *terminus ad quem*. Veiled, it arouses doubt; unveiled, it commands worship." Here, then, is the pivotal point in the disciples' experience of Jesus; it is resolved when, "By approaching them Jesus awakened faith in the doubters!" Immediately Jesus affirms, "All authority in heaven and on earth has been given to me."

The command that follows is dependent on what has preceded it; "this affirmation of power is the objective presupposition on the part of Jesus for the immediately following imperative." But this is good news for the missionary. Jesus himself "assures the execution of the command over against both the disciples' weakness and any interference by a third party." The command itself is good news: "Make them what you yourselves are! Have them learn here, with me, where you yourselves have learned! Call them into the twelve of the eschatological Israel! Let them share in its place and task in the world!"

Jesus' command envisages the founding of the apostolic Church. "This apostolic Church, existing not for itself, but 'for Christ,' on behalf of him, . . . is the decisive event of the *eschaton* that has broken into time." This "new eschatological community" is "gathered from among the Jews and Gentiles." Even as "the apostles are called to make apostolic Christians of all others," so, "to become a Christian means to become a Christ to others by participating in Christ's kingly, priestly, and prophetic ministry." Among the activities entailed by such a life are baptism and teaching.

Finally, "the Church of the *eschaton* which broke into time and now is manifest and recognized is not left alone." The promise of Jesus is the promise of the risen Lord; "As the apostles receive and grasp this promise and stand on this firm ground, they are the rock on which Jesus builds his church, stronger than the gates of Hades." Thus, "because of Jesus' presence, the sum and substance of our text, the Great Commission of the Risen Lord to baptize and evangelize is valid throughout the days of this 'last' age."[3]

The understanding of the Christian mission framed above can be seen in various shades elsewhere in Barth's theology. As early as 1921, in the second edition of *The Epistle to the Romans,* he wrote:

> For, where the grace of God is, men participate in proclaiming the transformation of time and of things, the Resurrection— however reservedly and with whatever scepticism they proclaim it. Where the grace of God is, the very existence of the world and very existence of God become a question and a hope with which and for which men must wrestle. For we are not now concerned with the propaganda of a conviction or with its imposition on others; grace means bearing witness to the faithfulness of God which a man has encountered in Christ, and which, when it is encountered and recognized, requires a corresponding fidelity towards God. The fidelity of a man to the faithfulness of God—the faith, that is, which accepts grace—is itself the demand for obedience and itself demands obedience from others. Hence the demand is a call which enlightens and rouses to action; it carries with it mission, beside which no other mission is possible.[4]

That way of speaking about mission gave way to more sophisticated expressions. In the *Church Dogmatics,* Barth again addressed himself to the Christian mission:

> It is because Jesus is Himself both the content and proclamation of Scripture that He makes the disciples what they could not be of themselves—witnesses to the content of Scripture, and therefore His witnesses. In Mt. 28:19a we are then given the simple commission which they are to execute as those whom He has enabled for the purpose: ... make of them what you yourselves are, my disciples. Let them learn what you yourselves have learned. ... The world, then, is to be summoned to faith in Him, to the recognition and acknowledgment of the repentance which He has completed for it, and therefore to the repentance in which the bearing away of sin which He has accomplished becomes recognisable and real for the world. This

is clear in Mt. 28:19b.... The command given to the apostles is simply the command to preach the Gospel. But they are to preach it... not in a vacuum, or without form, but in the specific form of its application to those who listen to it in the world.[5] The applied forms of preaching include baptism and teaching. All rests in the authority of the resurrected Lord who is with his disciples always. These various ideas resound throughout the *Dogmatics,* although they do not always appear together in the same context or as the point of focus. Rather, Barth's concept of the Christian mission is a part of the total harmony he constructs, just as it is but a part of the whole gospel. Barth allows the biblical doctrine of mission to inform and color his *Dogmatics* and avoids considering it in isolation.

In the maturity of his thought, Barth changed the title of his labors from "Christian" dogmatics to "church" dogmatics to reflect a new understanding. Toward the end of his life he adopted yet another title, "evangelical" theology. In the book by that title Barth once again discussed mission:

The community is confronted and created by the Word of God. It is *communio sanctorum,* the communion of the saints, because it is *congregatio fidelium,* the gathering of the faithful. As such, it is the *coniuratio testium,* the confederation of the witnesses who may and must speak because they believe. The community does not speak with words alone. It speaks by the very fact of its existence in the world; by its characteristic attitude to world problems; and, moreover and especially, by its silent service to all the handicapped, weak, and needy in the world. It speaks, finally, by the simple fact that it prays for the world. It does all this because this is the purpose of its summons by the Word of God.[6]

As before, the context of the Christian mission is the church. It is an "evangelical" mission, one that must "speak" but cannot limit that speech to mere words. The Christian mission can exist only as the *Christ*-ian mission; its basis is the Word of God.

In summary, Barth's understanding of the Christian mission incorporates the following ideas:

1. The *resurrection* of Jesus is the necessary prelude. It unveils the presence of the *eschaton.*

2. The *authority* of Jesus is both the basis of the Great Com-

mission and the guarantee of its fulfillment.

3. Jesus' *command* envisages the creation of a self-perpetuating community, the church.

4. Jesus' *church* exists for him. Its identity with him makes clear its participation in the *eschaton;* it is an eschatological community. This community is a witnessing community as it speaks by word and deed of its Lord.

5. Thus, the Christian mission begins with the Lord Jesus and ends with him; it is the task of the church within the limits of the world (its extent) and the *eschaton* (its duration); only the presence of the power of the risen Lord assures its continuation and success from the resurrection to the close of this age.

Reduced to its simplest form, the Christian mission is the work of Christ enacted in obedience by his body, the church. When the basis of evangelical unity is moved from Christ's command to preach the gospel, or loses sight of Christ's promise to return, or adds any other feature—good or bad—to these, the rock on which Christ builds his church is being replaced by sand which is washed away in the rains of every passing controversy. Evangelical unity predicated, for instance, on adherence to a doctrine of biblical inerrancy is a contradiction in terms: that which divides evangelicals cannot also bring them together. The only grounds for unity are the command and promise of Christ.

This understanding of the Christian mission and fidelity to its implications allowed Billy Graham and Karl Barth to assist rather than oppose one another during the 1960 Graham crusades in Switzerland and Germany. On two separate occasions they met, with Barth each time favorably impressed. He even attended the opening crusade meeting in Basel. Despite his reaction against Graham's style of presenting, as Barth put it, "the gospel at gunpoint," there was no opposition by him. Later, in 1962, while visiting in the United States, Barth again enjoyed a period of conversation with Graham.[7] Nor was the understanding Barth's alone. Graham, in a visit with Emil Brunner during Graham's stay in Switzerland, said that Brunner's theological impact had prepared the way for evangelism by its undermining of liberal theology.[8] In that regard, what was true of Brunner's work was also true of Barth's.

Karl Barth and Billy Graham obviously understood the Christian mission in somewhat different ways. Yet both were more interested in proclaiming the gospel in obedience to Christ and in light of the promise of his return than they were in conducting verbal warfare over otherwise important doctrines. The point is that evangelical unity consists of action undertaken in a common cause, namely, obedience to God.

Obedience to God is action enjoined by God on human beings and performed by them in the power of the Holy Spirit according to the divine will. Evangelical unity rests *solely* on such obedience and is ultimately vouchsafed *solely* by the promise of Christ's return. The nature of obedience and the fact of God's promise, however, are known *solely* through Holy Scripture. Accordingly, doctrinal differences do affect Christian unity. But, as Barth pointed out, although doctrinal differences may demonstrate a more or less willing obedience, or even prove a contrast between one person's obedience and another's rebellion, doctrine itself is not obedience. Rather, obedience is doing what one hears (Jn. 8:47; Mt. 7:24-27). As he wrote, "Man's action is good in so far as he is the obedient hearer of the Word and command of God. The hearing and obeying which proceeds from and by the Word of God is man's sanctification."[9] It is God himself who insures obedience and thereby maintains unity; there is no deprecation of human will here but only the final reminder of God's promise of Christ's return.

Because obedience is what it is, the instructions of the apostle Paul to the Romans speak to the evangelical need for unity in the face of temptations to seek unity in doctrinal standards. Paul touched the essence of the matter when he warned, "we shall all stand before the judgment seat of God" (Rom. 14:10). It is God who condemns—or justifies. What each person is called to is obedience predicated on the hearing of God's command: "Each of us shall give account of himself to God" (Rom. 14:12).

Does this, then, consign the community to an endless babble of subjective opinions? Not at all. Scripture, despite all the risks of error inherent in interpretation, is an objective standard by which the nature of obedience is disclosed. Doctrinal formulations derived from Scripture carry within themselves the ethical implications of Christian discipleship. Thus, although true obedience to God may entail a range of beliefs, doctrines and actions, all of them are enclosed by the perimeters established in the Bible. As an objective standard, the Bible is a broad arbiter in deciding what is within or without the already established bounds of Christian unity. The Bible is to be appealed to with reference to the effects of doctrinal differences on unity. But the Bible is rightly understood only when used to enhance unity, not to obstruct it.

## Validity

When the correct basis for unity has been perceived, the second proposition, on validation of evangelicalism, becomes viable. When a unity founded on the mission of the church is strengthened by the content of the gospel and actualized by proclamation, an apologetic of the Christian faith surfaces that has no need or use for philosophical hypotheses designed to safeguard the authority of the church's work. An evangelicalism united in the faithful proclamation of Christ need not claim authority—it *is* authority.

Challenges to the authority and veracity of the Bible are also challenges to the validity of evangelical existence. Some evangelicals, therefore, hold that it is imperative for the evangelical community to specify the locus and extent of that authority and the nature of that veracity. On the other hand, Klaas Runia has contended:

> With Barth we cannot emphasize enough that the divine revelation can only prove itself, and for that reason we have to renounce all human proofs. The authority of the Bible rests in itself. Rightly Bavinck says: "Holy Scripture is 'autopistos' (i.e., it brings out faith in itself) and therefore is the last ground of faith. The question: Why do you believe in Scripture?, can only be answered in this way: Because it is the Word of God. But if then it is asked: Why do you believe that Holy Scripture is the Word of God?, the Christian has no further answer."

Whoever wishes to call this a "logical circle" may freely do so. With good reason Barth is not at all afraid of this charge. He even openly admits that this is the only possibility.... The Christian faith and Christian theology need not be ashamed of this charge of a "logical circle." On the contrary! It is the very condition of their existence. As soon as they abandon it, there will not be any more *Christian* faith and *Christian* theology. Precisely this offense, this "skandalon" is the proof of their genuineness.

All attempts to explain this circle away, however well-intended they may be, actually mean an undermining of the basis.[10]

This view shared by Runia and Barth has been rejected by some as a "fideism" unworthy of theological integrity. ("Fideism ... refers generally to the doctrine that Christian assertions are matters of blind belief and cannot be known or demonstrated to be true.")[11] Clark H. Pinnock, R. C. Sproul and Norman Geisler among others deplore what Pinnock terms an "allergy" to Christian evidences. In response James Daane says:

Given his view of the Bible, the testimony of the Spirit, and faith, Pinnock is led to regard the church's preaching task not as the proclamation of the Bible's claims, but of the evidence of the Bible's claims. ... Seminaries whose professors successfully teach this view of the Bible, of the testimony of the Spirit, and of the Christian faith, will produce men for the pulpit who are apologetes rather than preachers, men who lecture in the pulpit on the evidences for the truth of the Bible, rather than men who preach the Bible itself.[12]

Daane further contends, "Reject a self-authenticating Bible, and we are left with a Bible that can only be validated by human judgment."[13] Yet does not such a view inevitably mean fideism? To this charge, Daane responds:

What arises out of God's grace and freedom, by the very fact of its origin cannot be put to the test of evidence or to the claims of rational judgment. It can be known and accepted only on its own terms. When such free and gracious actions occur, we can only react in stunned wonder and marvel that they did in fact occur, and break the silence of our amazement only to praise and proclaim.

Such faith is not fideism; it knows in whom it believes.[14]

Barth's position was much the same. He had learned from Anselm that theological knowledge works with what is given to it by its object. Such procedure is rational, not blind. When God is the object, faith—not fideism—is the specific mode of rationality, for faith alone is allowed by the object for the establishment and verification of knowledge. In the same way, the Bible can be known and accepted only on its own terms. Barth stated that "the truth and force of Holy Scripture in its self-attesting credibility is itself... a single and simultaneous act of lordship by the triune God, who in His revelation is the object and as such the source of Holy Scripture."[15]

The witness of Holy Scripture is... the witness of the Holy Spirit. He is indeed the power of the matter of Holy Scripture. By Him it became Holy Scripture; by Him and only by Him it speaks as such. In doing so it mediates revelation; it presents Jesus Christ; in the servant form of a human word it speaks the Word of God. Those who hear it, hear Him. Those who wish to hear Him must hear it. This is the Evangelical principle of Scripture as such: the universal, fundamental and self-sufficient thing which has to be said about the attestation and mediation of revelation.[16]

The authority of Holy Scripture rests in itself, which means it rests in God. There is thus no need to appeal to evidence substantiating the Bible's claims. It is even less rational to appeal to philosophical hypotheses to support the authority of Scripture. As Hans Urs von Balthasar has pointed out, it would be inaccurate to call Barth's position fideism, although it does share some likeness to fideism.[17]

Challenges to the authority and veracity of Holy Scripture are met by God. If it is not God who validates Holy Scripture, then evangelicalism's existence is invalid. But God does vindicate the Bible. He does so through the witness of the Holy Spirit. This view is not a theological cover for personal subjective decision by individuals as to where and how the Bible is or is not authoritative and truthful. Rather, it is God's own judgment on the Bible communicated to humankind.

According to Barth's thought, Scripture is Holy Scripture by virtue of the event of revelation. It is God's decision, his freedom, that establishes the Bible as the Word of God. Or, as one writer put it, "the Word of God contains the Bible."[18] The nature of God as subject and object prevents a rampant individual subjectivism and preserves a place for genuine subjectivity. James Brown has noted:

Barth talks a great deal about God as "Subject," "indissolubly Subject." But he very definitely allows that God is in certain respects "Object," if not "an object." God is Object to His own self-knowledge in the life of the eternal Trinity, Object of faith-knowledge to man in revelation, a disclosure which in turn presents God as Subject, the living Lord who calls for man's obedience, the active Subject in originating man's knowledge of Himself, both as to its form and its matter, its possibility and its substance.[19]

Again, it is only in faith that one may seek God and be found by him. Faith is from God but is also truly the individual's. The Holy Spirit imparts faith and confirms it. So-called existential encounter, where God meets a human being in the event of revelation, is rightful subjectivity. But it enhances the objective reality of Scripture as the divine, authoritative and truthful witness to God in Christ. The witness of the Holy Spirit to Christ when God meets a human being also corroborates Scripture as God's own Word.

God validates the Bible not only by the witness of the Spirit, but through the proclamation of the church. There is, though, a qualification here as well. Barth saw that proclamation is made possible by revelation and makes revelation known by pointing to it. But nonetheless it makes revelation known only through the Scripture adopted by the church in its preaching, that is, from church proclamation that is based on Scripture. Simply put, church proclamation is dependent on Scripture for its content.

Barth counted on the sufficiency of the gospel's faithful proclamation because God would validate the message in all the hearers who would listen. His insistence on that was a substantial reason for his resistance to apologetic endeavors to "prove" the Bible's claims. If evangelicals find that they cannot follow Barth in his "allergy" to Christian evidences, they must nonetheless follow him in responding to the challenge of evangelical validity by Christian proclamation. The point of contact between church and world is proclamation. Apologetics belongs properly to faith seeking understanding, rather than to understanding seeking faith.

As the content of church proclamation, Scripture stands in judgment over that proclamation. The development of dogmatics and the practice of exegesis refine as well as protect proclamation. As an exercise of obedience—with the true character of genuine obedience known only through Scripture—proclamation is subject to the Bible as its authority.

Barth's service to evangelicalism at this point is most evident in his unyielding commitment to church proclamation. By proclamation, evangelicalism can participate in God's response to the challenge of its validity. Evangelical unity rests in obedience to God's command to take the gospel to the whole world. The authority by which evangelical unity demonstrates its validity and purpose is manifested in its proclamation.

## Identity

Motive and content require context. Hence the third proposition: evangelicals must both broaden and sharpen their community identity. Among other things, this means determining the acceptable forms of communication to be utilized by those who call themselves evangelicals. Obviously, certain beliefs and actions comprising elements of the evangelical witness also provide identifying characteristics of that witness. Church proclamation based on the Bible characterizes evangelical proclamation and thus identifies it—at least in part.

In its broadest sense, Christian proclamation may be thought of as the totality of Christian witness. Proclamation thus includes all speech and behavior. To avoid making proclamation nothing by calling everything proclamation, the term is almost invariably restricted to verbal expressions of the gospel, particularly those most closely related to the reading or exposition of Scripture. In that narrow sense proclamation means verbal preaching.

Karl Barth entertained a livelier understanding of proclamation. He held a "high view" of proclamation, asserting that it was a form of the Word of God. He sought to maintain an awareness of the ongoing communion of God with humankind. That communion is in Christ (the Word of God), the Christ of Holy Scripture (the Word of God), the Christ to whom the church in every age bears witness by its speech and behavior, that is, by its proclamation (the Word of God). Because the church's proclamation bears witness to the Scriptures and to Christ, and because it is used by God for that purpose, it has authority. Yet that authority is not as great as the Bible's authority because proclamation is dependent on the Bible for its character as God-inspired proclamation. Thus the evangelical church cannot, in the name of proclamation, become an authority unto itself.

All proclamation bearing witness to Christ and built on the gospel is evangelical proclamation, assuming that it "rightly handles" the Scripture. If it does, it has authority. If proclamation is understood in its broadest sense as Christian witness, then the one who proclaims rightly must behave rightly for a genuine evangelical proclamation to exist. If only the narrower sense of proclamation is understood, not the speaker but his message alone must be considered.

Barth sought to end the questionable practice of separating ethics from theology. He broke from liberalism partly because the ethics of his teachers showed their theology to be a dead end. In contrast Barth devoted large sections of his *Church Dogmatics* to the ethical implications of various doctrines. He viewed ethics as obedience to the commands of God.

At the same time, Barth was open to hearing proclamations of a decidedly nonevangelical character. Even while separating such proclamations from his, he was willing to admit that the proclaimers—and perhaps even the proclamations themselves—were within the church.[20] Barth served as an example for American evangelicalism in his openness. He encouraged positive theology by practicing it. He listened to other voices in order to sharpen his own. More important, he tried to hear the Word of God, to allow it to stand in judgment on every human word. It cannot hurt evangelicalism to learn from his approach.

Evangelicals must hear such angry voices as that of the reader who wrote to *Christianity Today* and complained:

Barth's doctrine of Scripture makes for a magnanimity, but the doctrine of biblical infallibility makes for pusillanimity. Barth has a word for all Christians, but the inerrantists are in monologue. Barth is devoutly humble, but biblicist rationalism erodes both humility and true devotion....

Barth's doctrine of Scripture ... I have often used.... Whole sectors of modern life are open for the Christian witness by this approach, whereas the dogmatic approach produces an isolationist pride that cannot hold dialogue with the world because ... it is not really listening.[21]

Whether one agrees or not, it is imperative to listen; he might be right. If evangelicals listen, they can also begin to respond. Fidelity to the truth of the gospel demands listening because communication of the truth is dependent on some knowledge about the hearer. More important, the love of Christ that must accompany the communication of truth through proclamation is shown by the kind of listening that demonstrates genuine concern.

Barth similarly has given evangelicalism a solemn warning against "isolationist pride." In a certain sense, questions about a superiority in evangelical proclamation always risk such pride. Even the apostle Paul walked softly here (Phil. 1:15-18). But if the Bible is heard when it brings judgment on the proclamation of the church, all pride will be displaced by humble dependence on God—for Christians "do not know how to pray as we ought" (Rom. 8:26), much less proclaim the gospel.

How, then, can evangelicals broaden and sharpen their identity? First, they can broaden it by recognizing evangelical proclamation in its broadest sense. All who speak and live as witnesses to Christ in correspondence to the character of obedience pictured in Scripture can be recognized as evangelical. Such breadth transcends some areas of dispute while making others more important. Second, evangelicals can sharpen their identity by insisting that all their expressions be undertaken in witness to Christ and in conscious submission to the authority of Scripture. Differences in theological interpretations need not divide in most instances. Where interpretive differences mean a defiance of scriptural authority, a denial of Christ or a breaking of Christian fellowship, a nonevangelical spirit has gained entrance. Evangelical identity is dependent on a church clearly conscious of its mission and in submission to the content that sustains and directs it. Evangelical identity is manifested in proclamation established on the Holy Scripture. Above all, evangelical identity is Christ identifying with his church.

Thus as evangelicalism sets out into the future it can do so with authority. But it must return to the Scriptures and to Christ for that authority. Then its confession will *be* authority. Karl Barth, whatever his faults and whatever the deficiencies of his theology, can stand as an inspiration to excellence, as a guide to evangelicals seeking diligently to point ever and only to Jesus Christ.

# 14

# A Word
# to the Wise

Thus far I have said little from my own perspective concerning Barth's theological deficiencies. This has not been because I think Barth lacking in faults but because I fear that in the past critique has all too often displaced genuine dialog. My desire has been to give Barth a fresh hearing.

Faultfinding can be easy enough. Constructing a positive evangelical theology that is both true to the Scriptures and intellectually compelling to modern men and women is more demanding. I have argued earlier that a positive evangelical theology must be methodologically redemptive, and it is for this reason that I have sought to give Barth a fresh and sympathetic hearing. Nevertheless, though I remain convinced that Barth can serve as a useful model and guide for today's evangelicals, I do not mean to suggest that Barth ought not to be critically evaluated. In this chapter I intend to examine several further points at which Barth has been criticized in an effort to assess the degree to which they have been just.

In general four criticisms of Barth tend to recur: (1) he appears to be out of step with the witness of Scripture, (2) he is at odds with the Reformers, (3) he contends against essential evangelical theology, and (4) he is inconsistent, contradictory or simply obscure.

The first charge is the only ultimately significant one, but the criticisms easily overlap.

## Out of Step with Scripture

From the biblical perspective of historic Protestantism, Barth's doctrine of justification seems suspect to many. As Luther declared, the Reformation stood or fell on the correct understanding and appropriation of the doctrine of justification. Despite the many reconsiderations within both Protestantism and Roman Catholicism, the issue has remained a fundamental dividing point. Many evangelicals were surprised when the Catholic theologian Hans Küng, in a powerful book entitled *Justification: The Doctrine of Karl Barth and a Catholic Reflection* (Thomas Nelson & Sons, 1964), concluded that "there is no essential difference between the Barthian and the Catholic position."[1] More surprising still was Barth's commendation of the book in a warm letter which appeared at its beginning asserting that Küng understood Barth as he wished himself to be understood.

Küng, in a chapter on "The Declaration of the Sinner's Justice," summarized the doctrine with the formula "God's *declaration* of justice is, as *God's* declaration of justice, at the same time and in the same act, a *making* just."[2] Briefly, his reasoning is as follows:

The term "justification" as such expresses an actual declaration of justness and not an inner renewal. Does it follow from this that God's declaration of justice does not imply an inner renewal? On the contrary. It all comes down to this, that it is a matter of *God's* declaration of justice and not man's word: the utterance of the Lord, mighty in power. Unlike the word of man, the word of God *does* what it signifies. God said, "Let there be light" and there was light. . . . The sinner's justification is exactly like this. God pronounces the verdict, "You are just." And the sinner *is* just, really and truly, outwardly and inwardly, wholly and completely. His sins *are* forgiven, and man is just in his heart. The voice of God never gets lost in the void.[3]

That this does in fact represent Barth's position is evidenced throughout Barth's treatment of justification. Consider the following statement: "Certainly we have to do with a declaring righteous, but it is a declaration about man which is fulfilled and therefore effective in this event, which corresponds to actuality because it creates and therefore reveals the actuality. It is a declaring righteous which without any reserve can be called a making righteous."[4]

Is the difference simply between "declaring righteous" and "making righteous" simply terminological? Barth immediately continues his thought with the words: "Christian faith does not believe in a sentence which is ineffective, or only partly effective. As faith in Jesus Christ who is risen from the dead it believes in a sentence which is absolutely effective, so that man is not merely called righteous before God, but is righteous before God."[5] Has Barth, in the interest of demonstrating the union of justification with sanctification, actually fused them so as to confuse their genuine distinction?

Certainly if one is *actually* righteous before God, the *actual* character of that righteousness is *in Christ* (1 Cor. 1:30). Sanctification, too, is *in Christ,* but is distinct from justification (1 Cor. 6:11). To stress their genuine union in Christ, Barth speaks of the *one* act wherein Christians are both declared just and also made righteous. Although he is not speaking *against* the biblical testimony, neither is he placing the stress on *distinction,* a stress which in the eyes of the biblical witnesses is of even greater importance than the real union for showing forth the actuality of what takes place in Christ.

In this course of action Barth runs several unnecessary risks. He seems to be subsuming humankind into Christ in such a manner that he accentuates the objective character of Christ's work; that makes it seem that no real, inward change takes place. Or, viewed somewhat differently, what takes place for and in any one individual seems somehow to be the same in every other. Yet Barth explicitly says: "The Word of God is spoken to all. God's verdict and direction and promise have been pronounced over all. To that extent, objectively, all are justified, sanctified and called. But the hand of God has not touched all in such a way that they can see and hear, perceive and accept and receive all that God is for all and therefore for them, how therefore they can exist and think and live."[6]

Still, despite such disclaimers, Barth has left himself open for serious questioning. The ambiguity caused by Barth's treatment leaves dangerous room for misunderstanding the basis of God's

justification of man. Human beings are declared just on the basis
of God's justice revealed in Christ. Christ *is* the justice of God.
The making just of man is not the ground of justification—Christ
is. We are not declared righteous in view of the hope and prospect
that one day our earthly experience will prove us just. We are
declared just because Christ is righteous before God *for us*. Our
sanctification in Christ is our being made just in our earthly experience precisely because we are already accepted as truly righteous in God's eyes because of Christ, and because Christ's Spirit,
the Holy Spirit sent from the Father, is in us as well.

What might the evangelical community learn from Barth's
treatment of justification for its positive going forward? Exactly
where Barth is weak he is also strong. Justification and sanctification must not be made so distinct that they become un-
biblically separated, as has been the tendency in Wesleyan
thought. Rather, it must be kept clearly in view that the union
of justification and sanctification is in Christ. These doctrines are
not abstract church formulations but expressions of actuality, an
actuality revealed only in the Christ-event. There they are revealed decisively as the work of the God who is truly for us. If
Barth at moments seems to empty faith of some of its biblical
content, it should be remembered that faith can as easily be over-
filled with significance never granted it in Scripture. The only
proper course is to return to Scripture to hear it afresh.

## At Odds with the Reformers

Barth seems to be at odds with both Luther and Calvin on the
sacraments. Over the course of his life, this area of Barth's
thought displayed a dramatic movement. Roughly, his drift par-
alleled in many respects that of evangelicalism itself. Increasingly
he de-emphasized the strong sacramentalism of Lutheranism and
the Reformed tradition in favor of a position much more in line
with the Anabaptists. Criticism of Barth at this point may reflect
agreement more than disagreement among evangelicals. For
those who retain a strong view of the sacraments, Barth presents
a solid challenge to reflect whether or not the teaching and presentation of the sacraments in the church today actually promotes
a biblical understanding of God's work in Christ or militates
against it. But the sacramentalists challenge Barth with the

contention that his shift in thinking was more the product of an attempt to be consistent with his thought in general than to be honest with the biblical data.

## In Opposition to Evangelical Essentials

At times Barth seems to contend against essentials of evangelical theology. Although Barth's theology remained virtually continuous in character, certain particular facets did appear to undergo remarkable change. Less visible than his shift regarding the sacraments was his move from a sacramental understanding of Scripture, by which Scripture is seen as a vehicle and channel of the Word of God, to a Christomonistic understanding whereby Scripture becomes only a human witness to the Word, which remains essentially transcendent.[7] To the extent that such a shift reflects a move toward a theological system and away from Scripture it must be resisted. But again Barth is his own best friend. He insisted again and again that his intent was to move toward Scripture. Even in this criticism evangelicals may appreciate a submission to Scripture and a willingness to be corrected.

Perhaps the two greatest problem areas for American evangelicals in regard to Barth are Scripture and Christian experience, although the latter area is often ignored. Barth can be both praised and criticized for his provocative treatment of Scripture. On the whole, his acceptance of the full authority of Scripture and his insistence that it cannot be separated from God's revelation are to be heartily applauded. Even if full agreement is not reached with him on every matter, Barth's teaching easily falls within the range of genuinely evangelical thought. His stress on the Bible's character as a witness ought to be greatly welcomed as a biblical safeguard against "bibliolatry" and against a neglect of the purpose and center of Scripture: the presentation of the gospel of Jesus Christ. Yet Barth must be criticized for his doubtful handling of inspiration and his unclear presentation of Scripture's "fallibility."

Barth's handling of the infallibility-fallibility tension was admittedly often awkward. He demanded that no judgment be placed on the Scripture as to where it was in error. At the same time, he also demanded a clear recognition that fallibility meant the real presence of error. But, we may ask, of what practical hermeneutical value is it to say that errors are present but cannot be firmly delineated? The precise bearing of this tension on the exegesis of Scripture Barth never resolved satisfactorily.

Likewise, Barth's analysis of the history of the doctrine of verbal inspiration must be challenged. While his criticism of the doctrine is instructive, it is far from certain that it rests as firmly on historical evidence as he thought it did. Then, too, his exegetical underpinnings in this discussion are not as sound as they might be. On the whole Barth has left too many readers with the legitimate concern that the arguments advanced stem less from Scripture than they do from a rebellion against what Barth perceived as the devastating practical outworkings of the doctrine of verbal inspiration in conservative circles. Although we may heed his warnings, we must look to others for a better discussion of the issue.

When evangelicals turn to hear Barth on the Christian life, they are likely to be both pleasantly surprised and dismayed. On the one hand, Barth is outstanding in relating doctrine to life in ethics. But does he offer more than ethical possibilities envisioned for all people and realized only in Christ, or is there a genuinely visible change in any person who accepts and receives the lordship of Christ? Often it appears that Barth understands the essential difference between Christians and unbelievers strictly as a difference between those who have heard and received the gospel and those who have not—irrespective of demonstrable change in behavior. Perhaps Barth has not adequately separated the believer from the world. In Barth's stress on the objectivity and completeness of Christ's work, any subjective change in a believer almost seems to disappear. Justification swallows up sanctification. Of course, Barth denies that, and many texts might be adduced in his defense.

What is more to the point is the inconsistently evangelical character of Barth's treatment. Where he might criticize the evangelical community for its preoccupation with subjective experiences such as "being born again" and might warn of anthropocentricity, he might be criticized precisely for a lack of any real insistence on those matters in his own theology. If it can be seen that what Barth and evangelicalism have to say in this area are not mutually exclusive, perhaps a more biblical perspective may yet dawn in the theological consciousness. It is clear that evangelical theology can draw closer to Barth here, even while refusing to give up its distinctive emphases. The crucial matter is to affirm with Barth the centrality of the work of Christ *for man* in order that a work of God might take place *in man*. This is the heart of the Christian mission. It is time to rededicate the service of the church to the fruitful pursuit of this greatest of all commissions.

## Inconsistent, Contradictory and Obscure

Barth's writings often seem to be inconsistent, contradictory or simply obscure. The movement in Barth's theology makes it easy to complain that he was inconsistent, but the facts do not substantiate this charge beyond certain particular inconsistencies within the larger framework—which was characterized, as discussed earlier, much more by continuity than discontinuity. There is value in an almost monolithic presentation such as Calvin's *Institutes,* which despite continuous expansion remained the same even in the maturing of its author. Barth, on the other hand, changed the manner of his speaking. Dialectics and existentialism faded in favor of the language he used to reflect his thinking in the *Church Dogmatics.*

Still Barth can legitimately be criticized for the often obscure and laborious circuit of prose by which he thought around problems. His style left him exposed to questions about where he actually stood, and whether a particular stand was significantly different from the one he had once espoused but now disclaimed.

At the same time, evangelicals can profit from the example of a theologian more than willing to find better expressions for the gospel and eager to press on in the search for truth. There is no false pride in Barth which clings to an old thought or manner of speech when it is no longer appropriate. What is visible instead is a man of humility.

Such a cataloguing of criticisms of Barth might be longer or shorter, and each criticism might be presented more exhaustively. But the way has been indicated for producing helpful criticisms. If no one person agrees fully with another, that is no weakness but rather the normal state of affairs. Even those evangelicals who are undoubted and unchallenged in their orthodoxy may be profitably studied and criticized. To criticize Barth profitably does not mean to condemn him. It includes criticizing one's own self as well, and seeking to walk as Barth did in the light of the knowledge of God in Christ.

# 15

# Scripture— A Case in Point

Thus far I have tried to assess the present state of evangelicalism and to suggest in general how evangelicals might learn from Barth, particularly in the development of a thoroughly evangelical and positive theology. What I plan to do in this chapter is to put forward a concrete example of how evangelical theology might be enriched and illumined by interaction with Barth. Specifically, I intend to suggest the essential elements of a new statement on scriptural authority.

The issue of scriptural authority is of course at the heart of today's crisis. And it seems to me that if evangelicals are to push forward beyond the present impasse, such a new statement of scriptural authority is essential. Moreover, the need to validate evangelical theology as a truly biblical and rational alternative for modern men and women demands such a new formulation.

A new statement ought still to be an evangelical statement. It should be the consistent, recognizable product of the reforming evangelical church. Yet while drawing on the evangelical heritage, a new statement may also incorporate insights from Barth. American evangelicals would be mistaken if they thought Barth would demand a new understanding of biblical authority that set aside every echo of the old understanding. So the theses of a new statement may and ought to remain rooted in the evangelical tradition even while seeking to sharpen it in renewal. Barth's challenge is not to agree with him but to seek to reflect the Bible's own understanding of itself.

The doctrine of biblical authority divides evangelicals today as it never has before. But the doctrine should be reworked not because it is already decided that the present understanding is beyond being salvaged. Rather, it should be reworked as part of the church's continuing dogmatic venture. Every new generation is called to this task. It is a work to be undertaken in faith as a response to the Lord's command to take his news and name to every corner of the earth.

Barth's doctrine of the Bible has already been discussed briefly. But despite Barth's strong statements on the fallibility of Scripture and his awkward handling of the doctrine of inspiration, he has some salient points to offer in these areas also. Unfortunately these points are often lost amid the justifiable criticisms of Barth's position. He needs, however, to be fully heard.

## Significant Insights from Barth

There are four features germane to the task of reformulating the evangelical understanding of Scripture. First, it must be remembered that, for Barth, "not God alone, but God and man together constitute the content of the Word of God attested in Scripture."[1] Evangelicalism has gladly embraced this fact. The wonder of the Bible is in its existence as a joint enterprise between God and man, but with God as the senior partner. God utilizes Scripture in a unique manner: the Bible is the single source of knowledge about God's revelation. In Barth's view, "We have no right, then, to expect to impart into the reality of God's process of revelation to and among men any contribution learned from a source of knowledge different from Holy Scripture."[2] This alone makes Scripture determinative for the evangelical church.

Second, as a consequence of what we have seen, the Bible has authority which rests in itself. Barth expressed this by stating: "Scripture is recognized as the Word of God by the fact that it *is* the Word of God. This is what we are told by the doctrine of the witness of the Holy Spirit."[3] This is singularly important. It has been argued that the doctrine of the witness of the Holy Spirit is the one point at which the Reformers were in closest agreement. Whether that can be substantiated or not, it is clear that this doctrine, once so vital, has fallen into wide neglect. Here evangelicals can move closer to Barth and the Reformed tradition in general. This doctrine must be recovered.

The authority of Scripture means authority for the church that lives under the Word. Barth emphasized that "under the Word and therefore under Holy Scripture the Church does have and exercises genuine authority. It has and exercises it by being obedient, concretely obedient."[4] While this is decidedly affirmed by evangelicals, it is often softened in practice. Evangelicals have long led the way in proclaiming the authority of the Bible. Yet its practical consequences in the local church are still largely undefined. Although a new statement on biblical authority cannot be comprehensive enough to delineate every manifestation of that authority, it must both reassert Scripture's authority and indicate its scope more clearly than ever before. Evangelicalism today is faced less with the problem of the nonrecognition of biblical authority than with the grave situation of widespread practical neglect of the application of that authority.

Third, Barth maintained, "If God speaks to man, He really speaks the language of this concrete human word of man. This is the right and necessary truth in the concept of verbal inspiration."[5] This, however, did not lead Barth to the same conclusions on infallibility espoused by many evangelicals. He believed that "verbal inspiration does not mean the infallibility of the biblical word in its linguistic, historical and theological character as a human word."[6] This thesis was important to Barth. Being human means being fallible. A human word is a fallible word; to Barth it has a capacity for errors. Verbal inspiration meant to Barth, then, "that the fallible and faulty human word is as such used by God and has to be received and heard in spite of its human fallibility."[7]

Many evangelicals agree with Klaas Runia's claim that "however much Barth may pour out his wrath on the concept of 'inspiredness,' the scriptural data compel us to maintain its legitimacy in a Christian theology of Scripture. In our opinion Barth has made a caricature of it, and to a great extent his fight is against his own self-constructed caricature."[8] Barth's understanding of verbal inspiration and biblical fallibility is not a traditional evangelical understanding. But many of the evangelicals who criticize Barth on this matter nevertheless respect his efforts to relate the inspiration of Scripture to the continuing activity of the Holy Spirit.

Because the Bible is the work of God's free grace, the existence of Scripture as *Holy* Scripture rests not in the inherent nature of the texts but the decision and action of the Holy Spirit.[9] This is Barth's significant contribution to the discussion of Scripture's inspiration. Barth maintained that "in the so-called doctrine of inspiration the point at issue was and is how far, i.e., on the basis of what relationship between the Holy Spirit as God opening up man's ears and mouth for His Word and the Bible, the latter can be read and understood and expounded as a human witness of His revelation as the Word of God and therefore in the strict sense as Holy Scripture."[10]

The humanity of the Bible must be accepted. The church believes that the Bible is the Word of God despite the stumbling block of its humanity. Only by the miracle of God's free decision and act is this barrier overcome.[11] Only the Word of God itself can prove itself and "over-master" the belief of the church. As Barth wrote, "Believing is not something arbitrary. It does not control its object. It is a recognizing, knowing, hearing, apperceiving, thinking, speaking and doing which is over-mastered by its object."[12] Yet, Barth warned, "We must remember ... that the inspiration of the Bible cannot be reduced to our faith in it, even though we understand this faith as the gift and work of God in us."[13] Thus the church is returned once more to the "logical circle" of the Scriptures as the Word of God.[14]

The evangelical faith in Holy Scripture is neither fideistic nor irrational. In accepting the humanity of the Scriptures evangelicals affirm the miracle of God's free decision in making this human word the very Word of God. Yet evangelicals are often so anxious to defend the divine side of Scripture from critics that they subsume the human thus denying its true integrity. Barth must be allowed to challenge the evangelical community to see human and divine in genuine union *without* either *fusion* or the *subsuming* of the human into the divine. While conscientious evangelicals are anxious to avoid charges of a dictation-theory understanding of inspiration, they must be sensitive to Barth's warning that less than a full and open acknowledgment of the truly human character of Scripture will inevitably lead to the distortions of mechanical predetermined dictation.

At the same time, evangelical insistence on the proper relation of human to divine must be retained. The Bible is pre-eminently *God's* Word. If evangelicals sometimes seem to fuse the human and divine, Barth occasionally gives the appearance of separating these two elements. Certainly he recognized their distinction clearly enough. Barth's success in maintaining the union of divine and human rested not in the evangelical solution of verbal inspiration but in his understanding of revelation.

The fourth relevant feature of Barth's position is one often missed in expositions of his thought. Barth's same concept of inspiration that accepts and understands the human fallibility of the Bible also accepts and declares the divine *infallibility* of Holy Scripture. But is he restoring with the right hand what he has removed with the left? Many evangelicals have been rightly displeased with Barth's cumbersome handling of a fallible-but-authoritative Bible. There is, however, a valuable matter to be perceived in what Barth attempted.

In explaining biblical fallibility Barth prefaced his discussion of the biblical authors' "capacity for errors" by stating that such a discussion was necessary in light of the "distinction between inspiration and therefore the divine infallibility of the Bible and its human fallibility."[15] Following the line of Luther and especially Augustine, Barth had previously asserted, "We know what we say when we call the Bible the Word of God only when we recognize its human imperfection in face of its divine perfection, and its divine perfection in spite of its human imperfection."[16] The infallibility of Holy Scripture, for Barth, consists in its existence as the Word of God in the event of revelation. That is, of course, a denial of an infallibility based upon an inherent "inspiredness" of Scripture. Rather, contended Barth, the Bible is infallible only in light of and by relation to the work of the Holy Spirit. Stated somewhat differently, and perhaps too simplistically, the Bible is a fallible word witnessing to the infallible Word.

Barth qualified infallibility by relating it expressly to God and carefully distinguishing it from the fallibility of every human word. Barth's action constituted a hermeneutical qualification with regard to the infallibility of Scripture since it is only to the right exercise of exegesis that infallibility is related. Exegesis undertaken in the guidance of the Holy Spirit and in strict fidelity to the texts themselves is hearing what the Bible proclaims. That in turn is hearing the voice of God. This helps, in part, to account for Barth's oftentimes quite distinctive treatment of biblical passages. It relates the component facets of Barth's exegetical process closely to one another. Above all it keeps the exegete centered on the person of Christ himself. Thus infallibility is hermeneutically qualified by the event of revelation.

This facet of Barth's thinking must increase attention to the interface between inspiration and interpretation. For Barth, liberty must be granted to the interpreter to discern the infallible truth of God in the text of Holy Scripture. Barth's doctrine of inspiration includes the role of the Holy Spirit as the one who permits the interpreter to hear the Bible's message rightly. It is God who has elected the testimony of the biblical authors and who stands behind them and in their witness. Barth, however, saw the double dangers of an interpreter either pressing his understanding as a judgment over every other understanding, or abusing his interpretative freedom by refusing submission to the authority of Scripture. After all, Scripture is always its own best interpreter.

Barth maintained that the vital functioning of dogmatics as *church* dogmatics was needful to counteract such interpretive dangers. In the first instance, dogmatics is to resist popery by pointing to the freedom of God's grace; no one can control or possess God's Word through interpretation and decree. In the second instance, the church is the church only so long as it is submitted to the authority of the Bible as the Word of God. Dogmatics points to rebellion as sin by sharpening the church's right expression of true proclamation.

Both those who follow Barth's views on Scripture and those who maintain the more traditional understanding of inspiration can learn from each other. Why shouldn't we have the best insights of both? Evangelicals should recognize the often static form their presentation on Scripture takes for itself. Barth's almost complete actualism with regard to Scripture can be tempered to serve the evangelical understanding. The points of contact between Barth and evangelicalism are numerous and significant enough to warrant a realistic hope that Barth can be used as a resource for a new statement on biblical authority. I agree with Runia who, in spite of his many questions and reservations, has gladly stated, "We gratefully acknowledge that Barth presents the great principle of the authority (and sufficiency) of the Bible in a clear and convincing way."[17]

## A New Statement of Biblical Authority

How, then, are we to build on the dialog we have begun? I believe that having heard Barth and having addressed him positively with questions and criticisms, a step forward, however preliminary in nature, can be taken. I think the new form of a statement on biblical authority can incorporate as its center the following five theses:

1. *The authority of Holy Scripture is inherent.*

2. *The authority of Holy Scripture is apparent only within the church.*

3. *The authority of Holy Scripture is the witness to Christ for the church.*

4. *The authority of Holy Scripture is complete within the church.*

5. *The authority of Holy Scripture is given for the proclamation of the Word of God by the church.*

These theses form only the nucleus of a more comprehensive statement on biblical authority. They require elucidation to specify their orientation and meaning. I want in the following few pages simply to suggest the contributing influence of Barth on evangelical presuppositions and to elucidate briefly the character of each thesis. It is my conviction that each of these theses demands a corresponding thesis in each of the realms of biblical interpretation and biblical preaching. But here the issue is biblical authority alone.

*The authority of Holy Scripture is inherent.* Barth located this "inherent" authority in the *continuing* activity of God. Evangelicalism has found inherent authority in its doctrine of inspiration. I do not believe these must be mutually exclusive. The thesis itself affirms the independence of the Bible from apologetic proofs. Biblical authority rests, not in the church's ability to demonstrate the logic or the scientific accuracy of Scripture, but in the Bible's own ability to persuade men and women that it bears reliable testimony to the work of God in Christ. This singular ability stems from a once-for-all inspiration and a dynamic, moment-by-moment moving of God's Spirit.

The inherent authority of Scripture can only mean the authority vested in it by its author and, therefore, the author's own authority. Accordingly, the authority of the Bible rests in the authority of its human composers. But their authority is only that of witnesses, no matter how intimately involved; theirs is an authority invested in them by another. That it was God himself who gave them their authority is attested by their own acknowledgement and demonstrated by their testimony of Christ. That theirs is a right and true authority is proved by the witness of God's Spirit, who continually testifies to the reliability of the human testimony and the written record. No apologetic proof can supplant this testimony by the Holy Spirit.

Barth's return to the Reformers in an insistence on a perpetual, dynamic connection between Scripture and the Holy Spirit is an example to be followed. The evangelical understanding of inspiration has often served to sever Spirit and Word by rendering the personal decision and action of the Spirit as of little account in the face of the divinely inspired Scripture. The Spirit's witness, while inseparable from inspiration, is not to be identified with inspiration. Luther and Calvin united Spirit and Scriptures by recognizing that the witness of one was the witness of the other. The Holy Spirit seizes upon the Scriptures as the instrumentality of his witness to Christ. This means the confession of Scripture is completely dependent on the continuing act and decision of the same Spirit who first inspired it.

Articles IV and V of the Westminster Confession of Faith summarizes this doctrine:

Art. IV. The authority of the Holy Scripture, for which it ought to be believed, and obeyed, dependeth not upon the testimony of any man, or Church; but wholly upon God (who is truth itself) the author thereof: and therefore it is to be received, because it is the Word of God. Art. V. We may be moved and induced by the testimony of the Church to an high and reverend esteem of the Holy Scripture. And the heavenliness of the matter, the efficacy of the doctrine, the majesty of the style, the consent of all the parts, the scope of the whole (which is, to give all glory to God), the full discovery it makes of the only way of man's salvation, the many other incomparable excellencies, and the entire perfection thereof, are arguments whereby it doth abundantly evidence itself to be the Word of God: yet notwithstanding, *our full persuasion and assurance of the infallible truth and divine authority thereof, is from the inward work of the Holy Spirit bearing witness by and with the Word in our hearts.*[18]

The Reformation understanding, very dynamic in character, was blunted in later generations. Evangelical thought in the main followed the tactics set forth by Protestant scholastics in their debates with the Catholic Counter Reformation. Bernard Ramm has noted:

The subsequent history of the *testimonium* is a mixed one. Among the orthodox it suffered from four things: (i) it became identified with religious experience and so lost its real force as a persuasion; or (ii) in the development of a rationalistic apologetic there was no genuine place left for the *testimonium;* or (iii) a sense of balance was lost and the *testimonium* was interpreted as a formal validation of Scripture; or the validation of theological propositions without proper regard to Christ or salvation; or (iv) there was a failure to see its critical role in theological methodology.[19]

Barth points today's evangelicals back to this Reformation understanding. Interestingly, G. C. Berkouwer, who likewise urges a recovery of the Reformers' teaching on the witness of the Spirit, has been criticized for leaning too far toward Barth. The current furor over inspiration and inerrancy may be only got around by a reformed view of the Spirit's role beyond his work in inspiration. Yet this does not mean giving up an evangelical tradition; it means reforming it.

Inspiration is the vehicle by which God insures the reliability of the biblical witness. At the same time, inspiration points beyond its own existence as a vehicle of communication to the One who brings it into being: God himself. Inspiration substantiates the authority of what it has created, even as what it has created, by virtue of its inherent authority through the witness of God's Spirit, functions in such a manner as to point to inspiration. Both inspiration and the Spirit's testimony create the Bible's authority because each is rooted in the one work of God whose labor is to bear witness to man through Scripture to what has been done in Jesus Christ on behalf of man.

*The authority of Holy Scripture is apparent only within the church.* Because it is only within the church that God's work in Christ is known effectually, it is only within the church that the rightful nature and character of Holy Scripture is apparent. This thesis is hardly disputable. Evangelicals have based their claim of true church status on their recognition and submission to the manifest authority of the Bible in their midst. Yet few, if any, theologians have so thoroughly explored the relation of biblical authority and the believing community as did Barth.

Barth was far more interested in proclaiming the biblical message than in defending it, precisely because he knew that biblical authority is apparent only within the church. This fact constitutes a fundamental and permanent difference between the church and the world. The church confesses the authority of God, the author of Scripture, and gladly acknowledges the inspiration of the Bible. The world is generally content to allow the church an inspired book but wants no part of the authority which rules the church. When, as is frequent today, evangelical apologetics supplants the proclamation of the gospel, Barth's insistence on rightly understanding the relation of the church to the Bible, and especially the church's proclamation as the Word of God, becomes especially needful. Here he serves to call evangelicalism back to its rightful place.

*The authority of Holy Scripture is the witness to Christ for the church.* Biblical authority is known correctly only within the church, and it is known there by its function. If evangelical Christians owe no other debt to Barth, this is one that is great indeed. Barth fixed attention on an operative biblical authority that is firmly attached to the Scripture's avowed purpose of bearing witness to Christ. The evangelical doctrine of inspiration can only benefit tremendously by this. The central thesis of biblical authority is that this authority *is* the witness to Christ for the church.

The church established by Jesus Christ recognizes the Bible's authority for no other reason than the Scripture's unique function in witnessing to Christ. Certainly this accentuates the role of inspiration and makes the Spirit's witness indispensable. It also explains the place of Scripture as canon. As canon, as the rule or standard to which the church must base every final appeal in at least all matters of faith and practice, the Scripture functions as that authority designated by God as his own Word. But this is not merely a body of propositionally timeless truths given to solve problems and answer questions. The Bible, because of the abiding witness of God's Spirit, is functionally alive and relevant. The interpretive task, therefore, is the challenge to meet God afresh again and again in the event of Christ's self-disclosure to which the Scriptures bear witness.

This idea of biblical authority understood functionally may raise two questions. First, what becomes of the character of the Bible with regard to propositional truth? Since there are statements of a propositional nature within Scripture that are true and reliable, there can be hardly any argument against the notion of the Scriptures as a body composed to a significant degree by propositional truth. At the same time, while it may be admitted that any man may read and understand the words of Scripture, it must be disputed that any man can understand the Word of God apart from the ministry of the Holy Spirit.

Second, are there ever times when the Bible does *not* function as the authoritative Word of God? Barth's handling of matters like inspiration raised this question in spite of his strong statements that the Bible's *"becoming* the Word of God" means that it *is always* the Word of God. But joining Barth's emphasis on the Spirit's role to the evangelical tradition allows a definite and unambiguous claim that Scripture *always* functions as the Word of God both because it *is* the Word of God and is still *becoming* that Word as a new Word each moment. Any understanding that the Bible is the Word of God when it becomes the Word of God *to me* must be rejected. If we slumber or are hard of hearing the Spirit of God preaches no less heartily or with less authority.

Scripture's identity is so bound up with that Word in Christ to which it testifies that it too is a part of the revelation of God in Christ and must be called the Word of God. Because God by his Spirit continually bears witness to the Word in Christ and the Word in Scripture, the two are both rightfully called the Word of

God. But, of course, we cannot confuse the two since they are quite
evidently not the same. It took God's inspiration and it continues
to take his personal activity through the Spirit's witness to create
and sustain the Bible as his own Word. That God has done and still
does these things demands of the church the acknowledgment that
Scripture *is* and *is becoming* ever afresh the living Word of God.

*The authority of Holy Scripture is complete within the church.*
This does not mean that Scripture is exclusive of other authorities
within the church. Rather, the Bible lacks nothing for its authority
to be full and sufficient. This thesis ought to eliminate the tyranny
of the single authoritative interpreter of Scripture that plagues
some local churches. Barth's wrestling with fallibility-infallibility
and the interface between inspiration and interpretation should
prove instructive to evangelicals. There is a plethora of hermeneutical systems and a babble of interpretive voices in evangelicalism today.

Because the Bible's authority is inherent and complete, the
interpretation of Scripture carries the dual character of authority
and servanthood. The act of interpretation is the act of hearing.
The evangelical tradition has proven ready to listen to Scripture
and has heeded fine biblical expositors. But at times the practical
authority of Scripture in the church has been supplanted by the
interpreter who used his understanding as a standard by which
to judge all other interpretive efforts. Evangelicalism needs to
take its strongest stand in history today on the fact that Scripture
is its own best interpreter. Then Barth's contributions can be
weighed not as a competitive system but as a positive contribution
to the church.

Beneath the canon other authorities rightly have their place
in the life of the church. The rich tradition of the evangelical
church, the writings of the Fathers, the decisions of the councils,
the confessions of the creeds, the teachings of the catechisms and
the insights of present scholars all have a rightful place as guides
possessing an authority that is directly correspondent to their
faithful proclamation of Christ. The shepherding of pastors in
local churches also carries authority commensurate with their
faithful confession. Every office in the church has authority contin-
gent on its correct relation to the Word of God. All authority and
authorities within the church are subject to the one same standard

of the canon of Holy Scripture.

*The authority of Holy Scripture is given for the proclamation of the Word of God by the church.* Today the evangelical church is still known for its preaching. But the quality and intensity of that preaching has been called into question as seldom before. Barth called his own major work *dogmatics,* a sharpening of the church's proclamation in light of Holy Scripture. Evangelicalism is always in need of dogmatic reform. Fallible men preach the Good News. The gospel must constantly be presented in ways that are both faithful to Scripture and effective communication to the present generation.

The witness to Christ is given to those who not only can but will receive it. It is given for the creation of the church, its growth and its sustenance. Yet beyond these the witness to Christ that is embodied in the Bible and which constitutes its authority is given for the church to be used by the church as an instrument of life. The church has been commissioned, bestowed with a divine mission; this mission is inseparable from the existence and authority of Holy Scripture in her midst. While it is the purpose of Scripture to witness to Christ, it remains the peculiar character of the Bible that this witness is not fulfilled apart from the work of the church.

These theses may not prove acceptable as a starting point to many evangelicals. I do hope they can be a first word of some kind to the constructive task of building a better evangelical statement on biblical authority. At any rate, Barth has proven helpful to me and to others in coming to terms with this and other issues. My own fruitful interactions with Barth compel me to advocate developing a dialog with him far more substantial than what has occurred in the past.

# Notes

## Chapter 1

[1] Carl F. H. Henry, *Evangelicals at the Brink of Crisis* (Waco: Word, 1967), pp. 10-11.

[2] Carl F. H. Henry, *Evangelicals in Search of Identity* (Waco: Word, 1976), pp. 16-17.

[3] Harold Lindsell, *The Battle for the Bible* (Grand Rapids: Zondervan, 1976), from the Foreword by Harold J. Ockenga.

[4] Henry, *Evangelicals in Search*, p. 17.

[5] See Carl F. H. Henry, "Agenda for Evangelical Advance," *Christianity Today*, XXI (5 November 1976), 164. Here Henry addresses only the Bible controversy.

[6] This may seem an odd, even untrue, statement considering the number of recent books in evangelical circles that discuss change and offer programs for change. However, these efforts, needful as they are, occupy places on the periphery of formal theological study. The notable works of men like Larry Richards, Bruce Larson, Keith Miller and others are all outside the sphere described here.

[7] Donald G. Dawe, "Have We Said 'No' to 'Nein'?" rev. of David Tracy, *Blessed Rage for Order* (Seabury Press), in *Interpretation*, XXXI, (January 1977), 80.

[8] Karl Barth, *Church Dogmatics*, II/1, trans. T. H. L. Parker, W. B. Johnston, H. Knight, and J. L. M. Haire, eds. G. W. Bromiley and T. F. Torrance (Edinburgh: T. & T. Clark, 1957), p. 535. Inasmuch as Bromiley and Torrance are the general editors for the *Dogmatics,* subsequent citations, for the sake of brevity, do not reiterate this. *Church Dogmatics* hereafter referred to by *CD,* with appropriate volume and part number.

With reference to this passage, see Klaas Runia, *Karl Barth's Doctrine of Holy Scripture* (Grand Rapids: Eerdmans, 1962), ch. 1. Runia comments: "We cannot but express our hearty agreement with this starting point of Barth. It is not only in full harmony with the view of the Reformation, but also with the *clear teaching of the Bible about itself.* Nowhere does the Bible appeal to any external authority in order to vindicate its own authority, but it appeals directly to God Himself and presents itself as the Word of God" (p. 8).

[9]George Eldon Ladd, *The New Testament and Criticism* (Grand Rapids: Eerdmans, 1967), p. 10.

[10]Lindsell, *Battle,* Preface.

[11]Larry Richards, "Church Teaching: Content Without Context," *Christianity Today,* XXI (15 April 1977), 802.

[12]Colin Brown, *Karl Barth and the Christian Message* (Chicago: InterVarsity Press, 1967), p. 9: "Conservatives mistrust him, suspecting that his neo-orthodoxy is somehow a cover for twisting truths that they hold vital and dear." Yet Brown adds, "There is probably no thinker today from whom more could be learnt, whether it be from his insights or from his mistakes."

## Chapter 2

[1]William Nicholls, *Systematic and Philosophical Theology,* ed. R. P. C. Hanson, The Pelican Guide to Modern Theology, Vol. I (Baltimore: Penguin, 1969), p. 17.

[2]Martin E. Marty and Dean G. Peerman, eds., *New Theology No. 1* (New York: Macmillan, 1967), p. 11.

[3]John Macquarrie, *God and Secularity,* ed. William Hordern, New Directions in Theology Today, Vol. 3 (Philadelphia: Westminster, 1967), p. 13. It must be noted immediately that when Macquarrie makes reference to "God talk" he means something vastly different from the evangelical theologian. Macquarrie admits to some difficulty in saying just how "God" should be talked about (or with).

[4]Rem B. Edwards, *Reason and Religion* (New York: Harcourt Brace Jovanovich, 1972), p. 4.

[5]Paul Tillich, *The Shaking of the Foundations* (New York: Scribner, 1948), p. 119.

[6]Karl Barth, *CD,* I/1, trans. G. T. Thomson (Edinburgh: T. & T. Clark, 1936), p. 309. See the preceding discussion as well.

[7]Ibid.

[8]Ibid.

[9]Ibid., p. 308.

[10]Jaroslav Pelikan, "Dogmatics," in *Handbook of Christian Theology,* eds. A. A. Cohen and M. Halverson (New York: World, 1958), p. 82. Note Pelikan's observation that Barth "has written an explicitly ecclesiastical dogmatics, ecclesiastical both in its source and in its object" (p. 85).

[11]Karl Barth, *Dogmatics in Outline,* trans. G. T. Thomson (New York: Harper & Row, 1959), p. 9.

[12]Barth, *CD,* I/1, p. 1.

[13]Ibid.

[14]Karl Barth, *The Humanity of God,* trans. J. N. Thomas and T. Wieser (Atlanta: John Knox, 1974), p. 11. The first essay, "Evangelical Theology in the 19th Century," (pp. 11-33), is well worth reading in this regard.

[15]J. D. Douglas, ed., *The New International Dictionary of the Christian Church* (Grand Rapids: Zondervan, 1974). The contributor of the article "Evangelical" (pp. 358-59), is C. F. H. Henry.

[16]Barth, *The Humanity of God,* p. 11.

[17]Douglas, pp. 358-59.

## Chapter 3

[1]Sydney E. Ahlstrom, "From Puritanism to Evangelicalism," in *The Evangelicals,* eds. David F. Wells and J. D. Woodbridge (Nashville: Abingdon, 1975), p. 269.

[2]See Bernard Ramm, *The Evangelical Heritage* (Waco: Word, 1973), pp. 11-21.

[3]Bruce Shelley, *Evangelicalism in America* (Grand Rapids: Eerdmans, 1967),

p. 46.

[4]Ibid., pp. 51-52.

[5]M. Eugene Osterhaven, "American Theology in the Twentieth Century," in *Christian Faith and Modern Theology,* ed. C. F. H. Henry (Grand Rapids: Baker, 1964), p. 48.

[6]Harold Lindsell, *An Evangelical Theology of Missions* (Grand Rapids: Zondervan, 1970), p. 22.

[7]Sydney E. Ahlstrom, *A Religious History of the American People* (New Haven: Yale Univ. Press, 1972), p. 814. Hereafter cited as *RHAP.*

[8]Ibid., p. 815.

[9]This is all the more interesting in light of the common tendency to confuse *The Fundamentals* with the five points of the Niagara Bible Conference of 1895. There a statement affirmed five essential points of doctrine: the verbal inerrancy of the Bible, Christ's deity and Virgin Birth, the substitutionary atonement, the bodily resurrection of Christ, and his physical Second Coming. Moreover, while the twenty-nine articles of *The Fundamentals* speak in some respect to the issue of the Bible's authority they do so in a multifaceted manner that assumes inerrancy without being dependent on it.

[10]Harvie M. Conn, *Contemporary World Theology* (Phillipsburg, N.J.: Presbyterian and Reformed, 1976), p. 115.

[11]Ahlstrom, *RHAP,* p. 816.

[12]Conn, p. 115.

[13]Ahlstrom, *RHAP,* p. 816.

[14]It must be understood that when a conservative scholar wrote on inspiration he was discussing inerrancy. See James M. Gray, "The Inspiration of the Bible—Definition, Extent and Proof," *The Fundamentals,* III, 7-41. This article is a clear exposition of the subject that faces the problems squarely and provides an able rationale for the inerrancy position.

[15]J. I. Packer, *"Fundamentalism" and the Word of God* (Grand Rapids: Eerdmans, 1958), p. 29.

[16]Ahlstrom, *RHAP,* pp. 910-11.

[17]Frank S. Mead, *Handbook of Denominations in the United States* (Nashville: Abingdon, 1975), p. 227.

[18]Edward John Carnell, "Fundamentalism," in *Handbook of Christian Theology,* p. 142.

[19]Bernard Ramm, *A Handbook of Contemporary Theology* (Grand Rapids: Eerdmans, 1966), p. 53. Hereafter cited as *HCT.*

[20]Ibid., pp. 53-54.

[21]Carnell, p. 143.

[22]Ahlstrom, *RHAP,* pp. 958-59.

## Chapter 4

[1]Lindsell, *Theology of Missions,* p. 16.

[2]"Born Again!" *Newsweek,* 25 October 1976, p. 69.

[3]David Kucharsky, "The Year of the Evangelical," *Christianity Today,* XXI (22 October 1976), 81.

[4]*The Sunday Oregonian* [Portland], 26 December 1976, p. A19.

[5]"On Not Leaving It to the Liberals," *Eternity,* XXVIII (February 1977), 24.

[6]James A. Taylor, "Progeny of Programmers: Evangelical Religion and the Television Age," *The Christian Century,* XCIV (20 April 1977), 379.

[7]"Born Again!" *Newsweek,* pp. 70, 78.

[8]Ibid., p. 70.

[9]Lindsell, *Battle,* Preface.

[10]Clark H. Pinnock, "The Inerrancy Debate among the Evangelicals," *Theology, News and Notes* (Special Issue, 1976), p. 11.

[11]Lindsell, *Battle,* p. 23.

[12]Ibid., p. 25.

[13]Henry, *Evangelicals In Search,* pp. 50-51.

[14]Ibid., pp. 53-54.

[15]Lindsell, *Battle,* p. 210.

[16]Carl F. H. Henry, *God, Revelation and Authority,* I and II (Waco: Word), 1976.

[17]Ramm, *HCT,* p. 107.

[18]Bernard Ramm, "Carl Henry's Magnum Opus," rev. of Carl Henry, *God, Revelation and Authority,* I & II (Word), *Eternity,* XXVIII (March 1977), 62.

[19]Kenneth Wray Conner, "Legalism or Logos?" *The Christian Century,* XCII (17 December 1975), 1153.

[20]J. Randolph Taylor, "Here's Bright, America!" *The Christian Century,* XCIII (24 November 1976), 1030-32.

[21]"Born Again!" *Newsweek,* p. 78.

## Chapter 5

[1]The prominence of Bultmann surfaced more rapidly on the Continent than in the States, but even so the influence of Barth had waned quickly because it had never become truly dominant in the New World. In America Barth has been viewed more as a corrective to liberalism than as a theological alternative.

[2]Donald W. Dayton, "An American Revival of Karl Barth?" (I), *The Reformed Journal,* XXIV (October 1974), 17.

[3]Ibid., pp. 17-20.

[4]Donald W. Dayton, "An American Revival of Karl Barth?" (II) *The Reformed Journal* XXIV (November 1974), 24-26.

[5]*Union Seminary Quarterly Review,* XXVIII (Fall 1972), 111-15.

[6]For further information on the colloquium see H. Martin Rumscheidt, *Footnotes to a Theology: The Karl Barth Colloquium of 1972,* (Waterloo, Ontario: CSR Office, Wilfrid Laurier University, 1972).

[7]The Karl Barth Society of North America is under the auspices of the Toronto School of Theology. With regard to membership queries, Dayton can be reached by writing him at Northern Baptist Theological Seminary, Lombard, Illinois.

[8]Colin Brown, "Neo-orthodoxy," in *New International Dictionary of the Christian Church,* ed. J. D. Douglas (Grand Rapids: Zondervan, 1974), pp. 697-98.

[9]Van A. Harvey, *A Handbook of Theological Terms* (New York: Macmillan, 1964), pp. 162-64.

[10]Ramm, *HCT,* p. 89; cf. pp. 89-92.

[11]William C. Fletcher, *The Moderns* (Grand Rapids: Zondervan, 1962), p. 155.

[12]Langdon B. Gilkey, "Neo-orthodoxy," in *Handbook of Christian Theology,* eds. A. A. Cohen and M. Halverson (New York: World, 1958), p. 256.

[13]Robert T. Osborn, "Positivism and Promise in the Theology of Karl Barth," *Interpretation,* XXV (July 1971), 284.

[14]Ibid.

[15]G. W. Bromiley, "Karl Barth," *Creative Minds in Contemporary Theology,* ed. P. E. Hughes (Grand Rapids: Eerdmans, 1966), p. 51.

[16]Osborn, p. 284.

## Chapter 6

[1]Ahlstrom, *RHAP,* p. 944.

[2]Holmes Rolston, *A Conservative Looks to Barth and Brunner* (Nashville: Cokesbury, 1933), p. 7.

[3]Ibid.

[4]Ibid., p. 8.

[5]Ibid., p. 24.

[6]Ibid., p. 25.

[7]Ibid.

[8]Ibid., p. 28.

[9]Ibid., p. 27.

[10]Ibid.

[11]Ibid.

[12]Ibid., p. 29.

[13]Ibid., pp. 29-30.

[14]Ibid., p. 30.

[15]Ibid., pp. 70-101.

[16]Ibid., p. 86.

[17]Ibid., p. 75.

[18]Ibid., pp. 121-23.

[19]Ibid., pp. 122-23.

[20]Ibid., p. 121.

[21]Ibid.

[22]Ibid., pp. 184-206.

[23]Ibid., p. 188.

[24]Ibid.

[25]Ibid., p. 196.

[26]Ibid.

[27]Ibid., p. 54.

[28]Cornelius Van Til, *The New Modernism: An Appraisal of the Theology of Barth and Brunner,* 3rd ed. (Phillipsburg, N.J.: Presbyterian and Reformed, 1973), p. vii. The original 1946 edition was followed by a second edition in 1947. The third edition used here includes in appendixes four essays published subsequent to the 1947 edition.

[29]Ibid., p. viii.

[30]Ibid.

[31]Ibid.

[32]Ibid., p. ix.

[33]Ibid., p. 3.

[34]Ibid., p. 7.

[35]Ibid., p. 376.

[36]Ibid., p. 40.

[37]Ibid., p. 153.

[38]Ibid., p. xiii.

[39]Ibid., p. 27.

[40]Ibid., p. 68.

[41]Ibid., p. 77.

[42]Ibid., p. 351.

[43]Ibid., pp. 371-72.

[44]Ibid., pp. 9-130. This is, in fact, the substance of the first five chapters.

[45]Ibid., pp. 372-73.

[46]Ibid., p. 287.

[47]Ibid., p. 275.

[48]Ibid.

[49]Ibid., p. 106.

[50]Ibid., p. 366.

[51]Ibid., p. 378.

[52]E. T. Ramsdell, "Barth as Heretic!" rev. of *The New Modernism,* in *The Christian Century,* LXIII (7 August 1946), 964-65.

[53]Van Til, *The New Modernism,* p. 67. Monsma's book was *Karl Barth's Idea of Revelation* (1937).

[54]Peter H. Monsma, rev. of *The New Modernism,* in *Theology Today,* III (October 1946), 424-25.

[55]Ibid.

[56]Ibid.

[57]Ibid.

[58]E. J. Carnell, "Barth as Inconsistent Evangelical," *The Christian Century,* XXIII (6 June 1962), 714.

[59]John Warwick Montgomery, *Where Is History Going?* (Grand Rapids: Zondervan, 1969), p. 108.

[60]Bromiley, "Karl Barth," in *Creative Minds in Contemporary Theology,* p. 52.

[61]Colin Brown, *Karl Barth and the Christian Message* (Chicago: InterVarsity Press, 1967), pp. 155-56.

[62]Ramm, *The Evangelical Heritage,* p. 121.

[63]Hans Urs von Balthasar, *The Theology of Karl Barth,* trans. John Drury (New York: Holt, Rinehart and Winston, 1971), pp. 44-45. Von Balthasar refers to the second edition of *The New Modernism.* Note also that Von Balthasar's work is regarded as perhaps the best written about Barth's theology. Hereafter cited as *TKB.*

[64]G. C. Berkouwer, *The Triumph of Grace in the Theology of Karl Barth,* trans. H. R. Boer (Grand Rapids: Eerdmans, 1956), p. 386.

[65]Bromiley, "Karl Barth," in *Creative Minds in Contemporary Theology,* p. 52; see Eberhard Busch, *Karl Barth: His Life from Letters and Autobiographical Texts,* trans. John Bowden (Philadelphia: Fortress, 1976), p. 380. Hereafter cited as *Karl Barth.*

[66]Ramm, *The Evangelical Heritage,* pp. 118-19.

[67]Van Til, *The New Modernism,* p. 435.

[68]Ibid., p. 456.

[69]Cornelius Van Til, *Christianity and Barthianism* (Phillipsburg, N.J.: Presbyterian and Reformed, 1962), pp. 1-114.

[70]Ibid., pp. 115-200.

[71]Ibid., p. 446.

[72]Carl F. H. Henry, "Barth in the Balances," rev. of *Christianity and Barthianism, Christianity Today,* VII (21 December 1962), 303.

[73]Ibid.

[74]Ibid.

[75]James Daane, rev. of *Christianity and Barthianism,* in *The Reformed Journal,* XIII (January 1963), 29.

[76]Ibid., p. 27.

[77]Barth, *CD,* IV/2, p. xii. See *CD,* III/4, Preface.

[78]Ibid.

[79]Berkouwer, *Triumph of Grace,* pp. 384-93.

[80]Ibid., p. 384.

[81]Ibid., p. 386.

[82]Ibid., p. 388.

[83]Ibid., p. 10.

[84]Ibid., p. 19.

[85]Ibid., pp. 52-88, 89-122, 123-50, 151-65, respectively.

[86]Ibid., pp. 166-95.

[87]Ibid., pp. 23-51.

[88]Ibid., p. 49.

[89]Ibid., pp. 196-214.

[90]Ibid., p. 204.

[91]Ibid., p. 214.

[92]Ibid., pp. 215-61, 262-96, 297-327, 328-46, respectively.

[93]Ibid., p. 256.

[94]Ibid.

[95]Ibid., pp. 255-58.

[96]Ibid., p. 261.

[97]Ibid.

[98]Ibid., p. 288.

[99]Ibid., p. 290.

[100]Ibid., p. 380.

[101]Ibid., p. 381.

[102]Busch, *Karl Barth,* p. 381.

[103]Ibid.

[104]Mueller wrote his doctoral dissertation on Barth in the early thirties. This should not be confused with the work of his son, David (*Karl Barth,* in the Word Book series, Makers of the Modern Theological Mind).

[105]Advertising blurb used, *Christianity Today,* I (29 October 1956), 35.

[106]Gordon H. Clark, "Honest Criticism," rev. of *Triumph of Grace,* in *Christianity Today,* I (29 October 1956), 34.

[107]Brown, *Karl Barth and the Christian Message,* p. 155.

## Chapter 7

[1]Gordon H. Clark, *Karl Barth's Theological Method* (Phillipsburg, N.J.: Presbyterian and Reformed, 1963), p. 6.

[2]Ibid., p. 2.

[3]Ibid., p. 14.

[4]Ibid., p. 109.

[5]Ibid., p. 144.

[6]Ibid., pp. 146-50.

[7]Ibid., p. 184.

[8]Ibid., p. 224.

[9]John Gerstner, *Reasons for Faith* (Grand Rapids: Baker, 1967), p. 9.

[10]Clark, *Karl Barth's Theological Method,* p. 109.

[11]John Gerstner, "Warfield's Case for Biblical Inerrancy," in *God's Inerrant Word: An International Symposium on the Trustworthiness of Scripture,* ed. John Warwick Montgomery (Minneapolis: Bethany Fellowship, 1974), p. 128.

[12]Ibid., p. 123.

[13]See John Gerstner, *A Bible Inerrancy Primer* (Grand Rapids: Baker, 1965).

[14]R. C. Sproul, "The Case for Inerrancy: A Methodological Analysis," in *God's Inerrant Word,* p. 256.

[15]Ibid., p. 244.

[16]See, for example, Clark H. Pinnock, *Biblical Revelation: The Foundation of Christian Theology* (Chicago: Moody, 1971), p. 38.

[17]Norman Geisler, *A General Introduction to the Bible* (Chicago: Moody, 1968), p. 40, n. 7.

[18]Norman Geisler, *Christian Apologetics* (Grand Rapids: Baker, 1976), p. 55.

[19]Ibid., p. 56.

[20]Ibid., p. 59.

[21]Ibid.

[22]Ibid., p. 62.

[23]Pinnock, *Biblical Revelation,* p. 42.

[24]Clark H. Pinnock, *Set Forth Your Case* (Chicago: Moody, 1971), p. 133.

[25]Ibid.

[26]Ibid., pp. 132-33.

[27]Pinnock, *Biblical Revelation,* p. 21.

[28]Ibid., p. 96.

[29]Ibid., p. 166.

[30]Ibid.

[31]Clark H. Pinnock, "Prospects for Systematic Theology," in *Toward a Theology for the Future,* eds. David F. Wells and Clark H. Pinnock (Carol Stream: Creation House, 1971), p. 105.

[32]Ibid.

[33]Ibid.

[34]Ibid., p. 112.

[35]Ibid.

[36]Charles Caldwell Ryrie, *Neo-orthodoxy* (Chicago: Moody, 1956), p. 62.

[37]Ibid., p. 49.

[38]Ibid., p. 50.

[39]Ibid., p. 56.

[40]Ibid., p. 64.

[41]Francis A. Schaeffer, *The God Who Is There* (Downers Grove: InterVarsity Press, 1968), p. 53.

[42]Ibid., p. 52.

[43]Ibid., p. 54.

[44]Francis A. Schaeffer, *The Church Before the Watching World* (Downers Grove: InterVarsity Press, 1971), p. 20.

[45]Ibid.

[46]Francis A. Schaeffer, *The Church at the End of the 20th Century* (Downers Grove: InterVarsity Press, 1970), p. 21.

[47]Schaeffer, *The God Who Is There,* p. 53.

[48]Ibid., p. 80.

[49]Francis A. Schaeffer, *How Should We Then Live?* (Old Tappan, N.J.: Fleming H. Revell Co., 1976), p. 174.

[50]Schaeffer, *The God Who Is There,* p. 184, n. 1.

[51]Schaeffer, *How Should We Then Live?* p. 174.

[52]Schaeffer, *The God Who Is There,* p. 102.

[53]Harold O. J. Brown, *The Protest of a Troubled Protestant* (Grand Rapids: Zondervan, 1969), p. 55, n. 7; cf. Acknowledgments.

[54]Ibid., p. 183.

[55]Ibid.

[56]Ibid., p. 186, n. 8.

[57]Ibid., p. 187, n. 24.

[58]Montgomery, *Where Is History Going?* p. 108.

[59]Ibid., pp. 151-52.

[60]John Warwick Montgomery, *The "Is God Dead?" Controversy* (Grand Rapids: Zondervan, 1966), p. 31.

[61]Ibid., p. 23.

[62]John Warwick Montgomery, *The Suicide of Christian Theology* (Minneapolis: Bethany Fellowship, 1971), p. 134.

[63]Montgomery, *The "Is God Dead?" Controversy*, p. 57.

[64]Montgomery, *Suicide*, pp. 29-30.

[65]Montgomery, *Where Is History Going?* Preface.

[66]Ibid.

[67]Ibid., p. 101.

[68]Ibid., p. 104.

[69]Montgomery, *Suicide*, p. 161.

[70]Montgomery, *Where Is History Going?* p. 105.

[71]Ibid., p. 110.

[72]Ibid., p. 111.

[73]Montgomery, *Suicide*, p. 193.

[74]Montgomery, *Where Is History Going?* p. 113.

## Chapter 8

[1]Carnell, "Barth as Inconsistent Evangelical," p. 714.

[2]Ibid.

[3]Brown, *Karl Barth and the Christian Message*, p. 10.

[4]Ibid.

[5]Ibid., p. 9.

[6]Ibid., p. 12.

[7]James Daane, "Can We Learn from Karl Barth?" *The Reformed Journal*, XII (April 1972), p. 7.

[8]Ibid., pp. 8-9.

[9]The Chicago Call, addressed to the evangelical community, speaks directly to needs within evangelicalism as perceived by some of its members. See *Christianity Today*, XXI (17 June 1977), 1035-37.

[10]Donald Bloesch, *The Evangelical Renaissance* (Grand Rapids: Eerdmans, 1973), p. 7.

[11]Ibid., pp. 80-81.

[12]Ibid., pp. 81-83.

[13]Ibid., p. 83.

[14]Ibid., p. 84.

[15]Ibid., pp. 84-96.

[16]Ibid., pp. 99-100.

[17]Donald Bloesch, *Jesus Is Victor! Karl Barth's Doctrine of Salvation* (Nashville: Abingdon, 1976), p. 9.

[18]Ibid., p. 12.

[19]Ibid., pp. 23-31.

[20]Ibid., pp. 26-27.

[21]Ibid., p. 27.

[22]Ibid., p. 30.

[23]Ibid.

[24]Ramm, *The Evangelical Heritage*, pp. 108-10.

[25]Ibid., p. 108.

[26]Ibid., p. 109.

[27]Ibid.

[28]Ibid., pp. 109-10.

[29]Ibid., p. 110.

[30]Ibid., pp. 110-20.

[31]Ibid., pp. 111-17.

32Ibid., p. 118.

33Klaas Runia, *Karl Barth's Doctrine of Holy Scripture* (Grand Rapids: Eerdmans, 1962), p. 8.

34Ibid., p. v.

35Bromiley, "Karl Barth," in *Creative Minds in Contemporary Theology,* p. 59.

36Ibid., pp. 50-51.

37Ibid., p. 58.

38James I. Packer, " 'Sola Scriptura' in History and Today," in *God's Inerrant Word,* p. 60.

39Ibid., p. 57.

40James I. Packer, "The Necessity of the Revealed Word," in *The Bible: The Living Word of Revelation,* ed. Merrill C. Tenney (Grand Rapids: Zondervan, 1968), p. 41.

41George Eldon Ladd, "The Resurrection and History," *Dialog,* I (Autumn 1962), 55-56.

42Carl F. H. Henry, *Notes on the Doctrine of God* (Boston: W. A. Wilde Co., 1948), p. 114.

43Ibid., p. 121, n. 2.

44Carl F. H. Henry, *The Protestant Dilemma* (Grand Rapids: Eerdmans, 1948), p. 39.

45Ibid., p. 149.

46Ibid., p. 89.

47Carl F. H. Henry, *Evangelical Responsibility in Contemporary Theology* (Grand Rapids: Eerdmans, 1957), p. 55.

48Ibid.

49Ibid., p. 57. Henry understands Schleiermacher's doctrine as "God discloses no truths or doctrines concerning himself and his purposes."

50Ibid., p. 55.

51Ibid., p. 60.

52Ibid., p. 56.

53Ibid., p. 12.

54Ibid., p. 58.

55Ibid., p. 54.

56Carl F. H. Henry, *Christian Personal Ethics* (Grand Rapids: Eerdmans, 1957), pp. 132-42.

57Ibid., p. 93.

58Ibid., p. 137.

59Carl F. H. Henry, "Barth Among the Mind-Changers: Some Unresolved Issues," *Christianity Today,* IV (15 February 1960), 410.

60Carl F. H. Henry, "Graham Challenges Swiss Throngs to Decision," *Christianity Today,* IV (26 September 1960), 1057.

61Carl F. H. Henry, *Frontiers in Modern Theology* (Chicago: Moody, 1964), p. 30; cf. pp. 31-33.

62Ibid., p. 50.

63Ibid., p. 51.

64Ibid., p. 61.

65Henry, "Barth in the Balances," p. 303.

66Henry, *Frontiers in Modern Theology,* p. 68.

67Carl F. H. Henry, *Faith at the Frontiers* (Chicago: Moody, 1969), p. 154.

68Henry, *Frontiers in Modern Theology,* p. 111.

69Henry, "Barth in the Balances," p. 303.

70Ibid.

71Henry, *Evangelical Responsibility,* p. 66.

[72]F. F. Bruce, *Answers to Questions* (Grand Rapids: Zondervan, 1972), pp. 155-56.

[73]Klaus Bockmuehl, "The Latter Letters of Barth," *Christianity Today*, XX (27 August 1976), 1197.

[74]Ibid.

[75]Helmut Thielicke, *The Evangelical Faith*, I (Grand Rapids: Eerdmans, 1974), p. 60.

[76]Ibid.

## Chapter 9

[1]This study can only call attention to the problem. The resources for further exploration into this area have not been collected by anyone to date and the early influences on Barth have been largely left alone.

[2]Karl Barth, "On Systematic Theology," *Scottish Journal of Theology*, XIV (September 1961), 225-26. This article constitutes the authorized translation by Terrence N. Tice from *Lehre und Forschung an der Universität Basel zur Zeit der Feier ihres funfhundertjahrigen Bestehens,* dargestellt von Dozenten der Universität Basel (Basel: Birkhauser Verlag, 1960), pp. 35-38.

[3]Karl Barth, *The Word of God and the Word of Man,* trans. Douglas Horton (New York: Harper & Brothers, 1928), p. 100. Hereafter cited as *WGWM*.

[4]Karl Barth, *The Humanity of God,* trans. J. N. Thomas and T. Wieser (Atlanta: John Knox, 1960), p. 41. Hereafter cited as *HG*.

[5]Thomas F. Torrance, *Karl Barth: An Introduction to His Early Theology, 1910-1931* (London: SCM, 1962), p. 50. Hereafter cited as *KBET*.

[6]Barth, *WGWM,* p. 100.

[7]Barth, *HG,* p. 42.

[8]Von Balthasar, *TKB,* pp. 79-80.

[9]Barth, I/1, p. x.

[10]Barth, *HG,* p. 45.

[11]Karl Barth, *Evangelical Theology: An Introduction,* trans. Grover Foley (New York: Doubleday, 1962), p. xii. Hereafter cited as *ET*.

[12]Ibid., p. 3. Note not only the immediate context, but also the relation to pp. xi-xii, where Barth speaks of a "theology of freedom." The greater context of the book is an explication of this relationship.

[13]Karl Barth, "A Theological Dialogue," *Theology Today*, XIX (July 1962), 177. This article is a transcript of a question and answer period held in the Princeton University Chapel.

[14]Herbert Hartwell, "Last Thoughts of Karl Barth," *Scottish Journal of Theology,* XXVI (May 1973), 203.

[15]Frederick L. Herzog, "Theologian of the Word of God," *Theology Today*, XIII (October 1956), 317.

[16]Karl Barth, *The Epistle to the Romans,* 2nd ed., trans. Edwyn C. Hoskyns (London: Oxford Univ. Press, 1933), p. 1. Hereafter cited as *Romans*.

[17]Ibid., p. 9.

[18]Barth, *WGWM,* p. 104.

[19]Ibid.

[20]Ibid., p. 186. Cf. p. 212.

[21]Ibid., p. 213.

[22]Karl Barth, *Anselm: Fides Quaerens Intellectum,* trans. Ian W. Robertson (Richmond: John Knox, 1960), p. 57. Hereafter cited as *Anselm*.

[23]Karl Barth, *CD,* III/4, p. xiii.

[24]Barth, "On Systematic Theology," p. 226.

[25]Ibid., p. 227. Note: this thought was recorded by Barth in 1960.

26Barth, *CD*, IV/4, p. 802.

27Barth, *WGWM*, p. 199.

28William C. Fletcher, *The Moderns* (Grand Rapids: Zondervan, 1962), p. 150. Fletcher's chapter on Barth (pp. 110-28) is a somewhat different kind of introduction to Barth, dealing as much with literary concerns as with doctrine. One of the few intelligent studies of any length written by a scholar who is neither Reformed or Catholic; it is sympathetic and generally correct.

29Von Balthasar, *TKB*, pp. 151-52.

30Herzog, "Theologian of the Word of God," p. 376.

31Barth, *Romans*, p. 1.

32Ibid.

33Von Balthasar, *TKB*, p. 48.

34Barth, *Romans*, p. 10.

35Barth, *WGWM*, p. 196.

36Barth, *Romans*, p. ix.

37Torrance, *KBET*, p. 47.

38Barth, *WGWM*, p. 206.

39Von Balthasar, *TKB*, p. 59.

40Ibid., p. 67.

41Ibid., p. 63. Note the full discussion, pp. 58-73, for what is probably the best treatment of the subject of Barth and dialectics.

42Torrance, *KBET*, p. 83.

43See Torrance, *KBET*, pp. 88-89, and Von Balthasar, *TKB*, pp. 73-100. The summary by Torrance is helpful in describing this shift: "it is no longer a movement of thought setting men apart from God, but a movement referring man back to his source in the grace of God the Creator and Redeemer" (p. 89).

44Torrance, *KBET*, pp. 48-95, on "From Dialectical to Dogmatic Thinking." These five considerations should be compared with those identified by Von Balthasar who, as a Roman Catholic, focuses particularly on Barth's concept of the church.

45Von Balthasar, *TKB*, pp. 77-78.

46Torrance, *KBET*, p. 182.

47Ibid., pp. 183-93.

48Bernard Ramm, *Protestant Biblical Interpretation* (Grand Rapids: Baker, 1970), p. 69.

49Herzog, "Theologian of the Word of God," p. 321.

50Ibid., p. 322.

51J. C. Beker, "Reflections on Biblical Theology," *Interpretation*, XXIV (July 1970), 304.

52Krister Stendahl, "Biblical Theology, Contemporary," in *Interpreter's Dictionary of the Bible*, ed. G. A. Buttrick et al., I (Nashville: Abingdon, 1962), p. 420.

53Brevard S. Childs, *Biblical Theology in Crisis* (Philadelphia: Westminster, 1970), p. 110. See also *Interpretation*, XXXI (January 1977). The entire issue is devoted to the subject of Calvin and the Scriptures. With regard to Barth's impact, see James A. Wharton, "Karl Barth as Exegete and His Influence on Biblical Interpretation," *Union Seminary Quarterly Review*, XXVIII (Fall 1972), 5-13.

54Ibid., p. 52.

55Ibid., p. 110.

56Barth, *CD*, I/1, pp. 64-65.

57David L. Mueller, *Karl Barth* (Waco: Word, 1972), p. 146.

58Bernard Ramm, *HCT*, p. 57.

59Barth, *CD*, I/2, p. 716.

[60]Ibid.

[61]Ibid., p. 714.

[62]Ramm, *HCT*, p. 57.

[63]Childs, *Biblical Theology in Crisis*, p. 11.

[64]Ibid., p. 241.

[65]Ramm, *Protestant Bible Interpretation*, pp. 138-39.

[66]Barth, *Anselm*, p. 18.

[67]Fletcher, *The Moderns*, pp. 112-13.

[68]Georges Casalis, *Portrait of Karl Barth*, trans. and intro. Robert McAfee Brown (New York: Doubleday, 1964), p. 62. See, for example, *CD*, II/2 (on Rom. 9—11), and *CD*, III/1 (on Gen. 1—2).

[69]Herbert Hartwell, *The Theology of Karl Barth: An Introduction* (Philadelphia: Westminster, 1964), p. 15. Hartwell footnotes this statement to add, "It is at this point that many of Barth's critics fail" (p. 39, n. 64).

## Chapter 10

[1]John Godsey, "The Architecture of Karl Barth's Church Dogmatics," *Scottish Journal of Theology*, IX (March 1956), 236-50.

[2]Ibid., p. 248.

[3]Torrance, *KBET*, p. 32. See Fletcher, *The Moderns*, p. 112.

[4]Barth, *CD*, I/2, p. 293. Cf. pp. 4-7, where Barth claims that the roots of Neo-Protestantism (his term for liberalism) extend back to about 1700. See also Barth, *HG*, pp. 13-14.

[5]Barth, *HG*, p. 21.

[6]Barth, *CD*, I/2, p. 4.

[7]Barth, *CD*, IV/2, p. 119. Cf. p. xii.

[8]Ibid., p. 124.

[9]Barth, *CD*, I/1, p. 38.

[10]Ibid., p. x.

[11]Ibid., p. 16.

[12]Ibid.

[13]Ibid., p. ix.

[14]Ibid., p. xii.

[15]Karl Barth, *Dogmatics in Outline*, trans. G. T. Thomson (New York: Harper & Row, 1959), p. 9. See pp. 9-14.

[16]Barth, *CD*, I/1, p. 18.

[17]Ibid., p. 25.

[18]Barth, *Anselm*, p. 16.

[19]Ibid., pp. 16-17.

[20]Karl Barth, *CD*, II/1, p. 4.

[21]Barth, *Dogmatics in Outline*, p. 22.

[22]Ibid., p. 15. The phrase, "in spite of all that contradicts it," should not have any irrationality read into it. The humanity receiving God's revelation introduces all and any elements of contradiction. The revelation, "the word of grace," may be contradicted, but it is not itself contradictory.

[23]Barth, *CD*, IV/3a, p. 183.

[24]Ibid., pp. 183-84.

[25]Barth, *CD*, I/1, p. 263.

[26]Bernard Ramm, "Karl Barth and Analytic Philosophy," *The Christian Century*, LXXIX (11 April 1962), 453.

[27]Ibid., pp. 453-55.

[28]Ibid., p. 455.

29Clark, *Karl Barth's Theological Method,* p. 140.

30Ibid.

31Ibid.

32Fletcher, *The Moderns,* p. 113.

33Ramm, *HCT,* p. 129.

34Dietrich Bonhoeffer, *Letters and Papers from Prison,* trans. R. H. Fuller, ed. Eberhard Bethge (New York: Macmillan, 1962), p.168.

35Ibid., pp. 168-69. Cf. this: "In sum, his objections to Barth appear to be: (1) He identifies revelation with doctrine, so that faith becomes law. (2) Doctrine is understood not as the central articles of faith but as the whole dogmatic system. (3) The world is left alone, to its own devices, because Barth offers no suggestions for a nonreligious interpretation of Christianity. Altogether, this is orthodoxy." Robert T. Osborn, "Positivism and Promise in the Theology of Karl Barth," *Interpretation,* XXV (July 1971), 287.

36Hartwell, "Last Thoughts of Karl Barth," p. 197.

37Ibid.

38Barth, *CD,* I/1, p. 862.

39Ibid.

40Karl Barth, *CD,* IV/1, trans. G. W. Bromiley (New York: Scribner, 1956), p. 366. Cf. Ramm, *HCT,* p. 24; this is an instance of Ramm's repeated failure to do justice to Barth's dynamism by reducing concrete reality to an abstract "principle"— something Barth studiously avoids.

41Obviously much overlap exists among these features. For a more complete analysis, see Hartwell, *The Theology of Karl Barth: An Introduction,* pp. 20-37. Hereafter cited as *TKBI.*

42Oscar Cullmann, *Christ and Time,* trans. F. V. Filson (Philadelphia: Westminster, 1964), p. 60n. Cf. p. xiii. See also p. 1, where Cullmann reserves final judgment in anticipation of Barth's *CD,* V, never written but planned as the treatment of eschatology.

43See Hartwell, *TKBI,* pp. 30-32. Hartwell's analysis is good but some reference to Cullmann would have been helpful. However, the reader familiar with both Barth and Cullmann can discern differences on the basis of Hartwell's discussion.

44Childs, *Biblical Theology in Crisis,* p. 241n. This is in reference to Childs's observation that Barth "would have nothing to do with *Heilsgeschichte....*" and thus avoided a weakness that beset the Biblical Theology Movement (p. 110).

45Barth, *CD,* III/1, p. 60.

46David H. Wallace, "Oscar Cullmann," in *Creative Minds in Contemporary Theology,* p. 168.

47Otto Weber, *Karl Barth's Church Dogmatics: An Introductory Report on Volumes I:2 to III:4,* trans. Arthur C. Cochrane (Philadelphia: Westminster, 1953), p. 58. See also Barth, *CD,* I/2, pp. 45-70; Hartwell, *TKBI,* pp. 31-32.

48Barth, *CD,* I/2, p. 45; *CD,* II/1, p. 619.

49Barth, *CD,* III/1, p. 43.

50Ibid., p. 82.

51Klaas Runia, *Karl Barth's Doctrine of Holy Scripture* (Grand Rapids: Eerdmans, 1962), p. 92, citing H. N. Ridderbos, *Heilsgeschiedenis en Heilige Schrift* (1955), pp. 143-44.

52Runia, *Karl Barth's Doctrine of Holy Scripture,* pp. 92-93. Despite all this, Runia still states, "The whole idea of saga is to be utterly rejected" (p. 95). This, however, is unreasonable.

53Barth, *CD,* III/1, p. 84.

[54]"Faith, History and the Resurrection" (Appendix), *History & Christianity,* John Warwick Montgomery (Downers Grove: InterVarsity Press, 1964-65), p. 86. See also Lewis Smedes, "Does Karl Barth Believe in the Resurrection of Christ?" *The Reformed Journal,* XII (April 1962), 10-13.

[55]Karl Barth, "An Exegetical Study of Matthew 28:16-20," trans. Thomas Wieser in *The Theology of the Christian Mission,* ed. G. H. Andersen (Nashville: Abingdon, 1961), pp. 56-57.

[56]Ibid., p. 56.

[57]Ibid., p. 57. Here the words "style" and "historical" must be emphasized to retain Barth's thrust. The resurrection really did happen.

[58]"Faith, History and the Resurrection," p. 85.

[59]Ibid., pp. 86-87.

[60]See Barth, *CD,* II/1, pp. 128-78, esp. pp. 139, 143-44. Note also p. 4, on Barth's indebtedness to Anselm. See Hartwell, *TKBI,* p. 48 and Casalis, *Portrait of Karl Barth,* pp. xxi-xxvii.

[61]Henri Bouillard, "A Dialogue with Barth: the Problem of Natural Theology," *Cross Currents,* XVIII (Spring 1968), 208.

[62]Barth, *CD,* II/1, p. 168.

[63]Casalis, *Portrait of Karl Barth,* pp. xxi-xxii. Surprisingly, not many have explored this particular point. It is, however, another example of Barth's way of seeing theology actualized in history (in this instance negatively).

[64]Berkouwer, *Triumph of Grace,* p. 155.

[65]Henri Bouillard, *The Knowledge of God,* trans. S. D. Femiano (New York: Herder and Herder, 1968), p. 15. This is a nice summary statement of a primary critique offered by Barth, *CD,* II/1, pp. 128-78, esp. 137-40.

[66]Barth, *CD,* II/1, p. 165.

[67]Ibid., pp. 165, 137. "Everything depends on whether we really refer to Jesus Christ" (p. 165); this is the issue that when answered either dispels or protects the illusion.

[68]Ibid., pp. 97-98. Barth's exegetical portions concerning natural theology are primarily located here in II/1, pp. 97-128, and *CD,* I/2, pp. 303-7. Texts examined include Gen. 1-2, Psalms, Acts 17:22-31, Rom. 1:18-32; 2:12-13.

[69]Ibid., p. 99.

[70]Barth, *CD,* I/2, pp. 306-7; *CD,* II/1, pp. 119-21. The breakdown is as follows: Q, 2, 3, 6 (*CD,* II/1); 1, 4, 5, 7 (I/2). This harmony is not invalid inasmuch as: (1) the text being expounded is the same; (2) Barth, in II/1, refers to his earlier treatment for comparison; (3) the contexts in the *Dogmatics* are related.

[71]Barth, *CD,* II/1, p. 119.

[72]Ibid., p. 169; pp. 165-72.

[73]Ibid.

[74]Karl Barth, *The Heidelberg Catechism for Today,* trans. Shirley C. Guthrie, Jr. (Richmond: John Knox, 1964), p. 30. Note pp. 28-33 in this same connection.

[75]Von Balthasar, *TKB,* pp. 93-94, 147, et al. "Used badly, it may well be the invention of the Antichrist, as Barth said, but it is offered to man as a good tool. Barth might have been able to accept this idea without feeling that he betrayed his basic outlook" (p. 147).

[76]Berkouwer, *Triumph of Grace,* ch. 7, "The Triumph of Grace in its Antithesis to Rome," esp. pp. 185-90. "We are of the opinion that von Balthasar's interpretation ... is in error at a decisive point and that therein the fundamental fallacy of his masterful and in certain respects irenic book is to be found" (p. 186).

[77]Hans Küng, *Justification: The Doctrine of Karl Barth and a Catholic Reflection,* trans. T. Collins, E. E. Tolk, and D. Granskou, with a letter by K. Barth (New

York: Thomas Nelson & Sons, 1964), p. 193; see pp. 190-93.

[78]Barth, *CD,* I/1, p. 279. The term appears as early as p. 11.

[79]Ibid., see Von Balthasar, *TKB,* pp. 148-50; Berkouwer, *Triumph of Grace,* pp. 181-85; Bouillard, *The Knowledge of God,* pp. 97-104. Note the identification of other terms of analogy, e.g., *analogia relationis, analogia gratiae.* All of these speak to the same essential concern.

[80]Hartwell, "Last Thoughts of Karl Barth," p. 187.

[81]Karl Barth, *God Here and Now,* trans. and intro. Paul M. van Buren, intro. R. N. Anshen (London: Routledge and Kegan Paul, 1964), p. 28.

[82]Barth, *CD,* I/1, pp. 132, 352; II/1, pp. 297-321; III/1, pp. 265-66; III/4 is a comprehensive treatment of Barth's understanding of freedom.

[83]Brown, *Karl Barth and the Christian Message,* p. 76; see pp. 67-76; see Hartwell, *TKBI,* pp. 73-77; see esp. Von Balthasar, *TKB,* p. 74.

[84]Robert W. Jenson, *Alpha and Omega: A Study in the Theology of Karl Barth.* (New York: Thomas Nelson & Sons, 1963), p. 171.

[85]Barth, *CD,* IV/2, p. 264.

## Chapter 11

[1]See Karl Barth, *CD,* II/2, p. ix; esp. "May it not be that I have been too short and not too long at some important points?"

[2]Daniel D. Williams, *What Present Day Theologians Are Thinking* (New York: Harper & Row, 1967), p. 56. Note Williams's elaboration (p. 57): "Three things can be asked of any Christian theology. It must preserve and express the message of the Gospel. It should interpret the faith in a way which brings Christian belief into some kind of intelligible order with human knowledge and experience. Finally it should give an account of how faith may be presented to the unbeliever so that the way is opened for him to understand how it is related to his own experience. On all three counts Barth's theology stands impressively."

[3]"When Karl Barth decided to become a systematic theologian, Protestant historical scholarship lost a man who was potentially the greatest historian since Adolf von Harnack" (from the intro. by Jaroslav Pelikan), Karl Barth, *Protestant Thought: From Rousseau to Ritschl,* trans. Brian Cozens and Herbert Hartwell (New York: Simon and Schuster, 1959), p. 7.

[4]Ludwig Feuerbach, *The Essence of Christianity,* trans. George Eliot, intro. K. Barth, foreword by H. Richard Niebuhr (New York: Harper & Row, 1957), p. vii.

[5]Barth, *CD,* I/1, p. xiv.

[6]Gustaf Wingren, *Theology in Conflict: Nygren, Barth, Bultmann,* trans. Eric H. Wahlstrom (London: Oliver and Boyd, 1958), p. 108.

[7]Barth, *CD,* I/1, p. 104; pp. 98-111.

[8]Ibid., pp. 113-14.

[9]Ibid., p. 121.

[10]Ibid., pp. 122-23.

[11]Karl Barth, *Karl Barth's Table Talk,* ed. John D. Godsey (Richmond: John Knox, 1962), p. 41.

[12]Barth, *CD,* I/1, p. 123.

[13]Ibid.

[14]"Faith, History and the Resurrection," p. 86.

[15]Barth, *CD,* I/1, pp. 123-24. Cf. *CD,* I/2, p. 506.

[16]Ibid., p. 124.

[17]G. W. Bromiley, "Karl Barth's Doctrine of Inspiration" (paper presented at the 929th Ordinary General Meeting of the Victoria Institute, 18 April 1955), p. 69, cited by Brown, *Karl Barth and the Christian Message,* p. 32. See Barth, *CD,*

I/2, pp. 457-537.

[18]Barth, *CD,* I/2, p. 507.

[19]Ibid., p. 529.

[20]Ibid.

[21]Ibid., p. 531.

[22]Ibid., p. 534.

[23]Ibid., p. 537.

[24]Runia, *Karl Barth's Doctrine of Holy Scripture,* p. 74. Note his preceding comments, pp. 65-73 for his "cordial *agreement* with Barth's great stress upon the humanity of the Bible" (p. 65). For a review of Runia, see G. W. Bromiley, *The Reformed Journal,* XII (April 1962), 24.

[25]One must also ask why, if God did so produce such a document, he then allowed its inerrant autographs to perish. Surely, if he allowed this to happen to avoid bibliolatry, then why did he bother with inerrant originals of these books in the first place? The question must be raised afresh: are we more concerned than God himself about inerrancy?

[26]See Barth, *CD,* I/2, pp. 506-7, 512-14; in fact, ch. 3, "Holy Scripture" is pertinent to this whole area. The point is this, if inerrancy is to be held at all it must cease to concentrate on the Bible as an in-itself, for-itself entity. Instead, a review of the doctrine that does not separate ontology from function is needed.

[27]Barth, *CD,* I/1, p. 134.

[28]S. Paul Schilling, *Contemporary Continental Theologians* (Nashville: Abingdon, 1966), p. 23. This comment actually anticipates *CD,* I/2, where twelve references to John 1:14 occur.

[29]Barth, *CD,* I/1, 125.

[30]Ibid.

[31]Ibid., pp. 126-27.

[32]Wingren, *Theology in Conflict,* p. 108. This strange accusation makes sense in Wingren's framework because he has already found that "it is clear that Barth remains within the framework of Schleiermacher's theology . . . " (pp. 25-26). Not only that, but Wingren also believes that "the positions of Barth and Luther are incompatible and cannot be at all reconciled" (fn. 6, p. 26)! Cf. Von Balthasar, *TKB,* pp. 23, 65, 74, 134, 172, et al.; Torrance, KBET, pp. 96, 216, et al.

[33]Ibid., p. 34; "It is strange that we must make this statement, but it is necessary: in Barth's theology man is the obvious center."

[34]Ibid., p. 109.

[35]Ibid., pp. 110-28.

[36]For an alternate evaluation of Barth, see Küng, *Justification,* p. 279, who identifies various inherent "weaknesses" in Barth's theology, including his doctrine of sin, but who says, "these trends, while present in Barth's fundamental position, do not become errors nor irresponsible exaggerations." Cf. also Berkouwer, *Triumph of Grace,* pp. 215-61, who starts from a much different point from Wingren. Finally, cf. Hartwell, *TKBI,* pp. 116-23; Brown, *Karl Barth and the Christian Message,* pp. 119-23.

[37]Barth, *CD,* I/1, p. 136.

[38]Ibid. Barth states, "the doctrine of the Word of God in its threefold form is itself the sole analogy to the doctrine which will fundamentally occupy us in unfolding the concept of revelation; the doctrine of the three-in-oneness of God."

[39]Brown, *Karl Barth and the Christian Message,* p. 67.

[40]Bromiley, "Karl Barth," in *Creative Minds in Contemporary Theology,* p. 33. For an excellent presentation on Barth in a few pages, this is without a doubt the best.

[41]Barth, *CD,* I/1, p. 353.

[42]Barth, *CD*, I/2, p. 13.

[43]Ibid., p. 239; cf. pp. 203-79.

[44]Barth, *CD*, II/1, pp. 3-256, 257-678.

[45]Ramm, *HCT*, p. 40. Also see James Daane, "Can We Learn from Karl Barth?" *The Reformed Journal*, XII (April 1962), 7-9.

[46]Barth, *CD*, II/2, p. 13.

[47]Ibid., p. 3.

[48]A. D. R. Polman, *Barth*, trans. Calvin D. Freeman (Phillipsburg, N.J.: Presbyterian and Reformed, 1960), p. 34; pp. 33-34. Cf. Barth, *CD*, II/2, pp. 3-76, 127-45.

[49]Weber, *Karl Barth's Church Dogmatics*, p. 94. Cf. Barth, *CD*, II/2, pp. 18-22; (free, divine grace of God, p. 19; hidden and inscrutable divine resolve and decree, p. 20; God does that which is worthy of himself, p. 22).

[50]Barth, *CD*, II/2, p. 59.

[51]Bromiley, "Karl Barth," in *Creative Minds in Contemporary Theology*, p. 40.

[52]Weber, p. 94. Cf. Barth, *CD*, II/2, pp. 59, 63-64, 94-145.

[53]Barth, *CD*, II/2, p. 115.

[54]Ibid., p. 60. Here is Barth's exegesis of the text as well as citations of other passages. Cf. pp. 112-13, where Barth also discusses John 1:1-2.

[55]Ibid.

[56]Ibid., p. 353. Cf. pp. 340-409.

[57]Ibid., p. 125.

[58]Ibid., pp. 352, 449-506.

[59]Berkouwer, *Triumph of Grace*, p. 107.

[60]Ibid., p. 292; cf. pp. 262-96.

[61]Brown, *Karl Barth and the Christian Message*, p. 107. About this charge one must ask what criteria determine sufficient textual support. Barth is not interested in counting texts but expositing them. Besides, the texts he does adduce are several. It must also be remembered that Barth is always interested in the whole canon and its message.

[62]Ibid., p. 132. It must be noted that even Berkouwer hesitates in his criticism. Berkouwer comments, "Barth's opposition to all synergism has brought him to the verge of the apokatastasis" (p. 295, *Triumph of Grace*).

[63]Barth, *God Here and Now*, p. 34. Cf. Barth, *CD*, II/2, pp. 295, 417, 422, 476. He declares that "it is not legitimate to make the limitless many of the elect in Jesus Christ the totality of all men" (II/2, p. 422).

[64]Ibid. See Barth, *HG*, pp. 61-62.

[65]Weber, *Karl Barth's Church Dogmatics*, p. 98.

[66]Arnold B. Come, *An Introduction to Barth's "Dogmatics" for Preachers* (Philadelphia: Westminster, 1963), pp. 98-99.

[67]Barth, *CD*, II/2, p. 509; cf. pp. 509-51.

[68]Ibid., p. 552; cf. pp. 552-630.

[69]Ibid., p. 631; cf. pp. 631-732.

[70]Ibid., p. 733; cf. pp. 733-81.

[71]Ibid., p. 509. For further discussion on Barth's ethics see Robert E. Willis, *The Ethics of Karl Barth* (Leiden: E. J. Brill, 1971); Hartwell, *TKBI*, pp. 154-65; Henry Stob, "Themes in Barth's Ethics," *The Reformed Journal*, XII (April 1962), 19-23.

[72]Karl Barth, *Credo*, trans. J. S. McNab, foreword by R. M. Brown (New York: Scribner, 1962), p. 28. Cf. Barth, *CD*, III/1, p. 3.

[73]A statistic all the more amazing in light of Barth's comment, "In taking up the doctrine of creation I have entered a sphere in which I feel much less confident and sure" *(CD*, III/1, p. ix).

[74]Karl Barth, *The Faith of the Church: A Commentary on the Apostles' Creed According to Calvin's Catechism*, trans. Gabriel Vahanian, ed. Jean-Louis Leuba (London: Fontana Books, 1960), p. 40.

[75]Barth, *CD*, III/1, p. 42; cf. pp. 81-94 where Barth gives an extended treatment of saga and carefully differentiates it from other literary forms.

[76]Thomas W. Ogletree, *Christian Faith and History: A Critical Comparison of Ernst Troeltsch and Karl Barth* (Nashville: Abingdon, 1965), p. 192. Ogletree understands Barth as viewing *Historie* with a double usage: "On the one hand, it refers to a particular conception of the nature of the actual course of the events of history. On the other hand, it refers to a corresponding kind of portrayal of those events in history writing" (p. 192).

[77]Barth, *CD*, III/1, p. 94; the full discussion occupies pp. 42-92.

[78]Ibid., pp. 94-228, 228-329.

[79]Ibid., p. 97.

[80]Ibid.

[81]Küng, *Justification*, p. 19; cf. pp. 11-12.

[82]Barth, *CD*, III/1, p. 231.

[83]Ibid., p. 330. Creation is viewed as benefit (pp. 330-44), actualization (pp. 344-65), and justification (pp. 366-414). See Küng, *Justification*, pp. 18-27; Hartwell, *TKBI*, pp. 112-15; Von Balthasar, *TKB*, pp. 108-12.

[84]Hartwell, *TKBI*, p. 123; cf. pp. 123-31.

[85]Karl Barth, *CD*, III/2, p. 43.

[86]Ibid., p. 46; Barth states: "Hence in our exposition of the doctrine of man we must always look in the first instance at the nature of man as it confronts us in the person of Jesus, and only secondarily—asking and answering from this place of light—at the nature of man as that of every man and all other men."

[87]Karl Barth, *CD*, III/3, p. xi.

[88]Ibid., p. 12; cf. pp. 3-57.

[89]Ibid., pp. 58-288.

[90]Ibid., p. 289; cf. pp. 289-368.

[91]This term warranted a special footnote from the translators; in fact, it did in III/3 as well. It reads as follows: "Many terms have been considered for *das Nichtige*, including the Latin *nihil* which has sometimes been favoured. Preferring a native term, and finding constructions like 'the Null' too artificial and 'the negative' or 'non-existent' not quite exact, we have finally had to make do with 'nothingness.' It must be clearly grasped, however, that it is not used in its more common and abstract way, but in the secondary sense, to be filled out from Barth's own definitions and delimitations, of 'that which is not' " (p. 289).

[92]Barth, *CD*, III/3, p. 302.

[93]Ibid.

[94]Ibid., p. 349.

[95]Ibid., p. 353.

[96]Ibid., p. 363.

[97]Ibid., pp. 369-531.

[98]Barth, *CD*, III/4, pp. 3-685. The sections are as follows: first (pp. 47-115), second (pp. 116-323), third (pp. 324-564), fourth (pp. 565-658). On the doctrine of creation see Barth, "A Theological Dialogue," pp. 172-73; Berkouwer, *Triumph of Grace*, pp. 52-88; Von Balthasar, *TKB*, pp. 108-26.

[99]Karl Barth, *CD*, IV/1, p. 128; cf. pp. 157-780.

[100]Ibid., p. 130; cf. Barth, *CD*, IV/2, pp. 3-840.

[101]Ibid., p. 135; cf. Barth, *CD*, IV/3a, pp. 3-478; IV/3b, pp. 481-942.

[102]Ibid., p. 22.

103Bromiley, "Karl Barth," in *Creative Minds in Contemporary Theology*, p. 46.

104Barth, *CD*, IV/1, pp. 122-28.

105Ibid., p. 508.

106Ibid., pp. 359-60.

107Ibid., p. 413.

108Ibid., p. 568; cf. pp. 568-608.

109Ibid., p. 618; cf. pp. 608-42.

110Ibid., p. 620.

111Ibid., p. 596.

112Ibid., pp. 596, 599-602.

113Ibid., p. 594. On the doctrine of justification see Küng, *Justification*, about which Barth, in a letter to its author (published in the book), stated, "you have fully and accurately reproduced my views as I myself understand them." (p. xix). On a Catholic response to Küng, see Karl Rahner, *Theological Investigations*, IV (Baltimore: Helicon Press, 1966), 189-218.

114Barth, *CD*, IV/2, p. 500; cf. pp. 499-613. Barth, in regard to this doctrine, had the highest regard for Dietrich Bonhoeffer, *The Cost of Discipleship*, trans. R. H. Fuller (New York: Macmillan, 1963). See IV/2, pp. 533-34. Also on this doctrine, see Arthur C. Cochrane, "The Doctrine of Sanctification: Review of Barth's *Kirchliche Dogmatik*, IV/2," *Theology Today*, XIII (October 1956), 376-88.

115Karl Barth, *Christ and Adam: Man and Humanity in Romans 5*, trans. T. A. Smail, intro. Wilhelm Pauck (New York: Macmillan, 1956), pp. 34-35.

116Karl Barth, *CD*, IV/3b, p. 521.

117Barth, *CD*, IV/4, p. ix.

118Ibid.

**Chapter 12**

1Donald W. Dayton, "Fullest Impact Ahead?" rev. of H. Martin Rumscheidt, ed., *Footnotes to a Theology: The Karl Barth Colloquium of 1972*, in *Christianity Today*, XIX (8 November 1974) 150.

2Emil Brunner, *Dogmatics: The Christian Doctrine of God*, I, trans. Olive Wyon (Philadelphia: Westminster, 1950), p. 101.

3Emil Brunner, *Dogmatics: The Christian Doctrine of Creation and Redemption*, II, trans. Olive Wyon (Philadelphia: Westminster, 1952), p. 74, n. 1.

4Hugh Ross Mackintosh, *Types of Modern Theology* (London: Collins Press, 1964), p. 285.

5Karl Barth, *Church Dogmatics*, IV/2, p. 171.

6Ibid.

7Gabriel Vahanian in Karl Barth, *The Faith of the Church*, trans. and introd. G. Vahanian, ed. Jean-Louis Leuba (London: Collins Press, 1958), p. 7.

8Brown, *Karl Barth and the Christian Message*, p. 152.

9Ibid., p. 153.

10Torrance, "Karl Barth," *Scottish Journal of Theology*, XXII (March 1969), 1.

11Bromiley, "Karl Barth," in *Creative Minds in Contemporary Theology*, p. 59.

12Norman F. Langford, "How Barth Has Influenced Me," *Theology Today*, XIII (October 1956), 361.

13Karl Barth, *CD*, II/1, p. 265.

14Nels F. S. Ferré, "How Barth Has Influenced Me," *Theology Today*, XIII (October 1956), 361.

15Herbert Hartwell, "Last Thoughts of Karl Barth," *Scottish Journal of Theology*, XXVI (May 1973), 200.

[16]Ibid., p. 201.
[17]Ibid.
[18]Ibid.
[19]Ibid.
[20]Ibid., p. 202.
[21]Ibid.

### Chapter 13

[1]Barth, *Humanity of God*, p. 11.
[2]Karl Barth, "An Exegetical Study of Matthew 28:16-20," trans. Thomas Wieser, in *The Theology of the Christian Mission*, ed. Gerald H. Anderson (Nashville: Abingdon, 1961), pp. 55-71.
[3]Ibid.
[4]Barth, *Romans*, p. 311.
[5]Barth, *CD*, II/2, pp. 433-34.
[6]Barth, *ET*, p. 32.
[7]Busch, *Karl Barth*, pp. 446, 459.
[8]C. F. H. Henry, "Visit with Brunner," News, *Christianity Today*, IV (26 September 1960), 1067.
[9]Barth, *CD*, III/4, p. 4.
[10]Runia, *Karl Barth's Doctrine of Holy Scripture*, pp. 10-11.
[11]Van A. Harvey, *A Handbook of Theological Terms* (New York: Macmillan, 1964), p. 99.
[12]James Daane, "Faith or Fideism: What Authenticates the Bible?" *The Reformed Journal*, XXII (September 1972), 25.
[13]Ibid., p. 26.
[14]Ibid., p. 25.
[15]Barth, *CD*, I/2, p. 539.
[16]Ibid., p. 538.
[17]Von Balthasar, *TKB*, pp. 120-21. This is especially true with regard to the comment that fideism is "a view which assumes that knowledge originates in a fundamental act of faith, independent of rational presuppositions." J. D. Douglas, ed., *The New International Dictionary of the Christian Church* (Grand Rapids: Zondervan, 1974), p. 374.
[18]Walden Howard, "The Bible as Authority," *Keys to Creative Faith*, ed. Walden Howard (Waco: Word, 1976), p. 147.
[19]James Brown, *Kierkegaard, Heidegger, Buber and Barth* (New York: Collier Books, 1971), pp. 127-28.
[20]As an example of this kind of approach, see Karl Barth, *Protestant Thought: From Rousseau to Ritschl*.
[21]Willis E. Elliott, "Eutychus and his Kin," *Christianity Today*, VI (3 August 1962), 1065.

### Chapter 14

[1]Küng, *Justification*, p. 215.
[2]Ibid., p. 213.
[3]Ibid.
[4]Barth, *CD*, IV/1, p. 95.
[5]Ibid.
[6]Ibid., p. 148.
[7]See Donald G. Bloesch, *Essentials of Evangelical Theology*, I (San Francisco: Harper & Row, 1978), 79 n. 6, and II (1979), 271.

**Chapter 15**
[1]Barth, *CD*, I/2, p. 207.
[2]Ibid., pp. 207-8.
[3]Ibid., p. 537.
[4]Ibid., p. 586.
[5]Ibid., p. 532.
[6]Ibid., p. 533.
[7]Ibid.
[8]Klaas Runia, *Karl Barth's Doctrine of Holy Scripture* (Grand Rapids: Eerdmans, 1962), p. 160.
[9]Barth, *CD*, I/2, pp. 527-35, 538.
[10]Ibid., p. 514.
[11]Ibid., pp. 506-8.
[12]Ibid., p. 506.
[13]Ibid., p. 534.
[14]Ibid., p. 535.
[15]Ibid., p. 508.
[16]Ibid.
[17]Klaas Runia, *Karl Barth's Doctrine of Holy Scripture* (Grand Rapids: Eerdmans, 1962), p. 174.
[18]*Westminster Confession of Faith* (Glasgow: Free Presbyterian Publ., 1973), pp. 21-22.
[19]Bernard Ramm, *The Witness of the Spirit* (Grand Rapids: Eerdmans, 1959), p. 26.

# Bibliography

## Basic Bibliography (Topical) of Barth's Translated Works

### I. Dogmatic Works
A. Shorter Works

"The Christian Hope," *Episcopal Church News* (6 April 1952).

*Credo, A Presentation of the Chief Problems of Dogmatics with Reference to the Apostles' Creed.* Trans. J. Strathearn McNab. New York: Scribner, 1962.

*Dogmatics in Outline.* Trans. G. T. Thomson. New York: Philosophical Library, 1949. Harper Torchbooks, 1959.

*Evangelical Theology: An Introduction.* Trans. Grover Goley. New York: Holt, Rinehart and Winston, 1963. Garden City: Doubleday (Anchor Books), 1964.

*The Faith of the Church.* Trans. Gabriel Vahanian. New York: Meridian Books, 1958.

*God, Grace and Gospel.* Trans. J. Strathearn McNab. Edinburgh: Oliver and Boyd, 1959.

*God Here and Now.* Trans. and introd. Paul M. Van Buren. New York and Evanston: Harper & Row, 1964.

*God in Action.* Trans. E. G. Homrighausen and K. J. Ernst. New York: Round Table Press, 1936 and 1963.

*The Heidelberg Catechism for Today.* Trans. Shirley Guthrie, Jr. Richmond: John Knox, 1964.

*The Humanity of God.* Trans. J. N. Thomas and T. Wieser. Richmond: John Knox, 1960.

*The Knowledge of God and the Service of God.* Trans. J. L. M. Haire and Ian Henderson. New York: Scribner, 1939.

*Natural Theology* (with E. Brunner). Trans. P. Fraenkel. London: Geoffrey Bles, 1946.

"The New Humanism and the Humanism of God." Trans. Frederick L. Herzog.

*Theology Today,* VII (July 1951), 157-66.

"Protestantism and Architecture." *Theology Today,* XIX (July 1962), 272.

"The Real Church." Trans. J. W. Edwards. *Scottish Journal of Theology,* III (December 1950), 337-51.

"Revelation." In *Revelation.* Ed. John Baillie and Hugh Martin. Trans. F. O. Cobham and R. F. C. Gutteridge. New York: Macmillan, 1937.

*Theology and Church: Shorter Writings, 1920-1928.* Trans. L. P. Smith. Introd. T. F. Torrance. London: SCM, 1962.

*The Word of God and the Word of Man.* Trans. Douglas Horton. Boston: Pilgrim Press, 1928. New York: Harper Torchbooks, 1957.

B. Church Dogmatics

*Church Dogmatics.* Ed. G. W. Bromiley and T. F. Torrance. Edinburgh: T. & T. Clark, 1936-1969.

I/1 *The Doctrine of the Word of God,* Prolegomena, Part 1. Trans. G. T. Thomson, 1936.

I/2 *The Doctrine of the Word of God,* Prolegomena, Part 2. Trans. G. T. Thomson and H. Knight, 1956.

II/1 *The Doctrine of God,* Part 1. Trans. T. H. L. Parker, W. B. Johnson, H. Knight and J. L. M. Haire, 1957.

II/2 *The Doctrine of God,* Part 2. Trans. G. W. Bromiley, J. C. Campbell, Ian Wilson, J. Strathearn McNab, H. Knight and R. A. Stewart, 1957.

III/1 *The Doctrine of Creation,* Part 1. Trans. J. W. Edwards, O. Bussey and H. Knight, 1958.

III/2 *The Doctrine of Creation,* Part 2. Trans. H. Knight, G. W. Bromiley, J. K. S. Reid and R. H. Fuller, 1960.

III/3 *The Doctrine of Creation,* Part 3. Trans. G. W. Bromiley and R. Ehrlich, 1960.

III/4 *The Doctrine of Creation,* Part 4. Trans. A. T. Mackay, T. H. L. Parker, H. Knight, H. A. Kennedy and J. Marks, 1961.

IV/1 *The Doctrine of Reconciliation,* Part 1. Trans. G. W. Bromiley, 1956.

IV/2 *The Doctrine of Reconciliation,* Part 2. Trans. G. W. Bromiley, 1956.

IV/3 *The Doctrine of Reconciliation,* Part 3. 2 vols. Trans. G. W. Bromiley, 1961 and 1962.

IV/4 *The Doctrine of Reconciliaton,* Part 4. Trans. G. W. Bromiley, 1969.

## II. Exegetical Works

A. Commentaries

*Christ and Adam: Man and Humanity in Romans 5.* Trans. T. A. Smail. New York: Harper & Brothers, 1957; Collier Books (paperback), 1962.

*The Epistle to the Philippians.* Trans. James W. Leitch. Richmond: John Knox, 1962.

*The Epistle to the Romans.* Trans. Edwyn C. Hoskyns. Oxford: Oxford Univ. Press, 1933.

"An Exegetical Study of Matthew 28:16-20." In *The Theology of the Christian Mission.* Ed. G. H. Anderson. Trans. Thomas Wieser. New York: McGraw Hill, 1961, pp. 55-71.

*The Great Promise.* Trans. Hans Freund. New York: Philosophical Library, 1963.

*The Resurrection of the Dead.* Trans. H. J. Stenning. New York: Fleming H. Revell Co., 1933.

*A Shorter Commentary on Romans.* Trans. D. H. van Daalen. Richmond: John Knox, 1959.

B. Sermons
*Call for God.* Trans. A. T. Mackay. New York: Harper & Row, 1967.
*Come, Holy Spirit* (with E. Thurneysen). Trans. G. W. Richards, E. G. Homrig-
hausen and K. J. Ernst. New York: Round Table Press, 1934.
*Deliverance to the Captives.* Trans. Marguerite Wieser. New York: Harper &
Brothers, 1961.
*God's Search for Man* (with E. Thurneysen). Trans. G. W. Richards, E. G. Hom-
righausen and K. J. Ernst. New York: Round Table Press, 1935.

### III. Historical and Political Works
A. Historical
*Action in Waiting.* Ed. and trans. Society of Brothers. New York: Plough, 1969.
*Anselm: Fides Quaerens Intellectum.* Trans. Ian W. Robertson. Richmond: John
Knox, 1960.
"Feuerbach—An Introductory Essay." In *The Essence of Christianity.* By Ludwig
Feuerbach. Trans. J. L. Adams. New York: Harper Torchbooks, 1957, pp. x-
xxxiii.
"Liberal Theology: Some Alternatives." Trans. L. A. Garrard. In *The Hibbert
Journal,* LIX (April 1961), 213-19.
*Protestant Thought: From Rousseau to Ritschl.* Trans. B. Cozens and H. H. Hart-
well. New York: Simon and Schuster, 1969.
*Revolutionary Theology in the Making: Barth-Thurneysen Correspondence, 1914-
1925.* Trans. James D. Smart. Richmond: John Knox, 1964.
"Rudolf Bultmann: An Attempt to Understand Him." In *Kerygma and Myth,* II.
Ed. Hans Bartsch. Trans. R. H. Fuller. London: SPCK, 1962, 83-132.
B. Political
*Against the Stream* (Shorter Post-War Writings). Ed. Ronald G. Smith. Trans.
E. M. Delacour and Stanley Godman. London: SCM, 1954.
*The Christian Churches and Living Reality.* Trans. Elkan Allan. London: Hutchin-
son & Co., 1946.
*The Church and the Political Problem of Our Day.* New York: Scribner, 1939.
*Church and State.* Trans. G. R. Howe. London: SCM, 1939.
*The Church and the War.* Trans. Antonia H. Froendt. New York: Macmillan, 1944.
"The Church Between East and West." *Cross Currents,* II (Winter 1951), 64-77.
Also in *World Review* (June and July 1949).
*Community, State and Church.* Trans. A. M. Hall, G. R. Howe and Stanley Godman.
Garden City: Doubleday (Anchor Books), 1960.
*The German Church Conflict.* Trans. P. T. A. Parker. Richmond: John Knox, 1965.
*The Germans and Ourselves.* Trans. R. G. Smith. London: Nisbet, 1945.
*How to Serve God in a Marxist Land* (with Johannes Hamel). Trans. Henry Clark
and J. D. Smart. New York: Association Press, 1959.
"A Letter to American Christians." *Christendom: An Ecumenical Review,* VIII
(Autumn 1943), 441-58.
*Letter to Great Britain from Switzerland.* London: Sheldon Press, 1941.
*The Only Way.* Trans. Marta K. Neufeld and Ronald Gregor Smith. New York:
Philosophical Library, 1947.
*Theological Existence To-Day! A Plea for Theological Freedom.* Trans. R. Birch
Hoyle. London: Hodder and Stoughton, 1933.
*This Christian Cause.* New York: Macmillan, 1941.
*Trouble and Promise in the Struggle of the Church in Germany.* Trans. P. V. M.
Benecke. Oxford: Clarendon Press, 1938.

## IV. Miscellaneous

*Ad Limina Apostolorum.* Trans. Keith R. Crim. Richmond: John Knox, 1968.
*The Christian Life.* Trans. J. Strathearn McNab. London: SCM, 1930; Hodder and Stoughton, 1935.
*Christmas.* Trans. B. Citron. Edinburgh: Oliver and Boyd, 1959.
*The Church and the Churches.* Grand Rapids: Eerdmans, 1936.
"The Concept of the Church." In *Christianity Divided: Protestant and Roman Catholic Theological Issues.* Ed. D. J. Callahan, H. A. Oberman and D. J. O'Hanlon. Trans. U. Allers. New York: Sheed and Ward, 1961, pp. 153-69.
*The Holy Ghost and the Christian Life.* Trans. R. Birch Hoyle. London: Frederick Muller, 1938.
*How I Changed My Mind.* Introd. and epilogue John D. Godsey. Richmond: John Knox, 1963.
*Karl Barth's Table Talk.* Ed. John Godsey. Richmond: John Knox, 1974.
"A Letter from Karl Barth." In *The Christian Century Reader.* Ed. H. E. Fey and M. Frakes. New York: Association Press, 1962, pp. 102-5. (First printed in *The Christian Century,* 31 December 1958.)
"On Systematic Theology." Trans. T. N. Tice. *Scottish Journal of Theology,* XIV (September 1961), 225-28.
*Prayer.* Trans. Sara F. Terrien. Philadelphia: Westminster, 1952.
*The Preaching of the Gospel.* Trans. B. E. Hooke. Philadelphia: Westminster, 1963.
*Questions to Christendom.* Trans. R. Birch Hoyle. London: Lutterworth, 1932.
"Remembrances of America." *The Christian Century* (2 January 1963), pp. 7-9.
*Selected Prayers.* Trans. Keith R. Crim. Richmond: John Knox, 1965.
*The Teaching of the Church Regarding Baptism.* Trans. Ernst A. Payne. London: SCM, 1948.
"A Theological Dialogue." *Theology Today,* XIX (July 1962), 171-77.

## Basic Bibliography of Works on Barth

Andrews, J. F., ed. *Karl Barth.* New York: Herder and Herder, 1969.
Berkouwer, Gerrit C. *The Triumph of Grace in the Theology of Karl Barth.* Trans. H. R. Boer. Grand Rapids: Eerdmans, 1956.
Bloesch, Donald G. *Jesus is Victor! Karl Barth's Doctrine of Salvation.* Nashville: Abingdon, 1976.
Bouillard, Henri. *The Knowledge of God.* Trans. S. D. Femians. New York: Herder and Herder, 1968.
Brown, Colin. *Karl Barth and the Christian Message.* Chicago: InterVarsity Press, 1967.
Busch, Eberhard. *Karl Barth: His Life from Letters and Autobiographical Texts.* Trans. John Bowden. Philadelphia: Fortress, 1976.
Camfield, F. W. *Revelation and the Holy Spirit.* New York: Scribner, 1934.
Casalis, Georges. *Portrait of Karl Barth.* Trans. and introd. Robert McAfee Brown. New York: Doubleday, 1964.
Chapman, J. A. *Theology of Karl Barth.* London: Epworth Press, 1931.
Clark, Gordon H. *Karl Barth's Theological Method.* Phillipsburg, N. J.: Presbyterian and Reformed, 1963.
Come, Arnold B. *An Introduction to Barth's Dogmatics for Preachers.* Philadelphia: Westminster, 1963.
Fairweather, A. *Word as Truth.* London: Epworth Press, 1945.
Fries, H. *Bultmann-Barth and Catholic Theology.* Pittsburgh: Duquesne Univ. Press, 1967.
Hamer, J. *Karl Barth.* Westminster: Newman Press, 1962.

Hanson, W. G. *Message of Karl Barth*. London: Religious Tract Society, 1931.

Hartwell, Herbert H. *The Theology of Karl Barth: An Introduction*. Philadelphia: Westminster, 1969.

Hausmann, W. J. *Karl Barth's Doctrine of Election*. New York: Philosophical Library, 1969.

Heath, C. *The Challenge of Karl Barth*. London: Allenson, 1932.

Hoyle, R. Birch. *The Teaching of Karl Barth: An Exposition*. London: SCM, 1936.

Hunsinger, George, ed. *Karl Barth and Radical Politics*. Philadelphia: Westminster, 1976.

Jenson, Robert W. *Alpha and Omega: A Study in the Theology of Karl Barth*. New York: Thomas Nelson & Sons, 1963.

——————. *God After God*. New York: Bobbs-Merrill, 1969.

Karl Barth Colloquium, including J. A. Wharton, "Karl Barth as Exegete and His Influence on Biblical Interpretation"; John E. Smith, "The Significance of Karl Barth's Thought for the Relation Between Philosophy and Theology"; Robert W. Jenson, "Response"; Gabriel Vahanian, "Karl Barth as Theologian of Culture"; J. W. Deschner, "Karl Barth as Political Activist"; Paul L. Lehmann, "Karl Barth, Theologian of Permanent Revolution"; Frederick Herzog, "Response"; Philip Lee, "Karl Barth as Preacher and Pastor"; A. T. McKelway, "Magister Dialecticae et Optimarium Partium (Recollections of Karl Barth as Teacher)"; John C. Bennett, "A Non-Barthian's Gratitude to Karl Barth"; Horace T. Allen, Jr., "A Word in Commemoration"; *Union Seminary Quarterly Review*, XXVIII (Fall 1972).

Keller, A. *Karl Barth and Christian Unity*. New York: Macmillan, 1933.

Kent, F. *Karl Barth and His Teaching*. London: Independent Press, 1937.

Klooster, Fred H. *The Significance of Barth's Theology*. Grand Rapids: Baker, 1961.

Kuiper, R. B. *For Whom Did Christ Die?* Grand Rapids: Eerdmans, 1959.

Küng, Hans. *Justification: The Doctrine of Karl Barth and a Catholic Reflection*. Trans. T. Collins, E. E. Tolk and D. Granskou, with a letter by Karl Barth. New York: Thomas Nelson & Sons, 1964.

Leitch, J. W. *Theology of Transition*. London: Nisbet, 1952.

Lowrie, W. *Our Concern with the Theology of Crisis*. Boston: Meador, 1932.

Matczak, S. A. *Karl Barth on God*. New York: Society of St. Paul, 1962.

McConnachie, J. *Barthian Theology and the Man of Today*. New York: Harper & Brothers, 1933.

——————. *The Significance of Karl Barth*. New York: Harper & Brothers, 1931.

McCord, J. I. and T. H. L. Parker, eds. *Service in Christ*. London: Epworth Press, 1966.

Monsma, Peter. *Karl Barth's Idea of Revelation*. Somerville: Somerset Press, 1937.

Mueller, David L. *Karl Barth*. Waco: Word, 1972.

Oden, T. C. *The Promise of Barth*. Philadelphia: Lippincott, 1969.

Ogletree, Thomas W. *Christian Faith and History: A Critical Comparison of Ernst Troeltsch and Karl Barth*. Nashville: Abingdon, 1965.

O'Grady, C. *The Church in the Theology of Karl Barth*. London: Geoffrey Chapman, 1968.

Parker, T. H. L., ed. *Essays in Christology for Karl Barth*. London: Lutterworth, 1956.

——————. *Karl Barth*. Grand Rapids: Eerdmans, 1970.

Pauck, Wilhelm. *Karl Barth: Prophet of a New Christianity?* New York: Harper & Brothers, 1931.

Polman, A. D. R. *Barth*. Trans. C. D. Freeman. Phillipsburg, N.J.: Presbyterian and Reformed, 1960.

Robinson, James M., ed. *The Beginnings of Dialectical Theology*. 2 vols. Richmond: John Knox, 1968.

Rolston, Holmes. *A Conservative Looks to Barth and Brunner*. Nashville: Cokesbury, 1933.

Rumscheidt, H. Martin, ed. *Footnotes to a Theology: The Karl Barth Colloquium of 1972.*

_____. *Revelation and Theology: An Analysis of the Barth-Harnack Correspondence of 1923*. Cambridge: Cambridge Univ. Press, 1972.

Runia, Klaas. *Karl Barth's Doctrine of Holy Scripture*. Grand Rapids: Eerdmans, 1962.

Ryrie, C. C. *Neo-Orthodoxy: An Evangelical Evaluation of Barthianism*. Chicago: Moody, 1956.

Smart, James D. *The Divided Mind of Modern Theology: Karl Barth and Rudolph Bultmann, 1908-1933*. Philadelphia: Westminster, 1967.

Snyder, D. N. *Karl Barth's Struggle with Anthropocentric Theology*. Gravenhaga, Netherlands: E. Wattez, 1966.

Spencer, S. *Shall We Follow Karl Barth?* London: Lindsey Press, 1947.

Starkloff, C. F. *The Office of Proclamation in the Theology of Karl Barth*. Ottawa: Univ. of Ottawa Press, 1969.

Torrance, Thomas F. *Karl Barth: An Introduction to His Early Theology, 1910-1931*. London: SCM, 1962.

von Balthasar, Hans Urs. *The Theology of Karl Barth*. Trans. John Drury. New York: Holt, Rinehart and Winston, 1971.

Van Til, Cornelius. *Christianity and Barthianism*. Phillipsburg, N.J.: Presbyterian and Reformed, 1962.

_____. *The New Modernism: An Appraisal of the Theology of Barth and Brunner*. Phillipsburg, N. J.: Presbyterian and Reformed, 1973.

Weber, Otto. *Karl Barth's Church Dogmatics: An Introductory Report on Volumes I:1 to III:4*. Trans. A. C. Cochrane. Philadelphia: Westminster, 1953.

Willems, Boniface. *Karl Barth: An Ecumenical Approach to His Theology*. Trans. M. J. vanVelzen. Glen Rock: Paulist Press, 1965.

Willis, Robert E. *The Ethics of Karl Barth*. Leiden: E. J. Brill, 1971.

Wingren, Gustaf. *Theology in Conflict: Nygren, Barth, Bultmann*. Trans. E. H. Wahlstrom. London: Oliver and Boyd, 1958.

Yoder, J. H. *Karl Barth and the Problem of War*. Nashville: Abingdon, 1970.

Zerbe, A. S. *Karl Barth's Theology*. Cleveland: Central Publishing House, 1930.

## Representative English Reviews of Barth's Works

*Action in Waiting: On Christoph Blumhardt* (1969):
n.a., n.t., *Theology Digest*, XVIII (Autumn 1920), 279.

*Ad Limina Apostolorum: An Appraisal of Vatican II* (1968):
Rudolph J. Ehrlich, n.t., *Scottish Journal of Theology*, XXI (March 1968), 110-11.
n.a., "Three Views of Vatican II," *Christianity Today*, XII (7 June 1968), 891.
n.a., n.t., *Theology Digest*, XVIII (Autumn 1968), 261.

*Against The Stream: Shorter Post-War Writings* (1954):
Kenneth J. Foreman, "Multum in Parvo," *Interpretation*, IX (January 1955), 112-14.
Roger L. Shinn, n.t., *Theology Today*, XI (October 1954), 415-16.

*Anselm: Fides Quaerens Intellectum* (1960):

Gordon H. Clark, "Karl Barth: Teacher and Preacher," *Christianity Today*, V (5 June 1961), 784.

James W. Leitch, n.t., *Scottish Journal of Theology*, XIV (September 1961), 297-99.

Herndon Wagers, "Faith Seeking Understanding," *Interpretation* XVI (April 1962), 213-16.

*Call For God* (1965):

André Bustanoby, "Preaching to Prisoners," *Christianity Today*, XII (March 1968), 555-56.

n.a., n.t., *Theology Digest*, XV (Winter 1967), 296-97.

*Christ and Adam* (1956):

Cornelius Van Til, "Barth's View of Man," *Christianity Today*, II (3 February 1958), 34.

*The Church and the War* (1944):

John C. Bennett, n.t., *Theology Today*, I (January 1945), 552-53.

*Church Dogmatics* I/2 (1956):

Arthur C. Cochrane, "Ecumenical Theology," *Interpretation*, XI (January 1957), 98-100.

*Church Dogmatics* II/2 (1957):

George S. Hendrey, n.t., *Theology Today*, XV (October 1958), 396-404.

*Church Dogmatics* III/1 (1958):

J. I. Packer, "Barth's Dogmatics," *Christianity Today*, V (16 January 1961), 334.

*Church Dogmatics* III/2 (1959):

A. C. Cochrane, n.t., *Theology Today*, XVIII (July 1961), 221-23.

*Church Dogmatics* III/3 (1960):

Colin Brown, "Barth on Creation, Part 3," *Christianity Today*, V (31 July 1961), 949.

Daniel L. Deegan, n.t., *Scottish Journal of Theology*, XV (March 1962), 74-83.

B. A. Gerrish, "Creation and Covenant," *Interpretation*, XVI (April 1962), 216-20.

Geraint Vaughn Jones, "God and Negation," *Scottish Journal of Theology*, VII (September 1954), 233-44.

*Church Dogmatics* III/4 (1961):

Colin Brown, "Barth's Free Man in Christ," *Christianity Today*, VI (16 March 1962), 598.

Daniel L. Deegan, n.t., *Scottish Journal of Theology*, XV (December 1962), 400-12.

Charles West, n.t., *Theology Today*, XX (July 1963), 288-92.

J. Rodman Williams, "The Ethics of Karl Barth," *Interpretation*, XVII (January 1963), 84-89.

*Church Dogmatics* IV/2 (1958):

G. W. Bromiley, "The Doctrine of Reconciliation: A Survey of Barth's *Kirchliche Dogmatik* IV/2," *Scottish Journal of Theology*, X (March 1957), 76-85.

Arthur C. Cochrane, n.t., *Theology Today*, XIII (October 1956), 378-88.

*Church Dogmatics* IV/3 (1961):

G. W. Bromiley, n.t., *Scottish Journal of Theology*, XV (June 1962), 193-203.

Colin Brown, "Christ's Prophetic Office," *Christianity Today*, VI (22 January 1962), 949.

John B. Cobb, Jr., "The Strange New World—Real or Not?" *Interpretation*, XVI (October 1962), 472-75.

*Church Dogmatics* IV/4 (1969):

Herbert H. Hartwell, n.t., *Scottish Journal of Theology*, XXIII (February 1970), 96-99.
*Deliverance to the Captives* (1961):
Gordon H. Clark, "Karl Barth: Teacher and Preacher," *Christianity Today*, V (5 June 1961), 784.
McMurray S. Richey, "Preaching For All Prisoners," *Interpretation* XVI (July 1962), 319-21.
*Dogmatics in Outline* (1949):
D. M. Baillie, n.t., *Scottish Journal of Theology*, I (September 1948), 221-24.
J. Haroutunion, "A Debate With the Modern Mind," *Interpretation*, IV (April 1950), 221-23.
George S. Hendry, n.t., *Theology Today*, VII (April 1950), 114-16.
*The Epistle to the Romans* (1933):
n.a., n.t., *Theology Digest*, XVI (Winter 1968), 336.
*The Epistle to the Philippians* (1962):
E. F. Harrison, "Worth Waiting For," *Christianity Today*, VI (11 May 1962), 806.
E. Kenneth Lee, n.t., *Scottish Journal of Theology*, XVII (June 1964), 239.
*Evangelical Theology: An Introduction* (1963):
G. W. Bromiley, "A Theology That Walks the Earth," *Christianity Today*, VII (4 January 1963), 344-45.
Daniel L. Deegan, n.t., *Theology Today*, XX (January 1964), 568-70.
James D. Leitch, n.t., *Scottish Journal of Theology*, XVI (September 1963), 304.
*German Church Conflict* (1965):
n.a., n.t., *Theology Digest*, XIV (Summer 1966), 161.
*God Here and Now* (1964):
James Daane, "A Clear Overview," *Christianity Today*, VIII (5 June 1964), 847-48.
n.a., n.t., *Theology Digest*, XII (Winter 1964), 242.
*God In Action* (1936):
n.a., n.t., *Theology Digest*, XII (Autumn 1964), 210.
*The Heidelberg Catechism for Today* (1964):
n.a., n.t., *Christianity Today*, VII (22 May 1964), 803.
n.a., n.t., *Theology Digest*, XII (Winter 1964), 242.
*How I Changed My Mind* (1966):
n.a., n.t., *Theology Digest*, XIV (Winter 1966), 304.
*How To Serve God In a Marxist Land* (1959):
Charles C. West, n.t., *Theology Today*, XVII (October 1960), 404-5.
*The Humanity of God* (1960):
Daniel L. Deegan, n.t., *Scottish Journal of Theology*, XVI (June 1963), 195-97.
Nels F. S. Ferré, "Barth on Barth," *Interpretation*, XIV (October 1960), 455-56.
Charles C. West, n.t., *Theology Today*, XVII (January 1961), 553-56.
*Karl Barth's Table Talk* (1963):
n.a., n.t., *Theology Digest*, XII (Autumn 1964), 210.
*Natural Theology* (with Brunner, 1934):
Gwilym O. Griffith, "Natural Theology and the Ministry of the Word," *Scottish Journal of Theology*, I (December 1948), 251-71.
*Prayer* (1952)
Olive Wyon, n.t., *Theology Today*, XI (January 1955), 561-62.
*Protestant Theology in the 19th Century* (1972):

John McConnachie, n.t., *Scottish Journal of Theology,* I (December 1948), 332-36.

n.a., n.t., *Theology Digest,* XXI (Summer 1973), 156.

*Protestant Thought: Rousseau to Ritschl* (1959):

Robert D. Knudsen, "Brilliant Encounter," *Christianity Today,* IV (15 February 1960), 429.

*Revolutionary Theology In the Making* (1964):

G. W. Bromiley, "Crusade Against Demythologization," *Christianity Today,* III (8 June 1959), 34.

*The Teaching of the Church Regarding Baptism* (1948):

Floyd V. Filson, n.t., *Theology Today,* VI (July 1949), 262-68.

*Theology and Church: Shorter Writings* (1962):

F. W. Canfield, n.t., *Scottish Journal of Theology,* I (December 1948), 328-32.

Daniel L. Deegan, n.t., *Theology Today,* XX (July 1963), 298-303.

## Author Index